Praise for *Mindfulness: Living through Challenges and Enriching Your Life in This Moment*

"Mindfulness is a powerful tool for healing and growth. While timeless in its application, the medical community has only recently been captivated by the research demonstrating its beneficial effects. We have seen the work of Dr. Sears transform the lives of our patients, and are very pleased to see this type of information now become more widely available. Dr. Sears provides both inspiration and practical suggestions for dealing with serious challenges and for living a more fulfilling life."

Steve Amoils, MD, and Sandi Amoils, MD, co-medical directors of the Alliance Institute for Integrative Medicine, Cincinnati, Ohio, co-authors of *Get Well & Stay Well: Optimal Health through Transformational Medicine*

"Thank you Dr. Sears for a clear, concise, practical guide for weaving mindfulness seamlessly into your everyday life! Mindfulness is a simple concept but complex to describe and apply. Dr. Sears, a knowledgeable expert, guides by example with thoughtful and poignant stories from his personal and professional life in his new book, *Mindfulness: Living through Challenges and Enriching Your Life in This Moment*."

Susan Albers, PsyD, psychologist and author of *Eating Mindfully*

"This book is a practical guide to developing a better understanding of mindfulness and will be useful for anyone interested in discovering how this practice can help us lead wiser lives. Dr. Sears has written about mindfulness in a way that clearly shows how relevant this practice is for exploring and engaging in the joys and challenges of everyday life."

Susan L. Woods, MSW, LICSW, MBSR/MBCT Professional Educator and Mindfulness Meditation Teacher

"*Mindfulness: Living through Challenges and Enriching Your Life in This Moment* is a wonderful new book contributing an essential and most needed fresh new context for dealing with life's challenges, even when things go terribly wrong. It provides the reader with excellent tools and new scientific pathways, with cutting-edge neuroscience and mindfulness training. It is a wonderful, enriching guidebook for charting how to build the necessary new muscles for bringing an evenness to one's mind, self, relationships, and life."

Ronald A. Alexander, PhD, author of *Wise Mind, Open Mind*, Executive Director of the OpenMind Training Institute in Santa Monica, CA

"In a world where mindfulness teachings are now plentiful, Dr. Richard Sears offers a fresh perspective that is sure to interest and enliven you. Dr. Sears integrates a wide range of engaging personal and professional stories, mindfulness practices, and kernels of wisdom that have the potential to transform your practice and leave you with a deeper understanding and appreciation of yourself and others."

Ryan M. Niemiec, PsyD, author of *Mindfulness and Character Strengths: A Practical Guide to Flourishing*, Education Director of the VIA Institute on Character

"This is a clear, insightful book, showing how mindfulness can help us find our way through difficulties as well as how mindfulness can enrich our lives. Dr. Sears' experiences make the book personal and readable."

Thomas Bien, PhD, author of *The Buddha's Way of Happiness*

"MINDFULNESS is a tuning. Sears draws the reader into th̶ ̶f̶ ̶ ̶ ̶ ̶ ̶of Clear Mind and illumines the action-path. MINDFULNESS harmonizes one's o̶

Michael D. Fitzpatrick, world-renowned cellist and longtime the XIVth Dalai Lama

Mindfulness

Living through Challenges and
Enriching Your Life in This Moment

Richard W. Sears

WILEY Blackwell

3426550

This edition first published 2014
© 2014 John Wiley & Sons, Ltd.

Registered Office
John Wiley & Sons Ltd, The Atrium, Southern Gate, Chichester, West Sussex, PO19 8SQ, UK

Editorial Offices
350 Main Street, Malden, MA 02148-5020, USA
9600 Garsington Road, Oxford, OX4 2DQ, UK
The Atrium, Southern Gate, Chichester, West Sussex, PO19 8SQ, UK

For details of our global editorial offices, for customer services, and for information about how to apply for permission to reuse the copyright material in this book please see our website at www.wiley.com/wiley-blackwell.

The right of Richard W. Sears to be identified as the author of this work has been asserted in accordance with the UK Copyright, Designs and Patents Act 1988.

Library of Congress Cataloging-in-Publication Data

Sears, Richard W.
  Mindfulness : living through challenges and enriching your life in this moment / Richard W. Sears.
     pages cm
  Includes bibliographical references and index.
  ISBN 978-1-118-59757-6 (cloth) – ISBN 978-1-118-59758-3 (pbk.) 1. Mind and body. I. Title.
  BF151.S43 2014
  158.1 – dc23

                                                                          2014012632

A catalogue record for this book is available from the British Library.

Cover image: © Mitja Mladkovic / iStockphoto

Set in 10/12pt SabonLTStd by Laserwords Private Limited, Chennai, India
Printed and bound in Malaysia by Vivar Printing Sdn Bhd

1   2014

*To my daughters, Ashlyn and Caylee, my favorite
mindfulness teachers*

Contents

About the Author

Richard W. Sears, PsyD, MBA, ABPP, DMin, is a board-certified clinical psychologist, speaker, and consultant. He is a core faculty member of the PsyD Program in Clinical Psychology at Union Institute & University, where he is the Director of the Center for Clinical Mindfulness & Meditation. He is also Volunteer Associate Professor of Psychiatry & Behavioral Neurosciences at the UC College of Medicine, Clinical Assistant Professor at Wright State University School of Professional Psychology, and clinical/research faculty at the University of Cincinnati Center for Integrative Health and Wellness. He runs a private psychology practice in Cincinnati and conducts mindfulness groups at the Alliance Institute for Integrative Medicine. He is a psychologist contractor with the Cincinnati VA Medical Center, and is also working with the UC Center for Integrative Health and Wellness and Cincinnati Children's Hospital on projects involving mindfulness.

Dr. Sears is author of *Mindfulness in Clinical Practice* (with Dennis Tirch and Robert Denton), *Consultation Skills for Mental Health Professionals* (with John Rudisill and Carrie Mason-Sears), and *Building Competence in Mindfulness-Based Cognitive Therapy: Transcripts and Insights for Working With Stress, Anxiety, Depression, and Other Problems,* and *Mindfulness-Based Cognitive Therapy for PTSD* (with Kathleen Chard). He is editor of the book *Perspectives on Spirituality and Religion in Psychotherapy* (with Alison Niblick).

Dr. Sears is a fifth degree black belt in To-Shin Do/Ninjutsu, a licensed private pilot, and received past certification as an Emergency Medical Technician. He once served briefly as a personal protection agent for the Dalai Lama of Tibet with his teacher, Stephen Kinryu-Jien Hayes. He has studied and practiced mindfulness and the Eastern Wisdom traditions over 30 years, and was given a doctorate in Buddhist Studies from Buddha Dharma University. He received ordination in the Japanese Tendai lineage, Bodhisattva ordination and authority to teach *kōans* (*inka*) under Paul Wonji Lynch in the Zen lineage of Seung Sahn, and ordination in the Vietnamese Zen tradition of Thich Thien An under Suhita Dharma.

Acknowledgments

As with all things, this book is the product of a wide variety of influences, and it took many individuals to bring it into existence. I can't possibly name everyone who has inspired me, but I want to acknowledge some of the major ones.

I would like to begin by expressing my profound appreciation to Stephen K. Hayes, for 30 years of mentorship, growth, and friendship. I was also very inspired by the late Alan Watts (made available to the world through his son, Mark Watts). Both of these men have influenced me deeply.

I am very thankful for the love and support of my family, Carrie Mason-Sears, Ashlyn Sears, Jeremy Rogers (and for his photographs), Olivia and Brittney Taylor, Caylee Sears, and Charles and Elfriede Sears.

Many mindfulness mentors and friends have freely given their time and inspiration: Susan Albers, Ron Alexander, Ruth Baer, Andrew Bein, Thomas Bien, Sarah Bowen, Jon Kabat-Zinn, Steven C. Hayes, Marsha Linehan, Ryan Niemiec, Kevin Polk, Hank Robb, Elana Rosenbaum, Sharon Salzberg, Zindel Segal, Randye Semple, Dan Siegel, Jon Teasdale, Dennis Tirch, Mark Williams, Kelly Wilson, and Susan Woods. I have a special feeling of gratitude for Alan Marlatt, who read the manuscript of my last book and wrote an endorsement only months before he passed away.

I've been honored to work with a talented team of clinicians and mindfulness researchers: Kate Chard, Kristen Walter, and Lindsey Davidson at the Cincinnati VA; Steve and Sandi Amoils at the Alliance Institute for Intregrative Medicine; and Sian Cotton, Melissa Delbello, Jeffrey Strawn, Stefanie Stevenson, Lauren Stahl, and Tina Luberto at the University of Cincinnati Center for Integrative Health and Wellness and Cincinnati Children's Hospital.

I had the experience of a lifetime on the Dalai Lama security team with Stephen K. Hayes, David Piser, Steve Pavlovic, and Matt Woodard. I am also honored to have shared and learned so much from my ninja friends,

Jay Adler, David Allison, Marissa Birdi, Scott Bragg, Simon Clifford, Mark Davis, Johan D'hondt, Tori Eldridge, Kriss Elston-Hurdle, Rick Hansen, Rumiko Hayes, Hollie Hirst, Hakim Isler, Robert Johnson, Kathy Joseph, Phillip Lovell, Stacy Lynn, Dennis Mahoney, Hardee Merritt, Don Myochiriki Siclari, Paul Molinsky, Russ Nemhauser, James Norris, Leo Pimentel, Ian Pucek, Mark and Helen Russo, David Sink, Russ Sitz, Kim Stahl, Mary Stevens, Shane Stevens, Mike and Lori Stinson, and too many more to list.

Much appreciation to my Zen teachers and Dharma friends, who have profoundly opened me up to the moment, Paul Wonji Lynch, Suhita Dharma, James Myo Gak Foster, Robert Chong'an Denton, Sunyananda Dharma, Lawrence Do'an Grecco, Hwasahn Prajna, Charama Bhavika Prajna, Chasayk Kudhara, Haeja Prajna, Domun Prajna, Doshim Dharma, Beopbo Sunya, Chris Bonjok Hoff, Lama Kunga, Lama Pema Wangdak, Lama Surya Das, and so many others.

Many thanks to my colleagues, Joy McGhee, Jennifer Ossege, and Jennifer Scott, for their friendship, support, and assistance in making this book possible. Thanks also to Olivia Ossege for her beautiful photographs of Hawaii.

I have also been fortunate to receive support from inspirations and leaders like Philip Glass, Michael Fitzpatrick, Bill Lax, Rich Hansen, Larina Kase, John Rudisill, and Roger Sublett.

I am very appreciative for the support of Diane Baumer, for her careful reading and feedback on the manuscript, and for inspiring me by sharing her own natural writing style and persistence to work through challenges.

Thanks to Tara Robinson, editor of Cincinnati Whole Living Journal, for material inspired from our radio conversation, as well as Aarin Cox and A.J. McConnell, for their diligent transcription work.

Thank you also to Bob, Tom, Dean, Chick, and Kristi for starting my days with a laugh for the last 30 years.

And perhaps most importantly, thanks to the Wiley Blackwell team for bringing this book into reality: Andrew Peart, Olivia Wells, Karen Shield, Leah Morin, and those many others working behind the scenes.

I am grateful to all the individuals in my private practice and mindfulness groups, who have taught me so much. I present many of their stories in these pages, though the names and details have been changed to protect their privacy.

I apologize in advance for any omissions of credit. Many of my mentors had such a profound influence on me that I may have internalized some of what I've learned and forgotten from where I've learned it.

1

The Need for Mindfulness

Many of us have become so entrenched in getting things done, worrying about the future, ruminating about the past, and making comparisons that we don't spend much time in this moment.

The late Alan Watts talked about the trick that is played on all of us from the time we are children.[1] We are bombarded with the idea that some great thing will be coming in the future. When you're old enough, you get to go to kindergarten – won't that be great? Then first grade, then second grade. You can look forward to middle school, then high school, then college! Along the way, you long for the day you will meet that special someone who will make your life feel more complete, and perhaps start a family. Eventually you get to enter the world of work, where you can make and save money to get those things you've always wanted to make you happy. You fight your way up the ladder, believing that things will be so much better after you get that next promotion. And once you get that nice house and reliable car and perfect partner, life will be so much easier. Finally your kids grow up and get lives of their own. When you get to retirement, too tired to enjoy it from the stress of working so hard all those years, you realize that your life is almost over, and you were absent from most of it. As the saying goes, life is what happened to you while you were busy making other plans.

Mindfulness: Living through Challenges and Enriching Your Life in This Moment, First Edition.
Richard W. Sears.
© 2014 John Wiley & Sons, Ltd. Published 2014 by John Wiley & Sons, Ltd.

If we don't have much practice living in the moment we are in, how can we expect to enjoy that future we long for when it finally does arrive? Have you ever achieved a long sought-after goal, only to have the joy wear off after a few days, quickly setting your sights on your next future goal? If we are in the habit of always thinking of the next thing, we lose the skill of truly appreciating the present moment.

When we were young kids, the summers seemed to last forever, but as we grow older, time seems to slip away from us. The amount of time each of us has each day is the same as it has always been, but why does it feel like it moves so quickly? Why don't we have more time with all of the amazing technological advances we've made? With email and texting, I can now communicate with others instantly, anytime, anywhere. No longer do I have to write out a letter, walk to the post office, buy a stamp, and mail it. With instant access to databases on my computer and my phone, no longer do I have to spend hours researching information in a library on how to repair something in my house. With microwave ovens, I can cook my food in less time than it takes me to eat it.

How is it that our ancestors were able to sit on the porch every evening, watching the sunset, when they had to do things like prepare all their meals from scratch and wash their clothes by hand? Why does it feel like we seldom get a break from all the problems in our lives? Is it even possible to be more present, with all of our responsibilities, in the midst of all this modern chaos?

For many of us, it seems there is always "one more thing" to deal with, another problem to tackle, and we are waiting for things to calm down so we can start to live. Sometimes years can go by, and instead of the problems going away, they gradually wear us down, mentally and physically. It is difficult to accept that suffering is a natural part of life, and that how we relate to suffering makes all the difference. We get caught in vicious circles. We get stressed out that we are so stressed. We become anxious about our anxiety. We get scared of how afraid we feel. We feel depressed that we are so depressed all the time. We get angry about our anger. We hurt so much from our pain. We feel guilty about feeling so much guilt. We become addicted to our addictions. We are impatient with our impatience. We feel irritated about our irritability. We judge how judgmental we are. We rarely give ourselves permission to feel what we are truly feeling.

Though traumatic childhoods are all too common, most of us can remember how much easier it was to fully engage in our activities and relationships when we were younger. When we hurt, we cried and let it out, and usually felt better quickly. When we were happy, we could laugh from the very depths of our being. We explored with curiosity all the wonders in the world around us.

My preschooler notices the most ordinary things around her with amazement, things that most adults take for granted. My teenager, however,

Kids enjoying the beach. © Richard Sears.

has become indoctrinated and hypnotized into the realm of thinking and judgments, where not having an Internet connection is worse than death, one instant message can make or ruin her day, and comparison with peers is constant. Kids are being pressured to grow up very quickly these days, and too often leave behind some of their best qualities.

Mindfulness, the ability to pay attention in the present moment, is a natural human process that we are all born with, but tends to diminish as we grow older and get caught up in the world of thoughts. While thinking is important, when our lives are spent anticipating the future, or living in the past, we miss the richness of the moment we are in now. Fostering mindfulness allows us to more consciously participate in our lives, breaking us out of the mindless routines we often fall into automatically. When facing challenges, we can learn to step out of old habits that make the situation worse, consciously responding rather than unconsciously reacting. We can allow our emotions to rise and fall without getting as stuck in them. We can also choose to notice more often the beauty in the world around us, to appreciate the sound of good music, and to savor the connection we feel when we look into the eyes of those we love.

Although an ancient practice in many cultures, mindfulness is supported by hundreds of modern research studies that demonstrate amazing benefits for our mental and physical health. Medical imaging even shows growth in important areas of the brain after only eight weeks of practicing a mindfulness program like the one outlined in Chapter 7.

Of all the people I have met, one of the individuals who most embodies mindfulness is the Dalai Lama. Despite the many horrors he faced during the invasion of his native Tibet, resulting in the death of one million of its six million inhabitants, he captures everyone he speaks to with his genuine presence and his smile. When he stops to look and talk with you, you can sense that he is not thinking about other things. You feel as if you are the most important thing in the world at that moment.

The first time I met him, I was assisting Stephen K. Hayes with a security detail for a public presentation the Dalai Lama was giving. Mr. Hayes kindly assigned me to be backstage when His Holiness arrived. Another young woman waited beside me. Through my radio earpiece, I knew when he arrived, but still felt some surprise when he came in through the backstage entrance by himself. I immediately put my hands together in a gesture of respect, which he did also. He walked toward me, beaming with sparkling eyes. His translator walked in close behind, and I didn't understand what they were saying. All I could make out was the word "ninja," which His Holiness repeated with raised eyebrows and a questioning smile. For a moment which felt frozen in time, he looked at me as if nothing else mattered, despite the thousands of people waiting for him. He then gave both of us hugs before walking onto the stage to a cheering audience. I briefly shared a gaze of amazement with the woman beside me, then I followed him out to stand beside the stage and watch the crowd as he spoke to them.

Mindful awareness is a counter to our pervasive state of mindlessness. Have you ever found yourself pulling into your driveway at the end of the day, not really remembering how you got there? Perhaps you were deep in thought, or having an important phone conversation. It's likely you were driving safely, stopping at red lights, and avoiding the other cars, but you did not notice what you were doing with your conscious attention. We spend much of our lives in this "automatic pilot" mode.

Doing things automatically is not necessarily a bad thing. In fact, it is a wonderful time saver. If I am driving down the road and an animal jumps out in front of me, and I stop to consciously think, "Let's see now, how do I stop this car? Oh yeah, one of the pedals down here. Now which one was it?," it will of course be too late.

However, if we continuously operate on automatic pilot, we can get ourselves into trouble. My friend David Allison would say "My brain has a mind of its own!" whenever he found himself doing something he hadn't intended to do. I once was driving a friend home, and we got into a rich conversation. As I pulled into my own driveway, I remembered, "Oh yeah, I was supposed to take you home!"

The hardest automatic patterns to catch are those of thinking and feeling. Many years ago, a coworker walked by me, and I said, "Hey, good job on that project you did yesterday."

He stopped and glared at me for a moment, then said, "What do you mean by that?"

Confused for a moment, I simply repeated "I just thought you did a nice job on the work you did."

His stare intensified, and he looked angry. "What are you saying?"

I was perplexed for a moment, because he was not normally argumentative like this. I suddenly remembered that he had told me he was going through a divorce. It dawned on me that he probably had become accustomed to a lot of sarcasm from his soon to be ex-wife, so he assumed I was being sarcastic. I felt comfortable enough to say this to him, and he was able to laugh at himself and admit it was true.

You can imagine what would have happened had I not caught this. I could have thought, or heaven forbid, said out loud, "Excuse me, you jerk, I was just trying to give you a compliment!," thereby bringing to life the very thing he was defending against. Our friendship could have been strained or even ended due to a misunderstanding. Of course, it's often easier to catch the automatic thoughts, feelings, and behaviors of others, and harder to notice our own.

When I was a psychology trainee at a children's hospital, I worked with a young child who was very confused about why his mother brought him to this stranger to be given a lot of questions. I was able to engage him enough to get through the psychological testing, but every now and then, he would suddenly stop and look up at me with wide eyes, and ask in a loud voice, "What's going on?!"

Though this young boy was asking out of anxiety, we can learn to ask ourselves what we are experiencing right now as a way of getting more in touch with this moment. If we continuously forget to do this, we may just be engaging in outdated habits, or following along with what everyone else expects of us, without question. We can still choose to do what we were going to do automatically, but we can notice if it is moving us toward or away from the person we want to be and the life we want to live. In my psychotherapy practice, it is very common to hear someone stare off sadly and say, "I just don't know how my life ended up like this."

When we check into this moment, we often find more space for a wider range of conscious choices. The advice is often given that if you receive an email that really upsets you, you should wait at least 24 hours before responding. Have you ever responded to something hastily, only to regret what you said the next day? Perhaps someone was rude to you, but how you responded made it look like you were the one who was overly emotional and irrational.

I once worked with a student who did not follow this advice. I emailed him some feedback about a project he was working on, and he immediately fired back a five-page litany about all the things he didn't like about me and our agency. My immediate urge was to "counterattack," expressing how ungrateful he was for the time it took me to develop that feedback, all the years of support I had given him, and so on. However, sensing how strong my feelings were, I decided to sit with it and talk to colleagues. It actually took me days before I was ready to put the effort into composing a response that was professional and helpful, rather than venting to make myself feel better.

Even habits that we have worked hard to develop in the past can get in the way if they are done unconsciously. One of my therapy clients recently told me that his wife grabbed his arm, and he automatically thrust his thumb into one of her pressure points. Thankfully she was not hurt, but the man had said it was due to his military combat training.

Many years ago, when I was a new martial arts instructor, I too had worked hard to develop some automatic responses, but discovered I had to move beyond that, and always notice the situation as it is first. My school was on the corner of an intersection, with only a sidewalk between it and a busy highway. The all-glass construction made it easy for passersby to see what we were doing inside, which seemed good for marketing when I leased the place. One day, after class, I was standing in the lobby chatting with a friend and student named Phillip. I then began tidying up, when I heard a loud banging sound. I looked up, and a car was coming directly at me at high speed – it had been hit and pushed by another car running a red light. I turned away and ran across the floor of the school as quickly as I could. I then heard the sound of glass shattering behind me as the car smashed through the lobby doors. I turned around, and watched helplessly as Phillip was backing up and stumbling with the car headed right for him. Luckily, the car had been slowed somewhat by the door frames, and as Phillip reached the opposite wall and could go no further, the car came to a stop only inches away from him.

Amazingly, no one had been hurt. Tim, one of my other students, an Emergency Medical Technician, took charge of the scene until help arrived. What haunted me for weeks after that was the image of my friend backing away from the car. It could have turned out much differently. It was good that I had been able to save myself, but I had not given any thought to my friend in that moment. My training took on a whole new level when I realized that I had only been learning to protect myself, rather than keeping a broader awareness of the entire situation. Eventually, I became better at pausing, even for a fraction of a second, to prevent reacting in ways that could make things worse. I have learned that I can often process a situation more wisely without taking the time to think everything through in words.

Being in the present moment is very simple, though not necessarily easy. Many of us get inculcated by society into thinking that our sense of self-esteem rests on what we achieve or accomplish. Our lives can become more about "doing" rather than "being." As Alan Watts observed,[2] most of our activities are about getting something. We drive to get somewhere. We learn things so we can get a better job. We work to get money. We might even take time for ourselves because it will help us relax so that we can work better afterwards. However, most of us do recognize some exceptions, such as music and dancing. When you listen to music, you don't play it fast to get it over with. You enjoy the sounds. When you dance, you don't aim to arrive at a particular spot on the floor. You enjoy the dancing itself. When we realize that all we truly have is just this very moment, we can dance no matter what we are doing.

Is your life a march or a dance? Are you enjoying the journey, or only thinking about the "destination"? Being in touch with this moment fosters a sense of being, even in the midst of busy doing. As Kierkegaard said, life is a mystery to be lived, not a problem to be solved.

When our goal is to get something out of life, we always feel like we need more time. Despite research demonstrating that you can actually get more done if you focus on one thing at a time, we habitually multitask in the hope that we can "save" time and hence we are never fully present in what we are doing. Even having a nice conversation with a friend, there may be constant distractions of "dings" from text messages. Whenever you have "a free moment," you may immediately feel compelled to check your phone and email messages.

Being in a state of chronic busyness, or even crisis, is sometimes compelling and addictive – when I've got fires to put out, I don't have time to figure out what life is all about. Technology and busyness can become a way to avoid unpleasant feelings. Now that we can be "online" 24 hours a day, 7 days a week, if a little loneliness creeps up, we can text someone or check our social networking site. We never fully feel sad, and therefore never fully feel happy. We feel increasingly estranged from ourselves, from others, and from the world we live in.

I am certainly not suggesting that we give up technology, only that we need to learn how to use it wisely rather than having it use us. I am in awe that I have written most of this book on a computer tablet smaller than a piece of paper, and thinner than the width of my pinky nail. My phone can pay my bills and balance my checkbook, find my exact global coordinates, create spreadsheets and documents, and tune my guitar.

We can even use technology to enhance our relationships. The bulk of my work with students and colleagues is done online. When I am traveling, my youngest daughter and I can see each other while I read bedtime stories to her. Through social networking sites, I have been able to stay connected to childhood friends I had almost forgotten. I have tens of thousands of emails in my inbox, from people all over the world (yeah, I need to delete some).

But technology can create shallow, unfulfilling relationships, especially if we overly rely on it, and don't spend enough time in direct face-to-face contact with others. Have you ever seen teens sitting at a table and texting without looking at each other? What about the literally thousands of "friends" many have on their social networking sites? When she was 13, my daughter could not understand why I was concerned that she was spending hours on video calls with a 25-year-old-man in Brazil that she had never met in person.

This constant distraction, push for productivity, and lack of fulfilling relationships produces a serious strain on our stress response system. What was meant to be a short-term burst to help us survive a threat from a wild animal becomes a continuous bath of stress chemicals that causes long-term damage to our bodies.

Even when we are sleeping, our minds don't get much rest. Sleep is vital to our health, but whether you remember them or not, our nights are full of dreams. When I was a teenager, I read about lucid dreaming, and became fascinated. If I could consciously participate in or control my dreams, I would get so much more accomplished! For many of us, our sleep is a deep blank, and when we wake up the next day, we remember little if anything about our dreams. Following the advice of some books I had read, I got in the habit of keeping a dream journal, though early on there were many entries which said, "I do not remember any dreams this morning." Over the course of a year, I found that I could easily write many pages about my dreams each morning, and just didn't have the time to write them all down. It was an odd feeling to recognize that my mind never got a break! Even while asleep, I was continuously having all kinds of strange adventures, working hard to solve unimportant problems, and having a multitude of interactions with nonexistent people. While we are dreaming, we take what we are doing so seriously, but when we wake up, we realize it was all in our minds.

Incidentally, I was able to lucid dream several times. In the dreams, I felt just as awake as I do now, but slipped back into regular dreaming after a few minutes. I then wondered, was I dreaming that I was awake? Am I really awake now? The wisdom traditions say that much of our lives are spent in a sort of sleepwalking state.

As Woody Allen keenly observed, "Ninety percent of life is showing up." Yet we are often absent from our own lives. When we are talking with someone, we might be thinking about what we are going to say next instead of listening. While we are eating, we might be ruminating about something that happened yesterday. We can get lost in our daydreams, and get worked up over things that are only taking place in our heads.

Have you ever had the experience of talking on the phone, and suddenly stopping to ask, "Hello? Are you there?" You may not have even consciously known why you stopped to ask that, you just had a sense that they were not really there. They may have said, "Yeah, I'm here," but you just knew they must have been checking their email or something. Have you ever had a healthcare provider who barely made eye contact, and dismissed your questions before you even finished asking them? Research shows that providers who make a conscious effort to practice mindfulness, or to be more present in their interactions, not only reduce their own stress, but produce better outcomes for their patients.[3]

We have all experienced being fully present, though it usually happens in extraordinary circumstances. You break out of old routines when traveling in exotic places, having a new experience, enjoying yourself in an amusement park, or holding hands with someone you love while watching shooting stars under the summer sky. Our brains are also designed to pay attention to and remember things that could be dangerous. If you've ever been in a car accident, you know that you can become so present that things seem to be happening in slow motion. You are also much more aware of your surroundings the next time you drive.

Of course, we have all experienced many other, less dramatic moments in which we felt fully present and alive. Watching a child smile and say, "I love you," listening to a song that gives you goose bumps, enjoying the taste of a good meal. Practicing mindfulness helps us more consistently notice the richness in our lives, and helps us navigate more wisely through the tough times.

Mindfulness is like falling in love with the moment, over and over again. Just being with the person you love is enough – you don't have to get something from them. When you look in their eyes, you feel as if you have all the time in the world, for you can sense eternity in that moment. And just as going through tough times brings you closer to the ones you love, staying present when things are difficult builds a sense of intimacy with all of our fellow human beings and the world around us, though we may not appreciate it at the time.

Sometimes when I talk about the benefits of mindfulness, I feel like a snake oil seller, stereotypically featured in Hollywood movies about the Old West. Wagons traveled through small towns and sold their healing "elixirs" (often simply containing mineral oil, alcohol, and traces of odds and ends) for exorbitant sums of money. Claims were made that the elixirs could cure everything from bunions to snake bites. The wagons then mysteriously vanished the next morning before their customers could give feedback on the effectiveness of the treatment.

Mindfulness has also been touted to help an amazing range of problems, like stress, addictions, anxiety, depression, chronic pain, cancer, eating disorders, heart disease, irritable bowel syndrome, stuttering, post-traumatic stress disorder, psoriasis, and psychosis, to name a few. And did I mention that mindfulness also increases positive emotions like happiness, empathy, and self-compassion?

How can this possibly be? Is mindfulness some kind of hypnosis where people think they're better? Is it all placebo effect?

The placebo effect is a very real phenomenon. Our bodies sometimes have the seemingly miraculous capacity to get better just because we think we can get better. Drug manufacturers who are testing new products must also secretly give some of the test subjects a pill containing plain sugar, or some other inert substance, and they often get better too. A popular cartoon shows a patient shopping at a pharmacy, trying to choose between bottles labeled "placebo" and "extra-strength placebo."

Yet, in hundreds of high-quality, randomized studies that control for the placebo effect, mindfulness still shows significant improvements not only for mental and physical problems like those listed above, but for such things as relationships and quality of life as well. This is not snake oil. It is not placebo effect. We can measure significant positive changes in the lives of those who practice mindfulness, and even see growth in important parts of their brains using medical scanners.

It seems that more effectively managing our emotions, especially the stress response, is one of the key reasons why mindfulness helps in so many areas. Up to 90 percent of problems that bring someone to a primary care physician have at least some stress-related component. Of course, stress alone does not cause a disease like bubonic plague to spring up out of nowhere. But it does two serious things – it can make you more vulnerable to getting diseases, and it can make any current conditions worse by interfering with your body's ability to defend and heal itself. If we experience too much ongoing stress, it will manifest in different ways for different people, sometimes physical, sometimes mental, sometimes both.

A friend of mine's father, a very practical and conservative man, at times would feel so overwhelmed by his stress that he would say, "Time to move to Tahiti and paint nudes." But most of us can't escape our work and family responsibilities.

The good news is that we can begin having a richer, more fulfilling life starting right now, even in the midst of a busy life. A theme of this book is how to develop mindful awareness as an integral part of our everyday lives. If this becomes another "thing to do," it produces more stress than it solves. By letting go of old habits, we can shift from surviving to living, from doing to being.

I will be sharing material transmitted for thousands of years from person to person, in addition to the latest scientific evidence for how and why mindfulness works. To make these concepts useful and practical, I will share classic examples as well as stories from my own life and from the lives of those whose journeys I have been privileged to share through my clinical work.

As a young teenager, I read books about the ninja with fascination. Stephen K. Hayes was the first Westerner to venture to Japan in the 1970s to train with the last living ninja grandmaster. As a nerdy kid who had been picked on, I wanted to learn to protect myself and others, and was fortunate to be able to train regularly with Mr. Hayes. His brilliant modern adaptation, To-Shin Do, emphasizes the self-development aspects of the ninja arts. Though the techniques themselves are very useful from a practical point of view, they also serve as models for coming to a deeper understanding of how struggle happens, how we get in our own way, and how resistance can make things worse. It is about developing sophisticated strategies for achieving goals, and about understanding relationships and interpersonal dynamics. Most of all, the art of the ninja is about the human mind.

Our minds are far more powerful than any physical techniques, and can also do far more damage to ourselves and others than any external attacker. Though I considered some of the teachings of the Asian wisdom traditions strange at first, once I delved into them I found them fascinatingly profound. I was fortunate enough to find teachers who could separate out the deeply interwoven cultural aspects from the universal principles of the teachings. Without really intending it, I was ordained into a 2,500-year-old lineage when I was only 21 years old, the age I also received a black belt in our 900-year-old ninja art.

Once I was perceived as a teacher, I felt that my meditation training had not prepared me adequately to work effectively with many of the problems of modern society. Students would sometimes pay me for private lessons, but spend much of the time talking to me about their personal problems and relationships.

Having always been fascinated by science, I eventually chose to get a doctorate in clinical psychology, as it was more socially acceptable at the time than "meditation instructor." I had also found therapy very helpful when I had gone through some tough times. In graduate school, I eagerly studied the wealth of research about how the brain and the mind work. Interestingly, even the most concrete, scientific findings began to confirm for me many of the things I had learned from the Asian wisdom traditions.

To my delight, solid research began pouring out on the effectiveness of mindfulness. Having a depth of experience and training in both mindfulness and psychology, I could integrate them in a synergistic way, and I have greatly enjoyed sharing the principles I have learned with others.

How about you? How did you come to be reading this book? What are you hoping to get? What do you want to bring into your life? What is important to you? I challenge you to be more than a passive reader – I hope you can use this material to enrich your own life, starting right now.

You don't have to go on faith. There is plenty of scientific evidence to support giving it a try, and your own experiences and results will be reinforcement enough.

Mindfulness is often used as a spiritual practice, and you can certainly apply the principles in this book toward that end. Because there are many other books written from that perspective, I will focus on the secular and practical applications. However, you may come to experience a broadening of your personal spirituality, in the sense of finding more meaning, and of having a greater feeling of connection to the world we live in. Even a deep study of physics and of the brain can lead to profound realizations about the nature of the universe, who we are, and how we and everything are interconnected. As Carl Sagan noted, "We are made of star stuff."[4] The minerals in our blood and bones were literally created by the stars. We need air, water, earth, and other people just as much as we need our hearts, brains, and skin. By paying attention, we can more often notice and internalize the insight that our very existence is due to the contributions of countless other beings and processes. We are so much bigger than we realize.

Such insights are hard to come by, however, when we are feeling overwhelmed by life stressors. Sometimes mindfulness is presented as all rainbows and light, and therefore alienates people who are truly suffering and have very difficult life circumstances. These are the people I work with the most, so throughout this book I will give very concrete and practical suggestions for using this material to get through tough times, in addition to discussing the positive benefits of living life more fully.

It is easy to talk about being in the moment if you are a monastic in a beautiful, serene setting. But is it possible to learn and practice in the full swing of modern urban technological busyness? Can it be done while working 80 hours per week, trying to pay all the bills, raising children, dealing with a relative with schizophrenia, and managing a teen with addiction problems? I am here to tell you that it is possible, and urgently needed. I myself have these things in my life, and I and other therapists work with a broad variety of people with problems that would make soap operas look boring.

I have done work in hospitals, clinics, prisons, office buildings, homes, universities, morgues, cornfields, factories, and temples. I have worked with thousands of individuals, and have seen literally every disorder in the diagnostic manual. I have worked with police and security officers, members of all branches of the military, veterans of wars, and high level business executives, in addition to "ordinary" people. I find that most people don't realize how extraordinary they really are.

I have welcomed children into this world, and watched loved ones die in front of me. I have had guns pointed at me, and have survived physical attacks. I have narrowly escaped my own death a few times, and have been able to save a few lives.

I say these things not to impress you, but to let you know that I am not approaching this material from a naive or purely theoretical perspective. The challenges in your life cannot be easily dismissed, and I will not give pithy platitudes as if those things alone could transform your suffering.

The older I get, the less need I have for extreme experiences, and the more I enjoy all the little moments that constitute my life. My typical days now consist of work and child care, but I find it vivid and fascinating, and feel blessed to have a career that both engages me and helps others. I find it magical to feel the wind on my face, to hear the sound of the laughter of my daughter, and to feel heartbeats when I hold the person I love in my arms.

While my life is far from perfect, practicing mindfulness has made it richer than I would have previously thought possible. I have learned to more fully embrace the joy, the sadness, the good fortune, and the tragedies. I increasingly appreciate that without the horrible things I have experienced, I would not so treasure the wonders and love I have also experienced.

Practicing mindfulness does not make all of your problems go away, and it will certainly not "cure" all of your ills, but it can help you be more clear about what is actually happening moment-to-moment. With increased awareness, you can make more conscious choices about how to respond instead of falling back into old, unhelpful patterns. Of course, it will take some dedication and work to undo a lifetime of engaging in habits that may no longer serve you.

Tell me, if you became a little more present in your life right now, if you suffered just a little less, if your relationships deepened just a little, if you moved just a little closer to the things you value in life, wouldn't it be worth a little effort?

In the next chapter, we will explore more about what mindfulness is. The practice is very simple, but very rich in how it can transform our moments.

2

What Is Mindfulness?

We are born with the ability to be fully in our moments, but we can grow out of if we get overly caught up in the world of thoughts.

About 2,500 years ago, in a region that is now known as Northern India/Southern Nepal, there lived a prince named Siddhartha Gautama. As in most parts of the world at that time, suffering and death were everywhere, and Siddhartha's father wanted to protect his son from these harsh realities. When he grew into a young man, Siddhartha surreptitiously ventured out into the villages surrounding his palace, and was stunned by the sickness, old age, and death that he saw. How could he enjoy the pleasures of the palace knowing that so many others were suffering? What was the point of living such a life if disease and death could take it all away without warning?

Siddhartha decided to seek out the spiritual teachers of his time, most of whom taught a practice known as absorption meditation (*shamatha* or *samadhi*). This is a very blissful state to achieve. Practitioners describe it as feeling "one with the universe."

Interestingly, researchers such as Newberg and D'Aquili[1] have scanned the brains of those in this absorptive state. In the parietal lobes of the brain, they found reduced activity in a place called the Orientation Association Area. Basically, the left side senses "this is my body," and the right side senses

Mindfulness: Living through Challenges and Enriching Your Life in This Moment, First Edition. Richard W. Sears.

"this is outside my body." Babies have a hard time telling the difference until these regions develop more fully. So, imagine what it would feel like if your brain literally could not tell the difference between what is "me" and what is "outside me." Through related processes involving the Attention Association Area in the frontal lobes, the brain loses its sense of time. When this state of absorption is interpreted as a feeling of being "one with the universe," it is a literal subjective description of the experience of infinity and timelessness the person is having.

The problem, as Siddhartha discovered, is that once you come out of this blissful state, the world itself hasn't changed. It is useful as a tool for relaxation, and for gaining a broader perspective, but if you have to live in the world and interact with people, it does not give you insights into how to manage your anger, how to interact in your relationships, and how to deal directly with all of the suffering in the world.

Siddhartha decided to move on to another spiritual practice of the time, that of asceticism. It was thought that the more one denied the physical body, the more spiritual one would become. After trying all manner of extreme practices involving pain and starvation, he found himself no closer to any state of realization. In the end, he adopted a middle way, seeking balance instead of only pleasure or deprivation.

Siddhartha promoted a practice known as *vipassana*, or *sati*, which has been translated as "mindfulness." Rather than escaping into a blissful state, it involves moving into each moment as it is, and paying close attention. Through this practice, Siddhartha felt more awake and alive, which is why he was called "Buddha," which means "awakened one."

Siddhartha never claimed to be anything more than a human being who wanted to share what he discovered. He told others not to take his word for it, but to try it out for themselves. For thousands of years, millions of people have been doing just that, and now modern scientists are using all kinds of instruments to test out why mindfulness works so well. I believe that Siddhartha would have been fascinated with our discoveries about the brain and psychological science.

Of course, mindfulness does not belong to any particular religion, scientific field, association, or person. Mindfulness is not something I or anyone else owns. You do not need to be worthy to have it bestowed upon you. It is not something you can get from reading this book, or transmitted from a sacred teacher, because you have this ability already. What teachers and books can do is inspire you to make this natural ability more conscious and more consistent.

As I am writing this, I can hear the ticking of a clock downstairs, in between the clacking of my keyboard strokes. I feel some tension in my neck and lower back, and the thought is arising that I should go sit at a desk rather than lounge in this recliner. I notice a slight tension building in my head as the brightness of the morning sunshine builds up, and I close my eyes and let go of my resistance to it. A thought pops up about a challenge my family is facing right now, and I feel my chest tighten. I allow that thought and that feeling to linger for a few moments. Now a bird is singing outside my window. I open my eyes, and a soft breeze carries autumn leaves to the ground in my yard. I can feel my chest relaxing, and a sense of peace begins to move through me.

You may be thinking, "I just don't get it – mindfulness is only paying attention more? Why an entire book on that? Why an entire chapter on saying what it is? How is this going to help me with all my stress?" Mindfulness is simple, but when you fully grasp these concepts, you will discover an amazing range of implications and applications. Before we can bring it into our lives consistently, especially in the most challenging circumstances, we first need to clarify what mindfulness is.

Though sometimes used interchangeably, mindfulness is a specific type of meditation. Any practice devoted to the development of the mind or mental processes can be called meditation. Though this seems to be changing, when many people hear that word, they still think of the bizarre practices that tend to get negative publicity in the media. Perhaps one of the reasons mindfulness began getting more scientific attention is that it carries less emotional baggage.

When I owned a martial arts school, our brochure mentioned that we offered "optional meditation classes." A potential student came in to watch a class, and found the warmth of the atmosphere and the people to be very inviting. He told me he was very interested in joining our school, "But I don't want to do any meditation," he added emphatically.

"That's fine," I said, "We practice exercises for developing concentration, increasing focus, working more wisely with our thoughts and feelings, fostering compassion for others, and clarifying our values, goals, and sense of identity."

"Wow, that sounds great!" he smiled, "But I don't want to do any meditation!" Which is of course what I was describing.

When I was growing up, I was once told in Sunday school that meditation is evil, because if you clear your mind, the devil will jump in there. Actually, every religious tradition has some form of contemplative practice, but I believe there is a good reason for the misconception I was told, regardless of your views about the malevolent force explanation. When you first begin sitting down to watch your own mind, you will be surprised at the number and variety of thoughts swirling around in your head. It can seem like it must be coming from somewhere else, especially the really strange, random ones. However, you come to discover that they have always been there, but you were only aware of a small percentage of them. That constant mental chatter, slightly beneath the surface of our awareness, has an enormous impact on our daily moods and behaviors.

A Definition of Mindfulness

There are many, many definitions of mindfulness, from a single word to paragraphs full of scientific jargon. The one I find most useful for its elegance, simplicity, and breadth comes from Jon Kabat-Zinn,[2] one of the leading pioneers in the field. In the 1970s, Jon and his colleagues created a program called Mindfulness-Based Stress Reduction (featured on Bill Moyer's series "Healing and the Mind"). This eight-week program, designed to systematically develop mindfulness skills, paved the way for reproducible, well-controlled scientific studies to demonstrate its effectiveness.

Jon defines mindfulness as "The awareness that emerges, through paying attention, on purpose, in the present moment, nonjudgmentally, to the unfolding of experience from moment to moment." Because of the richness of this definition, we will explore each piece in turn.

The awareness that emerges ...

The first part of this definition refers to the "waking up" quality of mindfulness, that experience of recognizing that we are in automatic pilot mode. We experience this on a daily basis. We are off in a fantasy in our minds and then someone asks, "Did you hear me just now?" Suddenly our awareness of where we are, who we are with, and what we are doing right now emerges. "I'm sorry, I was off somewhere else," we respond. "Could you repeat what you just said?"

If you stop right now and allow yourself to notice your own body, you may just become aware of some tension somewhere, perhaps in your neck or shoulders. If so, you probably didn't just now create it. It was likely there for a while, and you just became aware of it.

When beginners start practicing mindfulness, they may become frustrated when they notice how often their minds wander off, or how much time they spend daydreaming instead of staying present. However, we encourage them to celebrate when they notice their minds are wandering, for that is a moment of waking up.

... through paying attention ...

One of the key components of mindfulness, which can be strengthened through specific exercises, is learning to consciously choose more often where to place your attention.

My Zen teacher, Paul Wonji Lynch, once told me a story about the "tree-sitting monk." After retiring from teaching, a Zen master chose to spend his days sitting in a tree, enjoying the scenery. Due to his fame, people still sought him out, and sometimes managed to find him. One seeker asked, "Great Zen Master, what is the ultimate secret?" The teacher looked down at the seeker and said, "Pay attention." The seeker stood still for a moment, thinking that perhaps something profound was about to be said. After a few minutes, the seeker said, "Great Teacher, I mean what secret truth can you tell me that you have learned from all of your years of experience and practice?" The teacher leaned a little more toward the seeker and said, "Pay attention." Again, the seeker was confused. "But Great Teacher, I have been studying self-development for many years, and am already well-versed in the basic teachings. I was hoping you could share the wisdom of the deep insights you have attained, so that I, too, may find peace." The teacher kept his gaze on the seeker, and again said, "Pay attention."

Attention is the vehicle on which mindfulness rides. It is the only tool we have to be present in the moment.

We all know how difficult it is to be engaged in what we are doing when we are tired. In fact, a very important component of attention, and therefore of mindfulness, is arousal. People drink coffee, or consume other stimulants, in order to wake up and to pay more attention. Mindfulness is about tuning into, not dropping out of, our experiences. Jon Kabat-Zinn describes this as "falling awake,"[3] instead of drifting off into a sleep-like state. Although relaxation is often a pleasant side effect of paying attention to our experiences and choosing to let go of our internal struggles, it is not the primary goal. Because attention requires energy, it is not something you should necessarily engage in 100 percent of the time.

It is important to note that this energy refers to brain activity, not muscle tension. Wrinkling your forehead, gritting your teeth, and clenching your fists will not help your attention, and in fact are likely to distract you. As Alan Watts[4] observed, this is like a passenger in a jet plane becoming concerned that the plane may not be able to get off the ground before the runway ends, so begins lifting and straining at the seat to try to help get the jet off the ground. This does not help at all – it only tires the person out.

When I was teaching a course in neuropsychology, I came across some theories of attention which I found very applicable to understanding the attentional processes in mindfulness. Each of these types of attention involves different brain pathways. Knowing this helps neuropsychologists interpret their test results to figure out where the functional problems lie for individuals with brain damage. Sohlberg and Mateer's clinical model[5] describes five types of attention: focused, sustained, selective, alternating, and divided.

Focused attention is the ability to hone in on one specific thing through one of your five senses. It is choosing to notice what you see, hear, feel, smell, or taste in the moment. Some also consider proprioception, or the feeling of the positioning of your own body in space, to be another sense, and some traditions even consider thinking as a separate sense, so these too can be focused upon. As you read this, you are focusing your visual attention on these words.

Sustained attention, also known as vigilance, is the ability to keep your focus on what you want to pay attention to. In order to get anything out of what you are reading right now, you have to keep your attention on the words as they are strung together here. If your mind keeps wandering off, you will not be able to read.

Selective attention involves choosing what to pay attention to in spite of all the other things that could distract you or pull your attention away. As you read this, you have to choose to ignore the sounds of traffic or birds, the smell of food cooking, the sensations in your body, or other distractions in order to keep reading.

Alternating attention refers to the ability to flexibly shift between different senses and different objects of awareness at will. It involves letting go of something when you choose to, rather than being stuck on it. As you read this book, you are alternating your attention between noticing the ink on the page (or digital screen), the meanings of the words, how this material might apply to you, and maybe checking the clock or listening for your phone to ring.

Divided attention refers to our ability to pay attention to and to do multiple things at the same time. Right now as you read this, you might be watching television, walking on a treadmill, or eating, and possibly doing all four simultaneously. Most of us don't need more practice with this one, as it is not uncommon to listen to the radio, talk on the phone, and drink coffee while driving to work.

Mindfulness actually exercises and strengthens all of these forms of attention. For example, in a practice called the body scan, you systematically move your attention through your body. You first choose what part to attend to, like the toes of your left foot (focused attention). You then practice staying with whatever sensations you find there (sustained attention). When thoughts or sounds distract you, you practice bringing your attention back to your body (selective attention). If strong sensations are felt in other parts of your body, or strong emotions come up, or persistent thoughts arise, you can choose to move your attention between those things (alternating attention). You are also remembering how to do the exercise and what is coming up next as you are actually doing the exercise (divided attention).

We can also make a distinction between narrowly focused attention and broadly focused attention. Alan Watts[6] referred to this as "spotlight consciousness" and "floodlight consciousness." In computer terms, we can describe it as "serial processing" (one thing at a time) and "parallel processing" (multiple things at a time). Our thinking brain, as with most computers, processes things one at a time. However, our brains process far more than words, which is why the human brain is so much more complex than any computer. When driving, we are taking in and processing an enormous amount of information at the same time. We are looking at the road, monitoring our speed, adjusting pressure on the pedals, making small adjustments with the steering wheel, noticing other cars, watching for traffic signals, and so on. It is important to take it all in and not get overly focused on one thing.

On the other hand, if you are attending a lecture on quantum physics, and your goal is to learn something from it, you had better focus on what the instructor is saying, and not pay attention to the sounds in the hall, the clouds outside the window, or what the people around you are wearing.

Practicing mindfulness develops both of these types of attention as well. Sometimes we place our attention on one thing at a time, such as when we move our attention to different parts of our own body, and sometimes we stay aware of a bigger picture, such as being in our entire body. Sometimes we may focus our attention on something we are reading, and sometimes we stay present with all the things going on within and around us as we talk and walk through the park.

… on purpose …

This refers to the conscious aspect of mindfulness, of making a purposeful, deliberate choice about what to attend to and which type of attention to use. It is about intentionally breaking out of automatic pilot, about choosing to notice more often. It is about catching our automatic reaction patterns, asking ourselves what is most appropriate for the current situation, and then making a more conscious response. Mindfulness practice strengthens our ability to use purposeful intention, fostering our willingness to move toward what we value in life. Our emotions are important guides, but we become less pushed around by them.

In order to notice anything, we have to choose to do so on purpose. Mindfulness is about noticing, and discovering that in fact we often have many more choice points in our moments that we usually recognize.

Even after all these years, I can be surprised at the power of purposefully coming back to the moment. Just this morning, after taking my 3-year-old to school in the rain, and trying to carry too much in from the car, I spilled her cup of breakfast cereal all over the floor of the garage, with the cup rolling under the car on dirty, wet concrete. I automatically reacted with a feeling of frustration and a sarcastic thought of "Oh, great!" But as I stood there for a moment, unable to move without stepping and crushing the cereal, I recognized that in that moment, the reality was just breakfast cereal on the floor. I realized how easily I could have slipped into a mode of, "This is going to be a bad day," which would then bleed over into my other activities and interactions. I simply bent down and picked them up one at a time. It actually turned out to be a very simple activity. By choosing to first pause, I recognized that all the frustration had only been in my mind.

Of course, we all have events, often daily, that are far more challenging than spilling cereal, but the principle is the same. We can purposefully choose to stop and look at what is actually going on in the moment. It is far easier to deal with difficult situations without automatically adding in harsh mental ideas and judgments. And it is a much better model to demonstrate for children.

We may also begin to notice how often we automatically go along with the expectations of other people. A friend of mine was once asked to pull forward when she was in a fast-food drive-through. Inspired by her husband's crusade of not sheepishly going along with such a request, which is often only done so they can lower their "time in line" statistics, she simply said, "No thank you." The stunned server hesitated for a moment, then made her beverage. Feeling victorious after her initial feeling of discomfort in not conforming to the social norm, my friend drove away, though she purposely decided to throw the drink away in case any special ingredients were added.

Salespeople are trained to take advantage of our automatic reactions. Telemarketers know that it is not polite to hang up on someone who calls you. It actually took me years to realize, "Hey, wait, you called me and interrupted my life, so I'm not going to feel rude about saying, 'no thank you' and hanging up." Actually, I did feel a little bad for the person calling me the first few times, but it passed. When I shared this insight with a friend, she also pointed out that I don't have to answer the phone just because it rings.

Something I have found of enormous importance is the choice of investigating intense thoughts and feelings versus letting them go. In the monastic traditions of many cultures, one was required to give up money, romantic relationships, and material goods to cultivate spiritual development. If strong thoughts or feelings arose, one would typically practice letting them go and returning to the breath, image, or words one was using in one's practice.

However, for those of us with active relationships and life commitments, when persistent thoughts and feelings keep arising, we can choose more purposefully to investigate them or let them go. There may be something important to learn from them, or they may be old past patterns that are no longer useful in the current situation.

I once had a participant named Joy in one of my mindfulness groups tell me that she really valued her alone time on her drive to work, and didn't really want to practice mindfulness during that time. She felt that her drive allowed her to just freely think about things. Of course, I told her that the choice was hers. The next class, she said, somewhat tongue-in-cheek, "Darn this awareness! I realized that as I was driving, my mind really wasn't wandering creatively. I was worrying about all the things I had to do at work, planning out what I would say if someone said this or that, and thinking about all the things I hoped wouldn't happen that day. I was actually getting myself worked up over things that hadn't even happened yet, and maybe wouldn't happen at all!" By choosing to check in on her thinking, Joy noticed that she was becoming anxious and irritated before she even walked through the door. After becoming aware of this pattern, she could decide whether or not she wanted to continue doing that, address the underlying anxiety, refocus on her driving, or think about something more helpful.

Thinking is of course not a bad thing. It is compulsive thinking that tends to create problems. You may well have an important meeting that you are mentally preparing for on your way in to work, so you can purposefully notice and decide if your thinking is helpful, or if it is just old repeated patterns of worry. The next time you notice you are worrying or ruminating, you can ask yourself, "Am I thinking this on purpose, or out of habit?" You can then choose whether to ponder it, do something about it, or let it go. How do you let go of thoughts and feelings that have you intensely hooked? By recognizing in the moment that they are likely symptoms of something going on within you. We will come back to that topic later.

Of course, one of the biggest challenges is remembering to remember to pay attention. Interestingly, the Sanskrit, Chinese, and Japanese words that are used for mindfulness also imply "remembrance." All of us can break out of automatic pilot when prompted. How fast are you breathing right now? You probably weren't consciously aware of it until I asked. The trick is, how do you remember to remember to check into this moment?

In the beginning, it is helpful to use prompts to remind yourself to be present. I once had a student who found a "mindfulness bell" program for her phone, which sounds a pleasant chime at random moments throughout the day. She said she often found herself hoping it would go off, looking forward to getting back in touch with the moment. Of course, I laughed, and told her teasingly that there was no need to wait for the bell! We can choose to get in touch with the moment whenever we like.

You could put this book down right now, and ask yourself what you are experiencing in your body, emotions, and thoughts. You can check in with all five of your senses and pay attention to what is going on in this moment.

You may also find it helpful to set up little reminders around your home or workplace, things that have personal significance to trigger more presence for you. It could be pictures of nature, inspirational notes, stimulating aromas, or a piece of jewelry.

Just as we can develop the habit of getting lost in our heads, we can develop a habit of tuning in to this moment more often. This requires consistent practice. Developing this new habit will seem artificial at first, but in fact, many of our habits of tuning out our experiences and grabbing onto old patterns are unnatural. Rather than gaining something, mindfulness is more

Hawaiian beach. © Olivia Ossege.

about letting go of things that get in our way, and becoming more natural once again.

Thirty years ago, when I first began studying the martial art of To-Shin Do, I thought I was pretty good at punching, and wanted to learn the "fancy" stuff. However, it quickly became obvious that I had a lot of bad habits. When my teacher watched me punch, he gave me a number of very helpful suggestions. "If you lower your elbow, your bone alignment will make the delivery more solid." "If you bend your knees, more of your body weight will be behind the strike." "If you line up your first two knuckles with your wrist, it will prevent you from hurting your hand." "Don't forget to exhale as you move." "Keep your back straight and head up so you can change your direction more quickly." "Try to let go of extraneous motions that might warn your opponent that you are about to move." "Don't tense your muscles too much or you will slow yourself down." "Be sure to push through the target." "Allow your arm to relax naturally so you'll be ready for whatever comes next." Literally hundreds of other suggestions came as I progressed.

The more I trained, the more I learned, and the worse I felt about my ability to punch. I became overly self-conscious, and my movements became awkward as I tried to remember everything. But eventually, the movements became very natural. I didn't have to think about them. I realized that I had been holding on to old bad habits that interfered with natural body movement. I had been relying on muscle and force instead of body weight, timing, and positioning.

In learning new habits, it may be helpful to know that we first learn movements in the thinking parts of the brain (known as the cortex), then, over time, internalize them into the lower parts (known as the basal ganglia). This is why consistent practice is necessary. Knowing this can inspire you not to give up too soon, and to be kind to yourself when you fall back into old habits without consciously knowing why.

Choosing to do things more often on purpose does not mean trying to control everything with our thinking (which is impossible anyway). Thinking is only one aspect of who we are. This is why when we become too self-conscious we get in our own way. When you are giving a presentation in front of a lot of people, or if you are around someone you find very attractive, you may feel awkward, because you are not just interacting, you are monitoring your own interaction. There have been a number of times where I have been playing guitar for a crowd of people, having a great time, and then I think, "Wow, I haven't played this well in a long time. I hope I don't forget how to play this song!" at which point I inevitably make a mistake.

Most people find it surprising to hear that research shows that the thinking brain is at least half a second behind reality. Our senses perceive reality, then thoughts arise. It can be an odd experience to realize that our thinking is not in the present moment, but usually a little bit behind what is going on around us.

… in the present moment …

So, if my thoughts are at least half a second behind reality, what is going on in this moment? The answer is very simple. What do you see? What do you hear? What do you feel? What do you smell? What do you taste?

One of our gifts as human beings is the ability to think abstractly. Learning from the past and anticipating the future give us a tremendous survival advantage. But if we have too much of this good thing, if we live in the past or continuously worry about the future, we may find it difficult to shift from surviving to thriving.

You can and should make plans for the future. But are you doing it compulsively? Are you constantly thinking about the future, which you can never fully prepare for anyway? Are you choosing to think about it, or are you compulsively trying to avoid feeling anxious or nervous?

Planners and to-do lists are wonderful tools, but can also create problems if not used well. I remember an important breakthrough I once had. When I looked at my planner, I saw that I had ten back-to-back meetings in one day, and it created a feeling of being overwhelmed. But the truth is, even though I was looking and thinking about all ten in that moment, I would only be in one meeting at a time. Each of those meetings would be unfolding only one moment at a time. I can just practice being in each now moment. I don't have to carry the entire day all day long.

The future that we long for, or fear, will be just another now.

Likewise, the past that we pine for, or regret, can only exist in memory. Some moments we want to hold on to – special times with loved ones, meaningful experiences that we want to cherish. We can certainly choose to savor memories, to enjoy the feelings they bring up, and to learn from the past. We could even choose to dwell there, but we will notice the tradeoff is a loss of quality of the moment we are in now.

We spend so much time dragging the past around, and trying to control the future. The truth is that we can't change them in this moment, and the constant attempts to do so only wear us out. We can learn from the past without becoming bogged down in it. We can plan for the future without being captured by thoughts about it.

Some of us define who we are by the past, by what we've accomplished or who we used to be, or by the future, by who we hope to one day become. It might be scary to loosen those anchors and ask ourselves who we are right now.

But this is also good news. We can keep the past as a reference point, but decide where to go in this moment. We are more like boats than trains on a track. We can see the past trailing away like the wake of a ship, but we don't have to keep going in the same direction. We can determine our life's compass heading right now.

Of course, the big joke is that you can't get out of this moment. Go ahead and try. Where else could you go? When else could you be? Even when you are thinking about the past and the future, you are doing it right now. Problems arise when we live in our thoughts, or over-identify with them, and confuse them with reality. Our thoughts are only one aspect of our present moment experience.

The practice of mindfulness is about starting fresh again in every moment, moment after moment. Where is your mind right now?

… nonjudgmentally …

I find this to be one of the most challenging things for those learning mindfulness. We habitually make continuous comparisons of how things are with how they "should" be. As with thinking, judgment is of course not a bad thing, but can get us in trouble when it's done compulsively. While I am judging, I am moving away from the moment. If right now you are thinking, "This author is okay, but I really wish I could be reading a better book right now," you will probably not get as much out of reading this. If while you are kissing your partner, you think, "This kiss isn't as good as the one I had last week," you are not feeling it as much. If you are watching a sunset, and think, "It's about time the weather became nice – it was awful how cloudy it was yesterday!" you will not fully experience the beauty of that sunset.

Judgments are of course important. We need to pay attention to what choices we need to make, what is helpful and not helpful for us, and what impact our behaviors have on ourselves and others. But few of us recognize how automatically we judge almost everything. We can't stop thoughts and judgments from arising, but we can learn that we don't have to automatically entertain them all when they show up. By noticing them more consciously, we can decide if they are important or if we want to set them aside to more fully engage with what we are experiencing in the moment. They don't completely go away, but with practice, they block the view less often.

Why is this so important? As the saying goes, we often judge a book by its cover, and therefore don't really know the truth about it. If I tell myself, "My back is killing me, and I can't stand it!" these are thoughts and judgments, and cause us to push away the experience. If I notice, "There is tension in my lower back, radiating out to my kidneys, with warm areas pulsating slowly, and a butterfly feeling in my stomach," I have opened up my experiences and know more directly what is going on, allowing me more informed choices about what to do next.

Interestingly, even positive judgments sometimes get in the way. While I'm telling myself how great a job I'm doing, I'm not as focused on what I'm doing. While I'm thinking about how much better this sunrise is than the one I saw yesterday, I'm not seeing this one as clearly. If I'm trying to feel myself feeling happy, I'm not fully present in my happiness.

Most insidiously, we often compulsively make judgments about ourselves. We can be our own harshest critics.

Our internal judgments often come from the voices of others. "A proper little girl should … ," "Good little boys mustn't … ," "You'll never amount to anything unless you … " One of my clients felt she was being "self-righteous" whenever something good happened to her. She eventually realized that this came from a family who put down anyone who achieved anything in their attempts to not feel bad about themselves. Noticing this helped her let the judgments go, so she could more fully enjoy the things she had worked so hard for.

Setting aside judgments helps us notice our experiences as they are. "I can't do this right!" is a judgment that shuts down further exploration. "My attention keeps wandering to memories of the argument I had yesterday, my shoulder muscles are tight, and my body feels tired all over" is noticing, which moves us into the present moment and opens up possibility.

Judging is our attempt to categorize or push away our experiences. Mindfulness fosters attitudes of inquiry, curiosity, wonder, and openness, which allow us to turn toward, or move into our experiences. We can practice giving ourselves permission to feel what we are feeling. We learn to become kind to ourselves. When sadness comes, we allow ourselves to feel it, and it passes. When happiness comes, we enjoy it, and let it go when it too passes. Of course we can plan to set up our lives with the conditions that foster more joy, but we learn to drop the struggle with feelings that are already here.

Ironically, even during mindfulness practice, we often "should" all over ourselves, as the late Albert Ellis would say. In formal practice, you are likely to find your mind wandering. "I'm daydreaming! I should be more focused! Wait, I just judged myself! I shouldn't do that. Oh no, I just judged my judging! Darn it, now I'm judging my judgments about my judgments!" This is why fostering an attitude of wonder is important. "Ah, isn't it interesting that judgment is here." Then you simply return your awareness to where you want it to be, as best you can. In all of this, I find a sense of humor is crucial, as it allows space for our feelings. It may sound strange at first, but you can even foster an attitude of "How curious, I am noticing that I am so angry that I'm having a thought of smashing my phone right now." Curiosity and exploration help counter habits of clinging onto our experiences too tightly or of compulsively pushing them away.

Learning to more often let go of compulsive judgments allows us to treat others, and ourselves, with more kindness and compassion as we move through our days.

… to the unfolding of experience from moment to moment.

This last part of the definition highlights the active component of mindfulness. It is not about stopping time or withdrawing from the world, it is about fully engaging with it as part of an active flow, recognizing the freshness of each moment as it springs into existence.

I have heard that if you exercise regularly, you will live ten years longer. However, if you count up all the time you spend exercising, it adds up to about ten years. While telling people this usually gets a laugh, no one has ever told me, "Well, in that case, I'll stop exercising!" The point of exercise is to feel more alive and more healthy in all the moments of your daily life. Likewise, the point of formal mindfulness practice is to exercise your mind, so that you can be more aware and present in your daily moments.

Only practicing being present in a formal meditation posture is like a musician who only practices scales, or a martial artist who can only perform a technique if the attack is prescribed in a certain way (and I've actually heard martial artists say "you attacked me wrong").

My martial arts training again provided a very concrete lesson in moment-to-moment awareness. At first, we practiced very specific techniques against very specific attacks, like a straight punch to the face. Then, we added simple in-the-moment decision making. The attacker could randomly punch straight in with either a right or a left punch. Over time, you learn to sense which side is coming. Then the punch could come in as a swinging punch, hooking around, which requires a different defense. At this point, the need for moment-to-moment awareness increases even more, as you could end up worse off if you move the wrong way for the wrong kind of attack. You learn how to detect if it will be a straight or hooking punch by the attacker's body positioning and movement. Gradually more attacks are added, until you learn to stay present for all of them, even ones by sophisticated attackers who are trying to feign one thing while they come in with something different.

The biggest challenge is in staying present moment to moment, and not overly anticipating the next thing or getting stuck in the past. If in my mind, I think, "Okay now, if he attacks with a high, hooking, right punch, I'll do this cool throw, and if he ... " I will get hit, as I'm not paying attention to what he is doing now. If I then think, "Oh, I should have been paying better attention! I should never have allowed that left to sneak in on me, I should've ... " I will get hit again. If I somehow manage to get his arm into a textbook perfect arm bar, but he then steps in a way that changes the angle and leverage, I have to realize that I am now in another new moment, and either make adjustments of my own or let it go and do something else.

It takes a lot of trust to stay in the moment, especially in ourselves. It is very seductive to think that it is better to keep slipping into the past or the future. Of course, after the encounter, I can reflect on what I've learned, or I can plan areas for future growth. But it is crucial to learn to recognize what is most appropriate for the situation I find myself in, moment to moment. Getting out of one's own way takes a lot of practice.

The more I was able to consistently stay present as things unfolded, the more seemingly "magical" things would happen. After many years of training, I became able to allow attackers to think they were winning, then use that against them at the last possible moment. I have learned to trust that whatever happens, I'll find a way to flow with it. What's the alternative? Worrying about it constantly?

Have you ever been talking with someone, and you were so busy thinking about what you wanted to say, that you were not listening to what they just said? Then you get busy trying to figure out the last thing they said, or debating internally whether or not you should just nod your head and hope it wasn't important, or if you should embarrass yourself by telling them you weren't paying attention. We have to trust ourselves that we can listen to the other person and not completely forget something important we need to say.

Of course you may have very good reasons for having trouble paying attention. You may be in an important job interview, or you may be feeling overwhelmed, or you may have something going on in your brain. You may need to do things like writing down a list of points to say. In any case, trying to anxiously remember to remember will not likely be helpful, and you cannot grab onto or stop time with your thinking.

In a sense, time doesn't really pass. A movie is actually composed of individual pictures that capture individual moments, but when you watch them sequentially, everything on the screen appears to be moving. Likewise, we are in this moment, then this moment, then this moment, and our brain creates the illusion of continuity. If you want to enjoy the movie, whether a comedy, musical, drama, or tragedy, it is important not to jam up the projector.

Similar to my martial training, in formal mindfulness practice, we start off staying present with one thing, like watching the breathing. We then practice moving our attention through our bodies. As our attention strengthens, we can attend to more subtle things, like sounds and thoughts. We then practice being aware moment to moment, through activities like stretching and walking. But by far the most important practice is integrating this quality of awareness into our daily activities.

Many people in my mindfulness groups choose tooth brushing as an initial moment-to-moment mindfulness practice, since it is something most of us do regularly. How often have you been in a rush and brushed your teeth so fast that as you were running out the door you had to stop and ask yourself, "Wait a minute, did I brush my teeth this morning?" Maybe you even ran your tongue along your teeth to see if you could taste the toothpaste.

If you choose to brush your teeth mindfully, you will discover that there are a lot of things going on. Even picking up the brush and reaching for the knob on the faucet requires sophisticated muscle coordination. Your hand squeezes the knob with just the right amount of pressure from your fingertips as you move it until the water begins to flow. A hissing sound begins as the water falls into the sink, bubbling, sparkling, splattering, and swirling around before going down the drain. A watery smell wafts up to your nose, and perhaps you sense a slight change in air temperature on your hand and arm. You feel the sensations in the muscles of your arm as you place the brush under the water and feel the pressure pushing onto the bristles, splashing over the fibers as gravity pulls it down against the barrier the brush has created …

Paying attention in this way does not necessarily mean that every single activity like taking out the garbage will become some kind of cosmic, sacred experience, although you might begin to notice that from time to time. Practicing staying present brings a richer quality of experiencing into more of the moments in our day-to-day lives, whether we are walking, having a conversation, eating, working, or making love. Then, even when we are very distressed, we will have practice in staying present, processing the experience, and letting it flow. Traditionally, there are four meditation postures: standing, walking, sitting, and lying down. In other words, we can do this anytime, anywhere, moment after moment.

Just this moment

So, putting that entire definition back together again, mindfulness is "the awareness that emerges, through paying attention, on purpose, in the present moment, nonjudgmentally, to the unfolding of experience from moment to moment."

You may be starting to see how simple yet profound this is. It really all boils down to noticing. That's all. In order to notice you have to purposefully pay attention, and awareness emerges. Everything you can possibly notice, including thoughts and judgments, exists in the present moment, and you notice how it all arises and passes away.

Just this moment.

In this space, you can choose to engage more fully in your life, whether you are facing horrible difficulties, embracing a loved one, or going about your day at work.

If this still doesn't make perfect sense to your thinking brain, that's quite all right. The more we explore the meaning and implications of mindfulness, and practice it in our lives, the more it will sink in, regardless of our word brain's capacity to understand.

Acceptance

The concept of mindfulness is intertwined with the concept of acceptance. The only way we can be fully present in the moment is to accept this moment as it is. This is often misunderstood. It means learning to accept the reality of each moment just the way it is, in order to let go of our internal struggles with it. It does not mean that we always like the way things are, or that we won't do everything in our power to change it in the next moment, but we can't change anything if we don't first accept the reality of it.

Alan Watts[7] told a story that illustrates how we don't like to accept where we are when we have a problem. A man was once lost in the English countryside. He eventually went up to a local and asked for directions to the town he was looking for. The local scratched his head and replied, "Well sir, I do know the way, but if I were you, I wouldn't start from here!"

Too often we are trying to start from a place other than the one in which we find ourselves. We want to be courageous after we've gotten some courage, we want to be more peaceful after we've found some peace, and we want to love after we've become more loving. We work hard to push away the past, the oftentimes horrible abuses we've suffered. We want to fix all of our problems before we move forward with our lives. However, if we cannot accept where we are currently, we will never find our way.

We waste so much time and energy wishing for things to be other than the way they are. We long for, regret, or grieve some past for which we selectively remember things, or that we recreate differently in our minds. Or we escape the reality we are in with the hope that all of our current work and suffering will be rewarded in a more peaceful and perfect future.

Acceptance is very difficult for the tragic things in our lives, such as childhood abuse, death of family members, and lack of resources. If you were abused, it was a horrendous thing to endure. It was not fair, and should never have happened. Those who loved you should have done something to prevent it or stop it. You may even try to convince yourself it wasn't that bad, or that somehow it was your own fault – which is our brain's constant attempt to make sense of things through comparisons and judgments. You can always think up worse scenarios, and sometimes that can be helpful. But if you have survived tragic circumstances, be kind to yourself, allow yourself to have the feelings (which it might not have been safe to have during the bad experiences), and let them flow through you.

If horrible things did happen, and we spend the rest of our lives wishing it had never happened, we will be missing our chances for a new life. Acceptance is starting fresh in this moment. We can feel the hurts from the past, which will come and go but probably never completely go away, and still choose where we want to go from here.

A woman once came to me for therapy, saying, "My partner doesn't treat me very well. I need to learn to accept it more." This is not at all the meaning of acceptance as we are using it here. It does not mean that you need to be okay with anything that anyone does to you, as if you were above the drama of the mundane world.

Perhaps what this woman really meant to say was, "Even though I don't want it to be true, and I keep hoping it will change, my partner is treating me very badly right now. I want to learn to accept that I really am in a bad relationship, because I do not want to admit it to myself. I kept believing that I could do something to change him, maybe by saying just the right thing to make him understand. I need help accepting how bad things are so I can decide what to do about this relationship."

It may well be true that you should not be where you are. It may not be fair. You may not deserve it. It may not be your fault at all. However, the only way to get to where you are going is to start from where you are.

Acceptance also involves acknowledging that suffering is a natural part of life, and you will not always be able to avoid it. The good news is that you can live a fulfilling life even with suffering in it.

The last thing we want to hear when we are suffering is how much we will grow from it. Yet, with time, and acceptance of the fact that it really did happen, as awful as it might have been, we can often find some gems. I would not have become a martial artist had I not been bullied growing up. I never would have become a psychologist, and written this book, had I not gone through a horrible relationship years ago. Of course, we should never use this as an excuse to hurt others, because "it's good for them." I once knew someone who called herself a "karma doler," who felt it her job to make the lives of other people difficult so they could grow. The world already has enough suffering in it. We don't need to create more.

Of course, the things we do to our children may sometimes seem horribly cruel from their point of view. "Why can't I watch TV until midnight? I don't feel tired!" "Candy tastes delicious, why can't I eat only candy for three meals a day?" Kids often don't appreciate those lessons until they are older.

After we learn to accept a difficult situation, we can open up to a new sense of freedom. Joy, the client I mentioned earlier, had been in a bad relationship for seven years. She continuously thought about how she could make things better. If only she could think it through, then she would know just what to say and just what to do to influence him to make the effort to improve their relationship. A very intelligent woman, she spent almost all of her free moments thinking about this.

One day, Joy was cleaning out old emails. She actually found messages she had sent to this man almost seven years earlier, near the beginning of their intimate relationship. She was stunned to see that she basically had the exact same thoughts then that she was currently having. Seven years of thinking had not changed anything. Seeing these thoughts so concretely in front her, she was able to begin to let go of them. Joy realized the thinking was her way of distracting herself, a way of staying with the all-too-familiar, low-grade feeling of depression. She didn't want to feel the intense grief of losing the relationship, didn't want to face the fear of being alone, and didn't want to accept a deeply held fear that she might be unworthy of love.

Accepting the reality of the relationship allowed Joy to let go of it and fully grieve its loss. It was one of the hardest things she had ever done, but she came out on the other side with much more freedom and integrity.

Ironically, your desire to read this book and "fix" some of the problems in your life may be a manifestation of wanting to avoid negative feelings. Or maybe your quest for a richer life is a subtle way to escape from problems that you don't want to accept are real. This is only natural, as no one wants to feel bad. If you say, "I'm accepting my feelings – why aren't they going away now?!," you're not really accepting your feelings. If unpleasant feelings are here, acceptance helps us to drop the struggles we may be having with them, so we can respond wisely rather than make things worse. After all, they are your own feelings. Why battle with yourself?

My first ninja teacher, Robert Johnson, taught me the power of acceptance in a couple of dramatic and memorable ways. Once he knew I was a serious student, he began randomly hitting me at unpredictable times, in unpredictable places. At first, it would be while we were standing in the classroom. Suddenly, with no warning, a full speed strike would hit my body, most often in the stomach, knocking my breath out for a few moments. He would simply smile and say, "So that in the end, there is no such thing as surprise for the ninja." Fortunately, my teacher had the skill and compassion to never cause any permanent damage to my body, but the physical sting and the mental embarrassment were pretty powerful. I took the lesson to mean that I needed to constantly be prepared, vigilant, and ready for anything. (In fact, Mr. Johnson nicknamed me "Ready," as when I began training I always came in with a friend, and he would say "Well, here come Rough and Ready." The first time I came alone, I voiced that I preferred the latter appellation.)

However, it did not take me long to realize that I could not possibly be vigilant at all times. My teacher would strike at random, sometimes even in public places outside of training. The harder I tried to be ready and defend, the more locked up I became.

After a while, something amazing happened. I told myself, "There is nothing I can do. He's just going to hit me." When I stopped trying, when I simply accepted that there was nothing I could do, I relaxed and became more fluid. Instead of tensing up and becoming frozen, I became more able to gently absorb the strike or let it roll off my body. That was a major turning point in my training.

I later learned that this was a very traditional approach to sword training in Japan. Someone who wanted to learn the art of the sword would live with the teacher, doing household chores. The teacher would randomly attack the student with a bamboo sword, and the student was expected to use pots, pans, towels, or whatever was on hand to defend. As the students tried to predict when the attacks would come, they were typically hit from behind, because it takes time to let go of the anticipated action and planned response and prepare for something else. Eventually, the students gave up, realizing there was nothing they could do but get hit. Once they reached that point, the teacher allowed them to begin training with the sword.

Though it may sound cruel in reading about it (as if the above story wasn't bad enough), another dramatic thing Mr. Johnson did also helped me to let go of internal struggle. After become proficient at falling to the ground safely, he had me stand in front of him, with a padded mat behind me on the ground. He would then smile and say, "Close those beady little eyes." I would then wait, sometimes only a few seconds, sometimes several minutes. Then he would throw a quick stomp kick right to my stomach. If I was relaxed, I could flow back with it, roll on the ground, and come back up on my feet. If I was tense, it would hurt a lot more, and I would be more likely to hit the mat with a thud. In the beginning, the anticipation was the hardest part. Knowing I was going to be hit with a kick from a black belt, but not knowing when, was quite anxiety producing. But again, I eventually learned that the anticipation did nothing to make the situation better, and in fact my resistance made it even worse. By accepting things as they were, I could be more present, and therefore better able to deal with whatever came at me.

As a concrete training exercise, it was invaluable to me, though I would not recommend it to most. Of course, later, I realized that the most advanced training is about not being there at all, and not putting myself in a position that makes me a target.

When teaching mindfulness, I do an exercise that leads to the same concept, but with less risk of physical injury. I have a pair of small brass cymbals, called *tingsha*, that are used for practicing mindful listening. They produce amazing harmonies and overtones, which provide a rich sound experience. Also, as the reverberations fade, thoughts often become quiet as well. Unlike bowl gongs, which produce a mellow sound, these brass cymbals emit a sharp, piercing tone, designed to arouse and awaken the attention. The sound can be quite jolting. Students often find themselves anticipating when the next ring will come. Noticing anticipation, they begin to see how it shows up in their thoughts, emotions, and body sensations. They begin to recognize how anticipation and expectation can interfere with direct perception. Eventually, they learn to stay present and observe all these processes without getting overly caught up in them.

Those who practice acceptance through formal meditation often reach a point where they have a profound feeling that everything is perfect just as it is. However, this description is not very appealing to those whose lives have been, or currently are, full of horrible traumas and tragedies. This experience is probably better described as a radical acceptance of the moment, a realization that things are as they are, and a letting go of internal struggle and resistance. Interestingly, the word that is often translated as "perfect" comes from the Sanskrit word *samyak*. This word is related to the English word "sum," meaning total or complete. So, to describe it another way, we can come to experience moments in which everything feels complete.

Four Foundations of Mindfulness

There are four areas that serve as foundations for developing mindful awareness. These four are inter-related, and affect each other, but we can learn to uncouple them, giving us a number of footholds to work from when we might otherwise get overwhelmed by a problem. Awareness of all four also allows us to engage more fully the entire range of human experiencing into more of our moments.

1. Mindfulness of body sensations

With the notable exceptions of people like dancers, athletes, martial artists, and yoga practitioners, most of us don't pay that much attention to our bodies, unless we're in pain or feeling really good. As James Joyce wrote in *Dubliners*, "Mr. Duffy lived a short distance from his body." Some of us live our lives almost entirely in our heads, and don't relate much to our physicality.

Choosing to get more in touch with our physical bodies can provide us with very important data. Go ahead and check in with your own body right now, performing a quick scan from your head to your toes. What sensations are you noticing? Is there any pain in your body? Are you noticing any muscle tension? Are there areas that feel warm or cold? What places feel relaxed or neutral?

I once did an exercise like this with a large audience, and someone raised her hand at the end and said, "Thanks a lot! I didn't notice before that my toe was hurting, and now it hurts a lot!" I told her that her toe had been hurting whether or not I asked her to notice it. Now that she was aware it was hurting, she could choose to take off her shoe, stretch it, massage it, take a pain reliever, or go back to ignoring it.

We often don't notice how much tension we hold in our bodies. We do things like furrowing our brows to concentrate, when this has nothing to do with concentration. A few days ago, I had a procedure done at the dentist. As I felt the pain in my tooth, heard the sound of grinding from the drill, and smelled burnt enamel, I noticed that my entire body was tense. This is a natural stress reaction – our bodies do this to prepare to fight or flee. However, if this is happening throughout the day, the tension gradually builds up, and we end up with a sore back or a headache at the end of the day. Stopping to notice can help prevent this cascade of tension from occurring.

The signals our bodies are telling us can be very important. I knew someone with diabetes who did not pay attention to his feet, which became infected, and eventually needed to be amputated. He later died because he was either unaware of or kept ignoring what his body was telling him.

People I work with sometimes tell me they don't feel anything when they begin to practice noticing their bodies, especially in certain areas. This is partially due to the fact that nerve sensors are in different concentrations in different body areas. Your lips, hands, and genitals, for instance, have lots of nerve endings. You back and thighs have relatively few. The other factor at play here is that nerve connections diminish when they are not used very often, just as you begin to lose muscle mass when you stop exercising. However, with practice, your brain will strengthen your sensory pathways and grow new ones.

Very often, I can feel a cold coming on several days before the major symptoms show up. My body just doesn't feel quite right as my immune system is fighting "behind the scenes." This allows me to take action, like getting more rest and taking vitamin C and zinc, which can often ameliorate or even prevent a full cold from coming on.

As we gain experience in noticing our physical sensations, we can become more aware of our emotional states.

2. Mindfulness of feelings

We are seldom given much education on emotional intelligence in school. In fact, many cultures pressure people not to show any emotion in public. This unawareness and denial makes it difficult for many of us to really know how we are feeling, unless the feeling gets very strong.

How are you feeling right now? Happy? Sad? Bored? Irritated? Tired? Not much at all? When I asked you that question, how did you decide? What information did you base your decision on?

All of our emotions will manifest in some way with a physical sensation in our bodies. If you cannot find one right now, either you are having trouble noticing it, or you may be confusing an emotion with a thought.

Most people gauge their emotions through a combination of body sensations and thoughts. In one classic experiment,[8] a woman was seen as more attractive when she gave men a survey on a shaky suspension bridge, in contrast to when she was on a solid bridge. The men interpreted their increased heart rate as sexual attraction.

In another well-known experiment,[9] subjects were given a shot of adrenaline (which they were told were vitamins), and asked to sit in a waiting room. A confederate (someone who is pretending to be a fellow subject but actually works for the researchers) began acting angry. Subjects in the room then tended to interpret the sensations they were getting from the adrenaline as anger. If the confederate acted happy, the subjects were more likely to think they were feeling happy too.

Fascinatingly, if the subjects were told that the vitamin shot could have side effects of increased heart rate and shakiness, they rated themselves as less angry or less happy, because they attributed what they were feeling to the shot.

This has profound implications for how we can work wisely with our emotions. If I can notice my body sensations as they are, I can watch the flow of thoughts that come up and interrupt them before they carry me away.

A colleague of mine had been working with a man who was very anxious without much success, and he asked me to come in and see if mindfulness might help get the client unstuck. He had already read about mindfulness, so was open to trying it. I asked him to close his eyes and rate his anxiety on a scale of 1 to 10. He said it was an 8.

"Where do you feel your anxiety?" I asked.

"It's in my head." He responded immediately.

"That may be a thought. Where in your body do you feel your anxiety?"

After a few moments of reflection, he stuck to what he originally said. "It's just floating around in my head."

"Actually, your brain doesn't have any feeling receptors in it," I informed him. "What you are experiencing are thoughts, ghosts, hologram projections. Instead of fighting the ghosts, we want to knock out the projector. Keep moving your attention through your body – it's the only place we can feel anything." I would not normally get so theoretical, but this client was very intelligent, and his knowledge of how anxiety worked was keeping him from feeling it.

After a few moments, he responded. "I can feel it in my neck."

"Very good," I said encouragingly. "Now, stay with those sensations. What are you feeling there? What did you notice about it that prompted you to rate your anxiety an 8? Is it still an 8, or has it changed?"

He appeared to be concentrating, then a look of confusion came over his face. "Actually, it feels more like muscle tension." His jaw then dropped a little, as he discovered an important breakthrough. "Wow. All these years, I think I've been confusing muscle tension with anxiety!"

Once we decide to move directly into an emotion, it is usually not as bad as our thoughts anticipate it will be, and once it has delivered its message, it doesn't need to knock as loudly at the door of our minds. This is why feeling emotions directly is usually much more helpful than avoiding them.

We can choose to compartmentalize our feelings, but it comes at a cost. There are certainly times we need to suppress our emotions, as when we are at work and have to keep up a professional face. If we are taking care of our children, we don't want them to worry about us too much (though expressing a little emotion in front of them may set a healthy example that it is okay to have feelings). But if stuffing our feelings down is our only coping mechanism, the feelings will become internalized, and eat away at us. It will take more and more energy to hold ourselves together all the time.

By giving ourselves permission to feel whatever we are feeling, we can process those feelings and let them go. Sometimes we fear that once we open the floodgates of emotion, they may never stop. Ironically, this causes us to both feel the emotion and fight it at the same time, which can keep it going even longer. Allowing ourselves a deep, healing sob, experiencing it fully in our bodies, and watching the thoughts and judgments come and go without clinging to them, permits an opportunity for true healing and emotional health.

Through mindfulness practice, we can learn to more consciously and consistently tease apart the physical components of our emotions from our thought components. This opens them up so we can work with our feelings much more wisely.

3. Mindfulness of thoughts

Thoughts are a funny thing. We are born with no language, but we pick it up as we grow older. We repeat what we hear others say, then we internalize the language, that is, we talk to ourselves. So, in our heads, we know what we want to communicate, then we translate it into words, then we tell ourselves those words, then we translate the meanings of those words back to ourselves. Thoughts themselves can of course be very useful, but we can get into trouble when we habitually over-identify with them, or confuse them with the reality they represent.

We tend to forget that words are representations of other things. Though they may be based in truth, thoughts are not facts, even the ones that tell you they are. This is at once hard to understand, yet obviously simple. Psychologist Hank Robb uses very clear, concrete questions to demonstrate this. If you are sitting down right now, go ahead and generate the thought "I am sitting in this chair" (or whatever you are sitting on). Once you have that in your mind, do you believe that thought is true? Most of us will say yes. Now, notice what it actually feels like physically to have your rump supported by what you are sitting on. Is the experience of sitting in the chair the same or different than your thought "I am sitting in this chair"? We would all agree that the feeling on your rump is not the same as the thought in your head. So, even "true thoughts" are not the same as the experience itself, and we can get ourselves into trouble if we forget that difference.

When thoughts feel real, they can produce a stress response or physical sensation, or even motivate us to do or say something, even though they are only in our heads. Thoughts have a tendency to spark more thoughts, so we can get lost in them for significant periods of time. We carry around so much in our heads and wonder why we are tired.

If you have suffered from anxiety, perhaps you have had the experience of noticing that your heart is beating fast. You then begin to worry. "Is my heart beating too fast? Maybe I should go to the emergency room. But what if I go there and they tell me it's all in my head? Then the next time I go, I might be having a real heart attack, and they'll send me home and I'll die! If I die, who's going to make sure the kids will get a good college education? I know my partner won't motivate them to go." So, you felt your heart beating, and then began worrying about the kids going to college!

Alan Watts[10] made an interesting observation. Someone who talks all the time can't hear what anyone else has to say. If we talk to ourselves all the time, which is what thinking is, we won't be aware of much else going on around us.

After you develop some skill with paying attention, you can more directly observe your own thoughts. We can become more aware of what we are thinking, how intense the thoughts are, and how much we think.

Many people find it curious that when they try to watch their own thoughts, they seem to disappear, or they have trouble finding them. Sometimes it is because by choosing to pay attention, you interrupt the automatic thinking cycle. Many times, however, it is simply because we don't have much practice doing this yet. It's funny to realize that when you think, "I'm not having any thoughts right now," that is actually a thought! We are so accustomed to being in the middle of our thoughts that it can be hard to "step back" and observe them.

Sometimes analogies or metaphors can help when we are learning to notice our own thoughts. We can picture our thoughts as cascading down on us like a waterfall, continually washing over us, knocking us around. Observing them is like stepping back behind the waterfall, and watching them flow past. Through the force of old habit, we will get pulled back into the current over and over, getting lost within our thoughts again. When we notice this has happened, we can "step back" again and return to watching them. The more we practice stepping back after getting pulled in, the stronger our "attention muscles" become, and the easier it gets.

When we begin to watch our thoughts, we are often surprised by how random they are. This quality can be very creative, which we sometimes might choose to foster, but it can also be very distracting. As we are working, we may be compulsively daydreaming about the weekend all week long, and we wonder why our lives are flying by so fast.

Noticing our thoughts allows us to become more aware of their patterns, and how much they influence our moods and behaviors throughout the day. With practice, we can learn to remember that we are having thoughts, but who we are is not limited to our thinking. We are so much more.

Of course, thoughts can be a very good thing. I always tell my mindfulness students to continue being thinking people. We just need to remember the limitations of thoughts and not treat everything as a nail for our thinking hammer.

Problems can arise when we get caught up, or "hooked," by our thinking. By becoming more aware of our thoughts and their patterns, we can pause to decide if these thoughts are helpful or not, thereby enabling us to choose our next response more wisely. We often get very stuck in our own way of thinking. I was once co-leading a workshop on spirituality variables in psychotherapy when someone approached me during a break.

"You were a bodyguard for the Dalai Lama?" he asked. He was an older gentleman, a psychologist with long white hair in a ponytail and with a long white beard. He was dressed in loose, artful clothing. I had an automatic, stereotypical thought that he was a peaceful hippie. I smiled and nodded my head. "Yeah, my 15 minutes of fame."

His next question took me by surprise. "Were you prepared to use lethal force to protect the Dalai Lama?" He looked quite serious. Perhaps he was wondering if I had a violent nature inside. I've given some presentations where, ironically, people have gotten almost violently angry when I talked about being a martial artist.

I smiled and said, "Since we were protecting a Nobel Peace Prize winner, we didn't want to make a big show of force."

"But if you had to," he continued, "would you shoot someone for the Dalai Lama?"

I wasn't exactly sure now where he was going with his line of questioning. "I'm not sure I would ever have to. Our charge was to protect the life of the Dalai Lama and his entourage, so our priority would have been to move him away from danger as quickly as possible."

He did not seem to like my answer, as he stared at me with piercing eyes and a flat expression on his face. He went on to talk about how he would use lethal force unhesitatingly, and that he owned two guns, keeping one on his person and one in his car. I simply reiterated that I would do everything possible to avoid taking a life, as the setting didn't allow us to have a deeper philosophical conversation. He didn't seem pleased at the end of our conversation.

In fact, I am authorized to carry concealed weapons in most areas of the country in which I live, and have studied and taught firearm shooting and disarming methods to police and military. Yes, if you are going to carry a firearm, you must mentally be prepared to take a life, as hesitation may allow the attacker to take the weapon and use it against you. But a true warrior acts out of what is best for the situation, rather than reacting out of fear. My job was to protect, not to kill those who may have been threatening him. Yes, it is conceivable that in some extraordinary circumstances, I might have had to damage a life to save others. But what a tragedy that would have been, after the worldwide message of peace and compassion the Dalai Lama continues to promote, despite the countless lives taken from the Tibetan people. As the Dalai Lama himself demonstrates, internal peace is a far more powerful tool than a gun.

It is easy to have a thought about what you "would" do, but countless social psychology studies show that we frequently don't actually do what we think we would have done in a real situation. There are so many factors to consider. In this case, how would I know if I was shooting an attacker, or shooting another agent who was about to protect us from an attacker behind me? What if the "attacker" had a plastic squirt gun? What if the bullet went through the attacker and killed innocent bystanders, or even a child?

It seems this man was fused with an idea that he felt was important to push on others. Sometimes this is helpful. Perhaps you have read something in this book that made you want to say, "Wow, my friend Joe needs to read this!" But too often we don't question our own ideas, and promote them to others in order to feel better about ourselves.

Of course, this is always easier to see in other people. This was also a lesson for me to continue to practice noticing my own assumptions.

As you become more aware of your own thoughts, you will begin to discover how often you have "automatic thoughts." I am fortunate to have a great boss. In fact, if I were to create a list of the things I would most want in a boss, it would describe him well. Yet, whenever he sends me an email or leaves me a voicemail which says, "Please call me as soon as you get a chance," I have an automatic thought that I might have done something wrong. I think back over the last few days and wonder what it could be. I then catch myself doing it, take a breath, and give him a call. Ninety-nine percent of the time, he is simply asking for my help with something, or updating me on something. However, because of that 1 percent, or perhaps because of past interactions with school principals, thoughts and feelings of being in trouble arise automatically. Imagine if I did not recognize this. I would probably sound defensive on the phone, starting off with, "What did I do wrong?," which would likely prompt my boss to say, "Uh, is there something you did that you think might be wrong that I should know about?," which would heighten my defensiveness even more.

By becoming aware of our own "top 10" automatic thoughts, we can use them as important information instead of fighting with them. If we notice a thought, "I can't do anything right," it is going to spark, or is the result of, something emotional, like stress. Instead of fighting the thought with more thoughts, we can check into how we are feeling and then do something to take care of the situation or ourselves in that moment.

Eventually, you may get down into some deeply entrenched thoughts or core beliefs about who you are. Too often we find negative core beliefs about ourselves and the world, such as "Life is supposed to be hard, and you're selfish if you are having fun," "I don't really deserve to be happy," "There is something fundamentally unlovable about me," or "You can never trust anyone, or you'll get hurt." These may have been internalized from society, parents, or perhaps even helped us survive tough times in the past. Uncovering these deep beliefs can be scary, but very liberating once we begin to recognize and diminish their influence. We can decide if these beliefs still fit for our current life. We can then begin to let them go, or at least not be so ensnared by them, and move closer to who we really are and where we really want to go in our lives.

With practice, we can become increasingly aware of even very subtle mental events. Thoughts are often not complete sentences, or even words. They may be images, colors, or phantasmal fragments.

It all begins with noticing.

Later, we will explore ways of working wisely with our thoughts, both for fostering creativity and for dealing with very difficult challenges.

4. Mindfulness of the nature of reality

When we develop our capacity for attention, we can understand ourselves more deeply and notice patterns in our interactions with the world around us. We become more in touch with reality, not in an abstract philosophical sense, but like a scientist who observes the nature of various phenomena and learns to predict cause and effect.

As we learn to engage all of our senses, we become more aware of the hindrances that get in our way. With increased clarity, we come to understand ourselves better. As our mindfulness practice blossoms, qualities arise in us like concentration, insight, energy, joy, tranquility, and equanimity.

By paying attention, we come to see how much suffering there is in the world. It is an integral part of the human condition. We can also see that our suffering comes from our attempts to hold onto our experiences, which is impossible. Once we know this, we can let go of our futile attempts to do so. Awareness of these principles informs us on how to live our lives.

The circumstances of our lives did not develop into the way they are by themselves. There were causes and conditions that made them the way they are. Understanding this, we blame others for our problems less often, and we can consciously work to set up the causes and conditions to make things different.

Although I don't take it overly seriously, I am amazed at how many synchronicities happen in my life when I pay attention. Sometimes I don't notice them right away, and sometimes they slap me in the face.

During my Zen training, I was once working on the "fox *kōan*." *Kōans*, which we will discuss in chapter 8, are Zen teaching stories designed to develop our attention and to show us how our thinking gets us into trouble. Basically, the story is that a ghostly figure approached a Zen teacher in ancient China and said, "Long ago, I was a Zen teacher, and someone asked me if an enlightened person is subject to cause and effect. I said, 'No.' For this, I have been reborn as a fox for 500 lifetimes. I ask you now, is an enlightened person subject to cause and effect?"

The teacher said, "Cause and effect are clear." Upon hearing this, the figure said he was freed, and asked the teacher to look for a dead fox on the grounds behind the temple and give it a respectful burial.

I had been working on this *kōan* for a little while, pondering the questions I was given about it, and finally gave the correct answers in a video interview with my teacher, Wonji. An hour later, I was driving home, and heard a voicemail message that said, "The old neighbors called and said they found a dead fox in our backyard." For several moments I was in a state of confusion and disbelief. We had just moved to a new house in the woods, but our old house, which we had not yet been able to sell, was in a suburban neighborhood. I had never even seen a fox in the nine years I had lived there. Sure enough, I drove there and found a dead fox in the small backyard.

When I arrived at the new home shortly thereafter, all the wooden floors had been cleared so we could apply a new finish. The only thing on the floor I could see was a small toy fox left there by my then 2-year-old. It was lying in front of the fireplace where the previous owners had hung a big portrait of a fox before we moved in. The next morning I drove by a local bookstore that changed its titles in the windows every week. The windows were full of books about foxes.

A little while later, I decided to look at a large book of *kōans* that had been sitting on my bookshelf for a while. I opened the book at random, and the one I immediately turned to was the fox *kōan*. Okay, I told myself, I had better pay attention to this.

As I read through the *kōan* carefully, I kept coming back to the line, "Cause and effect are clear." Many people think enlightenment is some kind of blissed out state, but if you are living in the world you will have an impact on the people and environment around you.

It suddenly dawned on me that I was not tuning in to how my feelings, as positive as they felt to me, were negatively impacting one of the most important persons in my life. Discussing this honestly created a major shift in the relationship.

When we learn to observe cause and effect, and notice the impact of our thoughts, words, and behaviors on ourselves and others, it leads naturally to a code of ethics. You could certainly choose to follow an established system with which you feel a connection, but if you are really paying attention you will know the best behavior for any given situation. You will begin to notice your old negative reactions more often when they come up, and determine if that is what is best to do in the moment. You will recognize how connected we are to each other and to the world we live in. Just as mindfulness helps you learn to treat yourself with more kindness and respect, you begin to treat our human and animal families and the environment in which we live with the same kindness and respect. After all, selfishness and unkindness come from not knowing how to handle difficult emotions. We all want to be happy, and remembering this, we become more patient with those who are trying to find happiness in ways that hurt others. We can still firmly set boundaries to protect ourselves and others as needed, but we more often feel compassion, or at least pity, instead of automatically reacting with anger.

Clearly seeing what is going on in the world around us, without automatically filtering through old thoughts and feelings, can reveal an amazing amount of wonders. It can also open us up to terrible heartbreak, when we recognize how much suffering there truly is in the world.

When I went to India and Nepal for six weeks, I had been told to expect a culture shock. I had read about and seen documentaries about these countries for years, but nothing could prepare me for the abject poverty and suffering that I saw. It was truly shocking. I could literally see the poverty even before my plane landed. As I was flying into Delhi in the evening, I could see many little fires out of my window. As I was driven to my hotel, I saw that each fire had been made by a homeless person or family, burning cow dung to stay warm. Almost everywhere I went in India there were countless families who were homeless or who created makeshift shelters out of tarps. The small children, especially those who were crippled, were the most heartbreaking to see. I will never forget the sad face of a very small girl, who couldn't have been older than 4 or 5, holding up a condom and looking at me as I walked by.

There was also such a stark contrast between those with and those without money. Very well-dressed men and women stepped over dirty, sick human beings as they entered their gorgeous homes, fancy restaurants, and beautiful temples. I myself felt like I had the resources of a god with the privilege I brought with me from my country. I carried on my person, in cash, double the amount of money the average person from that part of the world earned in an entire year. In the poorest part of India, I stayed in a decent motel room for over two weeks, with running water and my own bathroom, for less than what I often make for one hour of work. When I visited the Taj Mahal with a fellow conference attendee, we rented a car and two human beings (a driver and a tour guide) for an entire day for the price of one meal back home.

After a few weeks it became shocking that the poverty was no longer shocking, as it became a new "normal." Then, when I returned to the United States, I was surprised at how shocking it was to return to such a life of luxury, where people often take their privileges for granted and complain about relatively insignificant things.

There is some truth to the expression, "ignorance is bliss," but it comes at a price. Opening your heart exposes you to pain, but also allows us to take helpful action and change the world one moment at a time, one human being at time. I once heard a story about a high tide that had washed up thousands of starfish onto a beach, as far as the eye could see. An old man was trying to throw them back into the water before they dried out and died in the sun. A young man came along and said, "Why are you bothering? Just look at how many there are! You can't possibly make a difference!" The old man picked up another starfish, tossed it into the water, and looked at the young man. "I just made a big difference for that one."

Boy in Nepal. © Richard Sears.

We have to be careful to make sure our "help" doesn't make things worse. "Kindly let me help you, or you'll drown!" said the monkey, as he put the fish safely up a tree. True help must come from letting go of our own expectations and clearly seeing what needs to be done.

I have found that those who sincerely practice mindfulness are genuine, mature, and humorous people. When we recognize that suffering is every-where, we become more compassionate. When we see how everything arises, lingers, then passes away, we can more fully appreciate what we do have, and stop chasing after what we can't really possess anyway. Every moment, every experience, is full of wonder.

How the four foundations interact

After working with the four foundations of mindfulness, you will begin to see that in reality they are very inter-related and very interactive. Seeing something in the environment creates a thought, which evokes a tiny emotion, which sparks a tiny sensation in your body. This ability to notice and tease apart thoughts, feelings, and body sensations gives us a much wider perspective on our experiences. This holds profound implications, as it gives us a powerful tool for working with difficulties and for engaging with all our moments, which we will continue to explore throughout the rest of this book.

How Does Mindfulness Actually Work?

Mindfulness is growing in popularity within the professional and scientific communities because it fits so well with psychological principles we already know and have thoroughly researched. Of course, this is not to downplay the value of the other reasons people practice mindfulness, like for spiritual development. Mindfulness is a skill, a tool, and you can choose how and when to apply it. The same principles of mindfulness that help us enrich our lives also provide a way of effectively dealing with modern problems. In fact, many cutting-edge, evidence-based treatment programs now incorporate mindfulness. Although we will first focus on dealing with challenges, we will later explore how mindfulness can help us bring more richness to all of our moments.

Falling into vicious cycles

We all face significant challenges throughout our lives, but the biggest problems occur when we get stuck in vicious cycles. To illustrate how this happens, and how mindfulness can help break us out of them, let's use the development of an intense fear, or phobia, as an example. Later, we will talk about how these principles apply to stress, anxiety, pain, depression, and many other problems.

A wide variety of things can cause us stress, anxiety, or fear. Let's say that as I'm writing this, a massive bird flies into the window next to me and cracks the glass. Naturally, I will be startled and my body will have a fear reaction. Even after I fix the window, I am likely to remember that event the next time I sit down by that window, and my heartbeat will increase a little, and I'll feel at least a little anxiety. Ideally, I'll let myself feel that feeling, maybe smile at myself, and it will pass.

But if I decide to move away from that window, my anxiety level will drop. As a survival mechanism, our brains are wired to want to keep doing anything that takes away a bad feeling. If we discover that tigers are dangerous, and backing away from them saves our lives, we need that new brain programming to work quickly.

Because I felt better backing away from that window, I might get into a habit of backing away every time that memory produces a little anxiety. Over time, I could end up trying to avoid even thinking about that window as thoughts about it will make me feel bad. The more I try not to feel anxious, the more I end up avoiding anything related to the anxiety, and the worse it gets. Eventually, my fear may get generalized, and I might begin to back away from all windows. I may even stop driving out of fear that a bird will hit my windshield.

The reason why this cycle is so hard to break out of is because backing away in the moment really does lower the anxiety. Even if I tell myself, "This is silly. What are the odds that another bird will ever hit that window?," and I go ahead and sit by the window anyway, my body will still feel anxious. Because I don't like to feel anxious, I may fight it and will get anxious about my anxiety. As the anxiety gets worse, I decide that it really wasn't a good idea to sit by the window, so I back away and immediately feel better, never giving it a chance to go away on its own. Backing away becomes the only thing I do to deal with my anxiety, and I can end up living a very restricted life in my attempts to not feel anxious.

I could also turn to other unhealthy ways to deal with my anxiety. I could distract myself with lots of television, start drinking alcohol, or eat candy to help myself feel better. All of those things take away a little of the bad feeling while I am doing them, which seems better than feeling the anxiety at the time, but it doesn't permanently address the underlying problem, so I become caught in a trap of my own making.

Breaking out of vicious cycles

So how do we break out of such vicious cycles, ones that may even be affecting our whole lives, despite our own best efforts to fix them?

If you came to me and wanted treatment for a fear of windows (or if I had to go to your windowless home since there are windows in my office), I would first explain how we get stuck. Because backing away from something that causes us anxiety makes us feel a little better right away, we want to keep doing it. The reason we get stuck is because the way out of it, which involves feeling the anxiety more, is very scary and just doesn't seem to make logical sense at first.

A technique called exposure therapy has been proven time and again to be very effective at helping people with fear and anxiety. It basically involves exposing ourselves to whatever is causing the anxiety, and waiting for the feeling to pass on its own.

Once we decide to move closer to what makes us anxious, the anxiety of course goes up. Our fear is that the anxiety will go up and up forever and we'll explode or "lose it," or even die. If you've ever had a panic attack, you know they are very frightening, and you really want to avoid them.

But as we know from the laws of physics, there is no such thing as infinite energy. The anxiety can't go up forever because your body cannot sustain high levels of energy indefinitely. At some point, it will stop going up, level off, and begin coming back down again on its own. Your brain and body are designed to acclimate and readjust themselves.

Even though this is a solidly proven scientific concept, a leap of faith is required in the beginning. When I move into the anxiety and it gets worse, I have to trust that it will eventually come down by itself. It is scary for people to choose to expose themselves to high levels of anxiety, but chances are they have been living with terrible anxiety for many years already, and with this treatment it will be for a purpose.

I often find a swimming pool analogy helpful. Imagine yourself looking forward to a nice swim. When you get to the pool, you dip your toe in, and it feels cold. Sometimes you may decide that it's just too cold and you don't want to deal with it. But you also know that you can get used to the cold, and when you see other people in the pool having fun, from 2-year-olds to 90-year-olds, you know it's going to be okay. Your friends and family have jumped in and are urging you to come and join them.

So what do you do? If you stand there dipping your feet in and out of the water, it will never feel better. You could jump in all at once, making a big splash. You will probably shiver and shake from the cold after you jump into the water. If you run back out of the water right away, you will feel even colder because now you are wet. But if you stay in the water your body will adjust, and after a few minutes you will feel great.

You could also go in gradually (hoping that no one splashes you while you do that). You put your feet in the water until they acclimate. Then you go down one of the steps up to your knees until your legs feel fine. Eventually, your whole body feels great in the water, as long as you stay in it.

This is exactly how your body responds to anxiety. If you were afraid of windows, I would show you a picture of one from across the room. Naturally, your anxiety would go up and you would want to back away or close your eyes. But if you stood your ground and looked at the picture of the window, your anxiety would go up, level off, and come back down again. It might take a few minutes, which can feel like hours, but this always happens. Then, you take one step closer and the anxiety goes up again, you wait it out and it comes back down again. You keep doing this until you are touching the picture. Then you can repeat the process with a real window. The more you do this, the less high the anxiety level gets and the more quickly it passes. Eventually the anxiety, and therefore the need to avoid it, is extinguished. It's possible that you may still feel a little anxious about windows from time to time, just as water may still feel cold, but you learn that if you stay with it, it will pass.

It is important to note that this process only works if you allow yourself to feel the unpleasant feelings. If you close your eyes and think about a beach in an attempt to relax yourself, you are avoiding again. This would be like jumping out of the swimming pool, breaking the exposure process. The more we are able to let go of our struggle with our own feelings, the more quickly they will pass.

We sometimes go to great lengths to avoid feeling bad, so people are often amazed that they can move through a fear they have fought with for 30 years in just one or two exposure sessions. We can spend so much energy trying to avoid the monster that has been projecting such a large shadow on the wall. When we finally turn to face it directly, it often turns out to be just a small, harmless lizard.

How our thinking traps us

You may not be able to relate to a fear of windows, but the very same concepts apply to the way we relate to all of our unpleasant emotions. For now, let's stay with anxiety as an example to illustrate the principles involved.

By definition, anxiety is an unpleasant feeling, so we don't want to feel it. If it was not unpleasant, we would call it excitement. Therefore, we see it as a problem.

How do we fix problems? If there is a problem in the physical world, we think about it, and often come up with a solution. Just a few minutes ago, I got a nice cup of coffee from the downstairs hotel lobby. As I was writing, it began to cool. I much prefer my coffee to be warm, so that was a problem, albeit a small one, that created a small unpleasant feeling. I engaged my universal problem-solving device, known as thinking. I noticed a microwave, but thought my cup might melt if I tried to reheat it. I could have gone back down to the lobby and fetched a lid, but that would have wasted time and plastic. I then realized I could improvise my own lid. After looking around, I found a clean piece of paper and laid it over my coffee. Problem solved, worry gone, hooray for thinking!

Ideally, when this system works properly, a problem arises, feelings come up to alert me something is wrong, I take action to fix the problem, and the feelings go away. We get ourselves into trouble when we shoot the messenger.

Thinking is a wonderful tool for fixing problems in the physical world, but it doesn't always work so well for fixing thoughts and feelings. If we are feeling an unpleasant emotion like anxiety, we are likely to fall back on thinking as a way to fix it. We may try to come up with ways to reduce the feeling, like avoiding something that bothers us, or taking a drink of alcohol. We could also ruminate over something that happened in the past. "If only I had worn a tighter belt, people wouldn't have seen my underwear during that presentation." "I really wish I would have said something clever when they told me I was wrong." We could also worry about the future. "The next time that happens, I'm going to have the perfect comeback." "If Joe tells me he doesn't like me anymore, I'm going to pretend it doesn't bother me." We may even fall into patterns of beating ourselves up. "Why can't I control my anxiety?" "I'm such a worthless person."

Something very subtle is happening here. While we are thinking, we are not aware of our bodies as much, so our subjective feeling of anxiety is lower. Remember that when we do something that lowers a bad feeling, our brains say, "Do that more!," so our thinking goes on and on. Our brains are actually attempting to help us not feel the anxiety in our bodies. When we stop thinking we can feel the anxiety more, so we go back to thinking more. It lowers the felt anxiety a bit, so we keep doing it, but it doesn't usually make it go away completely, and we get stuck. This is why when something is really bothering us, we can end up lying awake at night, thinking about it for days.

Mindfulness as exposure therapy

So, how can we use mindfulness to disrupt this process?

It becomes a life-changing discovery when we realize that strong feelings are telling us something important and are not things to be avoided. When we practice paying attention, we also realize that strong thoughts are signs that something deeper may be going on.

When we find ourselves ruminating and worrying, we can stop and check in with our bodies. Chances are we will notice a feeling related to stress, anxiety, pain, or sadness. Instead of struggling with our thoughts, we can investigate the underlying emotion. Once we recognize the deeper feeling we can allow ourselves to feel it. After all, it's already there anyway. They will grow stronger once we stop distracting ourselves, so our brains will rebel and keep trying to pull us back into thinking. But we can thank our brains for trying to help and just keep escorting our attention back to the feelings. At that point we have opened up conscious choice. We can wait for it to rise and fall, we can do something to take care of ourselves, we can take some action in the physical world, or we can even go back to pretending it isn't there until we finish our work shift. Once the underlying feeling dissipates the compulsive thoughts lose their fuel and fade away.

A bigger sense of who we are

Thoughts can of course be very powerful, so learning to relate to them differently takes practice. We are usually "fused" to our thoughts, that is, our sense of identity is strongly tied to them. Mindfulness can teach us to relate to our thoughts differently. We can learn to "defuse" or "decenter" from our thoughts. Instead of feeling like we are in the center of a thought like, "I am a worthless person," we can sort of step back from our thoughts, and realize, "I am having a thought that I am a worthless person." Though it may not sound like much to read it here, this is a very significant shift.

Acceptance and Commitment Therapy (ACT)[11] refers to this as moving from "self-as-content" to "self-as-context." Instead of getting enmeshed in the content of our thoughts and feelings, we recognize that they take place in the larger context of who we are. In other words, we develop a capacity for flexible perspective taking. ACT often makes use of the chessboard metaphor. Instead of identifying who we are with the chess pieces, and getting involved with the battle of "good" versus "bad" thoughts and feelings, we recognize that we are the board itself, which holds the pieces. If you are a chess piece, you are quite invested in who wins. If you identify yourself with the board, you aren't affected by the struggles of the pieces.

This is why journaling or talking about our problems can often help. By putting our thoughts down on paper, or saying them out loud to another person, we can get some perspective on them and then make wiser choices about how to proceed.

A commonly used treatment intervention is called cognitive-behavioral therapy (CBT), which teaches a method for identifying and disputing irrational thoughts. If I recognize that I am having the thought, "I can't do anything right," we can challenge it directly. We can ask ourselves, "What is the evidence that I can't do anything right?"

However, I find that this technique, if too strictly applied, does not always work very well. You might dispute the above thought with, "My children came out right, there's something." But another thought might come back at you, like, "Well, maybe they're just smarter than me, or maybe they learned what not to do from my life." After all, these are your own thoughts – how can you out-think yourself? Yet, CBT has been very effective for a lot of people. Perhaps it is because by arguing with yourself, you are already stepping back from your thoughts and relating to them differently. Mindfulness does this more directly and explicitly. When we notice strong negative thoughts, instead of fueling them with more thoughts, or struggling with them, we step back from them. "I keep having the thought that I can't do anything right. It must mean I'm getting overwhelmed. I had better do something to take care of myself right now." You can then check in with your emotional state and how your body is feeling.

It is like being caught in a tug-of-war with your own hands, struggling harder and harder to win, and then realizing that both hands are yours. You can immediately let go and you stop struggling.[12]

This approach to working with difficult thoughts and feelings, stepping back and noticing them, represents a "second-order change." First-order change involves trying harder and harder to do what you've always done, regardless of whether or not we are making any progress with our increasing efforts, as when we keep fighting our thoughts with thoughts.

J. Scott Fraser[13] uses the analogy of a bird trapped inside a vestibule to illustrate the difference between first-order change and second-order change. When the bird tries to escape the building, it flies up into the windows above the doors. When the bird bumps its beak into the glass and realizes it can't get out, it continues to fly higher and to strike the glass harder. However, the bird only succeeds at exhausting itself. It eventually falls backwards and down, seemingly away from the direction it wanted to go, and finds itself on the floor of the building in front of an open doorway. When the bird flies forward at this point, it is easily able to escape the building.

It can be difficult for us to discontinue familiar ways of doing things and try new approaches to situations. How often have we just kept trying harder, metaphorically beating our heads against the proverbial wall, not realizing we could have walked around it? After all, you probably wouldn't have bought this book if the title was, "Feeling bad? Feel it more!," but that is basically what we have been discussing. Of course, the key lies in how you move into it and what you do next so that you don't make it worse than it already is.

Self-compassion

Interestingly, one of the underlying factors that keeps showing up in the research about why mindfulness is so helpful is self-compassion. When we practice noticing our own thoughts, emotions, and sensations, and suspend our automatic judgments and negative thoughts, we are learning to be kind to ourselves.

By treating ourselves more kindly, we are giving ourselves the unconditional caring we may not have received enough of in childhood. We can begin to let go of internalized messages that we aren't good enough, that we have to earn people's love, or that we don't deserve to be happy. This allows our sense of self-worth and self-esteem to blossom more fully.

You may need to read the above sections a few times for the concepts to fully sink in. They will provide an important key for working with almost every challenge in your life, and provide a foundation for enriching your moments. Even after you "get" these concepts intellectually, it will likely still take lots of practice to transform your old, more ingrained habits, so be patient with yourself.

Mindfulness and the Brain

You don't have to take my word for whether or not mindfulness works. For the first time in history, we don't have to rely on someone else's subjective report of how it works for them (though we can certainly learn things from that as well). Amazingly, we can actually see how and why mindfulness works using modern brain scanners.

Exercising the brain

Researchers like Sara Lazar[14] have demonstrated that people who practice mindfulness regularly show measurable changes in the brain, even after an eight-week program that meets only once a week with daily homework practice. And I don't just mean while they are doing it, but certain areas of their brains actually become measurably thicker! Even though I know the benefits of mindfulness first-hand, it still stuns me to know about these results.

Of course, if you were to tell me that you could measure my biceps, put me on an eight-week exercise regimen, and my muscles would be measurably larger afterward, that would not come as any surprise. The brain is very similar in this respect. Brain circuits that fire together, wire together. The more they are used, or exercised, the stronger, or more efficient, they become.

Also, just as muscles atrophy, or lose mass, if you don't use them, brain pathways that are not used regularly can lose their "tone," and become smaller. This is why those who "exercise" their brains do better in old age.

Research on the brain changes associated with mindfulness is growing exponentially. Currently, I am collaborating with Melissa Delbello, Sian Cotton, Randye Semple, Tina Luberto, Lauren Stahl and others on research involving brain scans of children and teenagers before and after a 12-week mindfulness course. It is an exciting time in mindfulness brain research.

Among the changes we see, one of the most important regions that shows significant development after practicing mindfulness is the middle prefrontal cortex.

The nine middle prefrontal brain functions

In his book, *The Mindful Brain*,[15] Dan Siegel describes the functions associated with the middle prefrontal cortex. Cortex means "bark," as it is the outermost area of the brain. The prefrontal cortex in general, in the very front of your brain behind your forehead, plays a vital role in what is known as "executive functioning," referring to the capacity to regulate other brain processes. It allows us to do things on purpose, plan for the future, make decisions, and over-ride strong feelings. The medial, or middle, areas of the prefrontal cortex are associated with the following nine functions. This is the area that thickens with mindfulness practice, and why those who practice mindfulness demonstrate more of these qualities.

Body regulation
If you have ever used biofeedback equipment, such as fingertip thermometers (also how "mood rings" work), GSR (galvanic skin response) sensors, heart rate monitors, or even brain wave monitors, you were probably amazed at your ability to change the functions of your own body. You were probably not even consciously aware of how you did it, as the language centers of your brain are not directly involved in the process. One of the functions of the prefrontal cortex is to help keep the body's systems in balance, particularly when recovering from stress.

Attuned communication
We all appreciate feeling connected, heard, and understood. Sometimes we meet people who don't seem to connect with us at all, giving us the feeling that they are talking "at" us. In some cases, it feels like we are only talking to a cardboard cutout of a person. People who can attune with others seem so warm and able to connect that we feel as if we have known them all our lives.

Emotional balance
Our emotions originate in several brain structures collectively known as the "limbic system." These structures operate separately from our cortex, which is where our thinking takes place. When feelings become overwhelming, the prefrontal cortex allows us to overcome or change the messages coming from the limbic system. However, we can also become too emotionally rigid. There is a clinical condition known as "alexithymia," which is characterized by

having only a limited range of emotions. Some would say that most men suffer from this condition, as many cultures have traditionally expected men not to show too much emotion. The continuous suppression of emotion comes at a cost – losing the capacity for the richness of emotional intimacy and passion in our lives.

Emotional balance, or maturity, is about feeling our emotions, and using them as guides, but not basing all of our decisions and behaviors solely on them.

Response flexibility

We have a number of reflexive, automatic responses built into our brains and spinal cords. For instance, if we touch a hot stove, our hand will pull back automatically. However, our frontal lobes can interrupt that process. If we are carrying a hot casserole, and it begins to burn through the hot pad, we can choose to quickly put it on the counter rather than automatically letting go and dropping it all over the floor.

This capacity to interrupt automatic patterns, which is also called psychological flexibility, is a crucial aspect of mindfulness training. We can more often recognize the choice points in our moments, even in the middle of a crisis. We can develop more flexibility in how we choose to respond to a situation, rather than being dominated by unconscious reactions.

Empathy

Empathy involves our capacity to feel what others feel. Young children under the age of four are often unable to do this, because their frontal lobes are still developing. If they take another child's toy, they don't understand why that child cries about it, because they look in their hands and see a toy, which makes them happy.

Individuals who are afflicted with antisocial personality disorder have a difficult time feeling guilt or remorse for what they do to others. They have been found to have less developed, or damaged, middle prefrontal cortices.

Insight

The ability to know ourselves is a very advanced skill, requiring the integration of a lot of information. Insight requires us to be aware of our own thoughts, feelings, and behaviors, as well as their consequences.

Fear modulation

Fear is regulated by a pair of structures in the limbic system called the amygdalae, which means "almonds," due to their size and shape. The middle prefrontal cortex can send calming signals to the amygdalae, and reprograms their response patterns to extinguish old fears.

Intuition

We have all had the experience of "knowing" something, without necessarily being able to explain it in words. This does not necessarily imply a mystical process. Our brain is collecting and integrating information and memories from countless sources, and this process does not need our conscious attention to operate. By getting out of our own way, we are able to sense much more than we can identify with words.

Morality

With the ability to sense and understand the feelings of others, and how we all want to be happy, we are compelled to do what is best for our fellow human beings. Recognizing our dependence on our environment, we take care of the world in which we live. Although traditions often enforce codes of ethics and morality, the practice of mindfulness fosters an internal code of behavior that facilitates living with integrity.

This is quite a list, don't you think? Wouldn't all of us like to develop these capacities further? While practicing mindfulness will not make us superhuman, we can help ourselves become more fully human. The effects of these changes are real and measurable.

Don't you wish these nine qualities could have been taught to us when we were kids? In fact, there is a growing movement to teach mindfulness in schools. Goldie Hawn has collaborated with Dan Siegel and others to produce an evidence-based mindfulness training program for schools called MindUP (thehawnfoundation.org). Just imagine the benefits of adding the development of the above nine areas to the curriculum of children around the world.

You will see that the qualities in the list above are often lacking for children and teenagers, because the prefrontal cortex does not finish developing fully until the late twenties. This is why teens can seem so impulsive and emotional, and don't often plan very well for the future. Challenges in these areas are also seen in disorders that involve disruptions in brain functioning, such as attention deficit/hyperactivity disorder (ADHD), autism spectrum disorder, and schizophrenia. Studies are underway to determine the impact of mindfulness training for these individuals, and are already showing promise.

In Chapter 7, I will outline an eight-week program that you can do on your own, based on the one that produced the brain changes we have been talking about, so you can experience them for yourself.

The good news is you don't have to memorize or even fully understand any of the things I have talked about in this chapter. By practicing mindfulness yourself, you will make all these discoveries on your own. My hope is that this book will inspire you to practice, set you off in a good direction, and save you time by learning from my mistakes and those others have made.

Now that we have explored what mindfulness is, we will look at the ways we can apply these principles for responding to challenges, both minor and serious, and for enriching our daily lives. But first, let's explore misconceptions about mindfulness, and what makes it different from other self-development techniques.

3

What Mindfulness Is Not

By paying attention, we can begin to notice how often our ideas can mislead us.

My martial arts teacher Stephen K. Hayes had a rare opportunity in the mid-1980s to go into communist-occupied Tibet and visit some of the temples and sites there. When he came back out, he went to Dharamsala, India, for an audience with the Dalai Lama who wanted to hear details of what he saw in Tibet. After their conversations, the Dalai Lama asked Mr. Hayes where he was from. It turned out that the Dalai Lama's oldest brother, Dr. Norbu, was a professor at Indiana University, and he suggested they get together when Mr. Hayes got back to the States.

Later, when the Dalai Lama came to visit Dr. Norbu, Mr. Hayes was asked to assist with security. At that time, the US government would not recognize His Holiness as a special dignitary, due to the political tensions with China, so would not provide Secret Service protection. Ever since then, Mr. Hayes has been a friend of the Dalai Lama's family, and still occasionally helps with security. A couple of weekends in the mid-1990s, he invited me to go along with him. It was a magical experience. It was one of the times when I was most mindful, and it also helped me become more aware of what mindfulness is not.

Wherever we went, our team was quite diligent about searching all the rooms for potential explosives or hidden weapons, paying particular attention to where sniper rifles could be positioned. Since the Dalai Lama was a

Mindfulness: Living through Challenges and Enriching Your Life in This Moment, First Edition. Richard W. Sears.
© 2014 John Wiley & Sons, Ltd. Published 2014 by John Wiley & Sons, Ltd.

Dalai Lama security team, 1996. Author is far left, Dr. Norbu far right. © David Piser.

walking advertisement that his country had been invaded, it was a very real possibility that he could be a target for assassination. However, our team most often dealt with fervent fans who wanted to be near His Holiness.

Our biggest job was to keep him moving in order to get him to the next venue on time. People strongly desired to touch and talk to the Dalai Lama, who would often try to stop, shake hands, and make eye contact with individual well-wishers. Our team had to be the bad guys and move him along. Of course, considering that the Dalai Lama is a recipient of the Nobel Peace Prize, we could not yell at the fans, or apply force in any way. From our training in the ninja arts, we could employ very subtle body movements to gently disrupt balance. Rather than pushing someone back forcefully, I could carefully use footwork to place my body in just the right spot to cause the person to slightly lose their balance, creating a need for them to take a small step back to regain their balance. In that small opening, I could move forward to gently nudge the Dalai Lama along. The highest level of protector is invisible, doing what must be done without being noticed, without becoming a target, without generating resistance.

Each venue we traveled to was completely sold out, with people lined up outside the doors. Sometimes, we could slip past people before they realized he was coming, or who he really was. Local police would do their best to set up barriers and block off roads to keep the crowds back, but sometimes swarms of people would descend upon us.

The Dalai Lama had a knack for quickly slipping through the openings we created for him, surging forward ahead of us while we were held back by the crowds. I quickly figured out that if I started far out ahead of the Dalai Lama, he would eventually catch up to me. There were many times when I ended up alone with him as we made our way onward.

On one such occasion, I was out with the Dalai Lama on a street in Chicago after a sold-out presentation. A few clever people had noticed the police tape and stood there on the chance that they might be able to catch a glimpse of His Holiness. Seeing the sincerity of those people, the Dalai Lama stopped to shake hands with them.

Keeping the Dalai Lama in my peripheral vision, I continued to scan the environment. This was a public street. There were no metal detectors and no security screening process. A hand moving toward His Holiness could be holding a flower, a knife, or a pistol. Purses and bags could contain anything. It was impossible to focus on any one possibility, and I most certainly would not want to tackle an old woman who only wanted to shake hands with the Dalai Lama. I had to keep my awareness very broadly open, and trust that my entire brain would process the scene and alert me to any suspicious developments.

I quickly caught site of a man who had crossed the cones and police tape, lingering in the street. He was dressed in somewhat ragged clothes, wearing a hooded sweatshirt and old sneakers. I did not see any bulges in his clothing, and didn't sense any immediate threat. Since it wasn't my job to go and tell him what the rules were, I stayed by the Dalai Lama's side, maintaining a broad awareness as best I could.

The event coordinator then appeared, dressed in a fancy suit, and walked up to the man in the sweatshirt and greeted him with a big smile and hug. Using what I then thought were my well-honed powers of observation, the thought arose that he must be the coordinator's teenage son.

A couple of minutes later, the Dalai Lama caught sight of the man in the sweatshirt. A huge grin came over the face of His Holiness and he quickly moved toward him with arms wide for a big hug. They chatted for a minute or two with arms entwined. I found that a bit confusing, but then the Dalai Lama is quite a kind and loving person. Perhaps they had shared a nice dinner at the coordinator's house the night before.

When the rest of the security team caught up with us, Mr. Hayes quickly guided the Dalai Lama to his police cruiser for the motorcade escort to the next venue. After a last, quick survey of the surrounding environment, we each shuffled for empty seats in the police cars as if we were playing a game of musical chairs. The man in the hoodie ended up sitting right next to me. I immediately had the thought that I should reach out my hand and introduce myself. I'm still not really sure why I didn't, other than perhaps being hypnotized by the excitement of the motorcade moving through the streets of Chicago as police cruisers blocked the intersections for us, sirens blaring, people staring.

Mr. Hayes also wrote about this scene later, after hearing about the passing away of this man in the hooded sweatshirt.

Mid-1990s in Chicago. I was coordinating Illinois police with Tibetan security agents of His Holiness the Dalai Lama for the Tibetan leader's visit. I noticed a quiet young guy who appeared to be a homeless person in a faded car wash hoodie with a badly shaved head who somehow infiltrated the Dalai Lama's entourage. He appeared harmless, and Tibetans went over and spoke to him, so I figured his presence had been handled.

Time to move, and our police motorcade pulled up in front of the building. I got the Dalai Lama in his car, split up the Tibetans in other cars, and then with two monks got in the police cruiser I had been assigned.

The little homeless guy tried to get in my car too. Politely but firmly I told him, "Sir, this is a motorcade vehicle. You'll need to get your own transportation." He said in a confused voice that he had been told to get in this car. Losing valuable time, I told him no. The police driver made it worse by looking over the seat at the young guy and saying to me, "It's OK. We have room." I ignored the driver and repeated that he could not ride in that car. Wordlessly, the young homeless guy backed out and closed the door and we sped away with siren and lights.

The next day I escorted the Dalai Lama to a speaking venue and spotted the same little guy in the same faded car wash logo hoodie. I asked the Dalai Lama's younger brother if he knew who that was. He looked over and then back to me and smiled, "That's Adam Yauch. His Beastie Boys did a benefit concert and raised millions of dollars for the free Tibet cause."

My heart sank. That was the "homeless guy" I threw out of my police cruiser yesterday.

I knew I had to apologize, and so braced for a rock star blast of ego and rage, and walked over to Adam Yauch. "I am so sorry for what happened yesterday in the motorcade confusion ... "

He looked me in the eye and cut me off mid-sentence. "No, it's OK. I completely understand. Yours has got to be the most difficult job of all," he said in a firm and sincere voice. "Thank you for all you are doing to keep the Dalai Lama safe."

20-some years later I am still moved thinking about that classy rock star bright light. RIP MCA. You made a big impression in the world and never stopped giving. You will be missed.

If trained ninja teachers can get caught by the misleading appearance of a famous rock star, after decades of practicing mindfulness and being in the company of some of the most compassionate people in the world, it is an important reminder of the power of thoughts. It is important to stay safe, and to set boundaries, but let's not wall ourselves off. We can practice staying in the moment and greeting every human being for who they are within, whether potential or actualized. It is of course natural and okay to make mistakes, but we can learn to catch them sooner, or at least become more aware of them, and then make conscious efforts to repair our mistakes.

In this case, we thought we were paying attention to the moment, but did not recognize that our thoughts were interfering with what we were actually seeing. Mindfulness has to be more than just being present. We are also thinking, feeling human beings, and it is important to engage all of our faculties consciously.

Of course, a conscious choice was made in the above scenario to prioritize safety. It was better to make a small mistake and apologize later, than to be too "accepting" and allow a tragedy to occur. Increased awareness helps us to balance compassion and assertiveness.

When reading about mindfulness, we can begin to form a number of idealistic concepts about what it is. In this chapter, we will explore what mindfulness is not, to clear our minds before we apply it to the most challenging of human problems in later chapters. We will then explore how we can enrich all of the moments of our lives.

Noticing Our Ideas

Whenever I give presentations on mindfulness, people inevitably approach me afterwards, and say, "Mindfulness is just like _____." You can fill in that blank with literally thousands of words. Naturally, our human brains are programmed to try to fit new ideas into the framework of what we already know. This can be a useful survival mechanism, making it easier to learn new things, but it can also cause us to be biased and prevent us from reaching a deeper understanding. Of course, this is what mindfulness is all about: recognizing when we are using mental shortcuts, and consciously choosing to let go of the ones that are not serving us in the moment.

One of the reasons people see mindfulness as being similar to other things they do or have seen is because mindfulness is a natural human capacity that we all possess, so of course it is everywhere. No one has a copyright or trademark on mindfulness. But since we so often add extra ideas onto simple concepts, it is important to distinguish it from other methods. In mindfulness, we practice acceptance and the suspension of judgment when we choose to do so, but we retain our ability to consciously notice differences. In the sections below, we will explore these differences and misconceptions in greater detail.

I want to emphasize that "different" does not mean "wrong," and certainly doesn't make mindfulness "better" than another approach. The point is not to go on a crusade for mindfulness, or feel righteous because you now know the "right" way to do it. Don't throw away other things that work! Life becomes richer with more flexibility, not less. If you only have a hammer in your toolbox, everything will look like a nail. If you want to construct a beautiful and meaningful life, it is best to keep a large number of tools handy. The hardest challenge, and the part that mindfulness can help with, is knowing when to use which tool, and for what purpose.

Not Always Rainbows and Butterflies

In books and articles on mindfulness, you will often see lovely pictures of clouds, mountains, water, and rainbows. These are inspiring images to help bring us into the moment, because we don't need to add a lot of words or interpretations onto those images. However, because mindfulness is

Dolphin leaping. © Olivia Ossege.

simply noticing, we could just as well use pictures of storms and lightning. For many people though, such scenes can bring up unpleasant memories and feelings.

Mindfulness is about being with whatever is happening in this moment, not about "making" yourself happy. If you are only trying to be in this moment because you want it to change, you are not really in your present experience – you are in your head, thinking and judging how it should be different. If strong unpleasant feelings are here, we can learn to stay present with them, then either wait for them to pass or make a conscious choice about how to proceed. Ironically, chasing after happiness to escape negative feelings tends to push the happiness away. Letting go of our struggles with how things are in this moment allows more space for happiness to blossom.

It's easy to be mindful in beautiful landscapes surrounded by loved ones, but it takes practice to be able to stay present during difficult times. As a therapist, I have listened to clients graphically describe suicide attempts, murders, and horrible sexual abuses from their childhoods. Mindfulness helps me stay present with these individuals without naively trying to put a positive spin on it.

Recently, I sat on the floor of my office with a client who was speaking from her three-year-old self. She courageously described a murder she had witnessed at that age, and how she was forced to help bury the body. She had never told this to anyone before, and in fact, had been told at the time that if she ever talked about it or cried about it, she would be buried too. After decades of holding it in, she sobbed with her full being. What she needed most at that time was my presence, to stay with her, to validate her feelings. My mindfulness practice helped me to do that, which will help her learn to do that for herself. As she was telling me these awful things, it would not have been helpful at all to tell her to "stay positive" or "look at the bright side," and in fact it would have interfered with the healing process.

Mindfulness is not necessarily about thinking positively. There is actually research that suggests that trying to tell yourself something positive can make you feel worse, because your brain knows that you are only telling yourself that because it is not true. Saying it to yourself can highlight the fact that you are "falling short" of where you want to be. Though it may seem only a superficial difference, instead of trying to escape how you are now, you can practice first accepting where you are in this moment. This helps to ground you, which allows you to set a positive direction that draws you toward what you value.

Mindfulness is also not necessarily about silence and inactivity. Though we often practice mindfulness exercises sitting still, it is actually a very active process. I've heard stories of people leading a group by saying something like "Let's all be mindful," then sitting in silence for a long period of time. This is fine for experienced practitioners, but can lead beginners to think that mindfulness is a type of zoning out. While there is a practice Jon Kabat-Zinn calls "choiceless awareness," in which we are simply open to whatever experiences are happening moment to moment (see Chapter 7), most beginners find it very challenging.

Some meditation teachers artificially speak slowly in a monotone voice, as if to imply that the goal is to be emotionless, or always blissed out. If you've lived a life of chaos, you may think it would be nice to be always calm, but most of us would find that boring after a while. Of course, it is understandable to not want to be stuck in chaos, or to be soaring and crashing all the time, but you do still want to feel alive. Learning ways to make the waves more moderate, and learning to surf the ups and downs of life, makes it far richer and zestier.

Mindfulness also does not mean always moving at a slow rate. Slowing things down can help us pay more attention, but maintaining awareness moment to moment does not require us to move like zombies. In considering things like making love, being fully present while shifting between moving slowly and quickly makes for a sublime experience.

Mindfulness and acceptance also does not mean that no matter what happens, you sit back and say, "Hey, that's groovy." Noticing how things are in this moment, you may need to set some firm boundaries, or engage in hard love or "fierce compassion." Mindfulness can help us be more clear in the moment to ensure our next choice is what is best for ourselves and others, rather than an unhelpful automatic reaction.

My four-year-old sometimes thinks I'm mean when I don't give her a lollipop when we are about to eat supper. Accepting how things are doesn't mean I automatically give her one. It does mean that I accept that she wants one in that moment, because her four-year-old brain is still growing its self-regulation parts. I don't take her demands and threats personally, so I am better able to model containing her emotions without reacting harshly, and making good choices in spite of strong feelings.

When guiding the Dalai Lama through a crowd, my heart melted to see the faces of so many people wanting so desperately to touch him. I wished that everyone could just sit down with him and have tea, but thousands of others were waiting at the next venue. My job required very active mindfulness. Sometimes I noticed small gaps in space and time through which we could slip. Sometimes I needed to prevent a gap from closing by placing myself between an individual and His Holiness. Other times, when gentle words were ineffective, I created gaps by gently leaning on someone, or by surreptitiously placing my knee in just the right spot, so that a slight imbalance created a subtle human domino effect away from us.

Avoiding and Letting Go

So what do we do with unpleasant feelings? Should we always move into them? Don't we all want to avoid suffering and be happy?

Ideally, we would all set up our lives to minimize suffering and maximize happiness. However, the reality is that at least some suffering is unavoidable. I'm certainly not suggesting that we should go searching for suffering and dive into it wherever we find it. The important question is, what do we do when we are suffering in this moment?

Because no one wants to suffer, when it shows up, we want it to go away. But as we have already discussed, and will explore further in the next couple of chapters, avoidance has a way of making unpleasant feelings worse, because it can lead to an internal vicious cycle of struggle.

This is most obvious for things like substance abuse or cigarette smoking. These things really do make us feel a little (or a lot) better immediately, but of course, when overly relied upon create more problems in the long run in terms of our relationships and physical health.

Less obvious are the very subtle forms of avoidance. Almost anything we do to try not to feel our feelings as they are right now can keep them stuck. By their nature, feelings are giving us important information, so they can become stronger when we ignore them or push them away. Ironically, we can even attempt to use mindfulness as a way to escape unpleasant feelings. When you mindfully feel your breathing, it can help you anchor into the moment, allowing you to let go of internal struggles. A nice "side effect" of letting go of struggle is relaxation. However, if you "can't stand" the way you are feeling, and try to focus on the breath to make the bad feelings go away, you become hooked in the struggle.

People can miss this point even after many years of practice. A woman who attended one of my mindfulness workshops told me that it was a major epiphany for her to realize that for 20 years, she had been practicing yoga and meditation as a way to avoid feeling anxious, and had not been able to figure out why she still struggled with it.

You can become completely absorbed and present in an activity, such as gardening, which provides a wonderful opportunity to feel the earth, smell the flowers, and breathe fresh air. But if you are gardening because you are trying to avoid something, that something will likely still be there after the gardening is done. If thoughts and feelings come up while you are gardening, you can notice them, then choose to either feel them for a moment, or return to your gardening. Of course, it's perfectly fine to choose to do something like gardening to get more into the moment when your thoughts become overwhelming and you want to get them out of your head.

Though avoidance in general tends to make things worse, when you do it as a choice rather than an automatic reaction, it can actually be helpful. For example, escaping a stressful and ambiguous situation is sometimes a healthy thing to do, but maybe not in the middle of an important business deal. By first noticing what is, you can consciously decide how you want to handle it, rather than habitually running away from unpleasant feelings. You could still choose to avoid. The point is to develop psychological flexibility so that avoidance is not your only option.

Joseph LeDoux talks about a concept called "proactive avoidance," using the example of social anxiety. If you are afraid to be around people, spending a great deal of time trying to avoid people will keep that anxiety going. On the other hand, forcing yourself to go to lots of parties might traumatize you if you can't stay with it long enough to wait for the exposure effect, the natural rising and falling of anxiety, to occur. Using proactive avoidance means that you would choose to go to some parties, but purposefully plan out ways you could retreat when you wish in order to have a sense of control over the mounting anxiety. For instance, you could plan to tell people you needed to go outside to make a phone call or choose to escape into the restroom for a little while.

If you have a headache, you might choose to take an aspirin to make it go away. We would not say that you are "avoiding" the headache, and that you should feel it more. However, if you are camping in the wilderness, and forgot to pack aspirin, you would probably want to have more options than "freaking out" if you get a headache. If you are suffering from daily headaches, and mindlessly gobble down aspirin all day long, you will likely develop long-term problems. Instead of only relying on aspirin, you could choose to pay more attention to the stress in your life, do more neck stretches, seek medical consultation, and so on.

Mindfulness is not necessarily a way to "feel better." If you are feeling bad, you are feeling bad. This does not mean you become masochistic. It involves fostering an attitude of curiosity and exploration. It may sound strange at first, but what do you even mean when you tell yourself you are feeling "bad"? Moving into it allows the experience to break up a bit, which allows you to loosen your resistance to it. Hence, you don't push aside your feelings, but you also don't have to chase after or dive into every single feeling that comes along. Through practice, your thoughts and feelings tend to flow more freely, sticking to you less. You can find a balance between avoidance and over-analyzing every whimsical feeling that blows by.

In the space created in this way, we can more easily choose to let go. Letting go means letting go of our resistance to what is happening right now. It does not mean pushing away.

You could be aware in this moment of how much you miss a loved one, or how much you are hurting from the loss of a relationship. Rather than push away those thoughts and feelings, acknowledge they are here. If you can, allow yourself to feel them fully, and notice the thoughts in your mind. If you need to go to work and meet your other responsibilities, just let them come and go in your mind as best you can. If you are in the middle of an important meeting, after you notice them, you can re-direct your attention to what is happening in front of you, letting yourself know that you will attend to them more fully later on if they are still present.

We get into trouble when we continuously fight our own emotions, not realizing that our brains are simply trying to help by distracting us with something else to focus on. Strong emotions grab our attention, but we may not notice how often we mix in thoughts, memories, and unrealistic expectations. Noticing allows us to move into and explore what is really going on, and prevents those feelings from negatively impacting how we are treating ourselves and others. The best decisions are made when we know what is really happening in this moment.

When strong feelings and thoughts are overwhelming and persistent, feeling "nothing" becomes attractive. This is why suicide becomes an attractive option for many, the ultimate way to avoid tortuous thoughts and feelings. It certainly works, but that method is irreversible, and it causes immeasurable pain for those around the person who committed suicide. It takes a degree of faith, developed through practice, to experience that "this too shall pass."

The goal is not to become blank, emotionless, and thoughtless. We can become less "sticky," letting thoughts and feelings flow more freely from moment to moment. It all comes down to noticing. Noticing our thoughts, emotions, sensations, and the world around us. Noticing our judgments and reactions to what we notice. We can learn to more often feel whatever feeling is already here, acknowledge it, and let it go.

There is a popular Zen story of two monastics taking a long journey. Along the way, they came to a river that had become very difficult to cross after days of rain. A beautiful woman was standing there, looking worried, unsure if she would be able to cross. Without hesitation, one of the monastics approached her respectfully, picked her up, carried her across the river, and put her down on the other side. The woman expressed her thanks and went on her way. As the two monastics continued on their journey, one of them couldn't stop thinking about what had happened, and became increasingly irritated at the one who had picked up the woman. Finally he could stand it no longer, and said, "Why did you pick up a woman like that? You know that is not becoming for a monastic." The other man looked surprised, and said, "I put her down on the other side of the river. Are you still carrying her?"

Sometimes we can put her down easily, sometimes she sticks to us, sometimes we cling to her desperately. Before you decide what to do with her, you'd better recognize where she is first. We can't let go of her if we don't acknowledge she is there.

Problems arise through habitual, compulsive avoidance. Awareness brings freedom of choice. You can still choose to avoid whenever you want. Sometimes I just enjoy a glass of wine and a mindless science fiction movie. Mindfulness is not the boss of us. We must be careful not to put it on a pedestal.

Not Mindfulness with a Capital "M"

Although I'm sure I inadvertently do this from time to time, I have noticed a tendency for some people to talk about Mindfulness as if it were spelled with a capital "M," as if it were something to revere. Although it is often an important part of spiritual practices and is present in various forms in almost all spiritual traditions, mindfulness itself is not a religion.

Of course, it is a natural human tendency to revere things that are special to us. Some people spend their whole lives following a sports team, religiously watching each game, wearing the team's colors, and surrounding their living and work spaces with sports paraphernalia. Their moods may rise and fall based on their team's performance. Losing a beloved player to retirement can induce a period of mourning.

My Fender Stratocaster guitar is very special to me. It is a tool for deep emotional expression. I get a little uncomfortable if strangers put their fingers all over it, and it is a showing of deep respect if I ask someone if they want to play it. When my daughter picked it up and dropped it on the floor when she was two years old, my heart stopped for a moment, but I did not yell at her. It is really only metal, wood, and plastic, and she was just doing what two-year-olds do.

Mindfulness is a natural human process. What makes it special is its ordinariness. It is not a set of commandments. It does not require a commitment to any belief system. However, it can be very helpful for informing us about what to do. As Alan Watts said, you are absolutely free to put your hand in the fire, but you should know that you will get burned. If it so happens that you don't want to get burned, you might just choose not to put your hand in the fire.

The practice of mindfulness is more about asking, "How's this working for me?"

When I conducted psychotherapy groups on an inpatient psychiatric unit, the nurses would tease me about getting their PRNs ready, meaning that after my groups, patients would frequently ask for something to calm them down. Because I could stay present with them without fear of how extreme their conditions were, I could ask direct questions. A woman named Dora once came in to the group with bandages wrapped all around one of her arms. She explained to the group what had happened that morning. Having just arrived on the unit yesterday, she had not yet been cleared for the privilege of being escorted out of the locked down unit to the outside courtyard for a cigarette break. Creatively, she managed to disconnect a "J" pipe from one of the sinks, and used it to bash into the wire-mesh-supported small window of one of the exit doors. She had managed to push her arm through the small opening she made, badly cutting her arm on the glass, and was about to release the door when the orderlies grabbed her. She was now on a 24-hour watch, and had everything removed from her room but a mattress.

I asked Dora a "how's that working for you?" kind of question, something like, "Was it worth it?"

Dora stared at me unblinkingly with a smirk. "Obviously, you are not a smoker!"

If you are willing to accept the consequences, you can choose to do whatever you want to do. Mindfulness does not tell you what you "should" do, it just helps you become more aware of how things are, and of how things evolve as a result of your actions. Dora did not like the way her body was feeling from nicotine withdrawal. Her automatic habit was to smoke a cigarette, no matter what it took. By noticing more directly what she was feeling, she could have still chosen to smash a window, but she could have also chosen to ask for something from the nurses, to take a walk through the corridors, or to just allow herself to feel uncomfortable until it passed.

Mindfulness is about conscious awareness. It does not dictate what you should do. However, clearly seeing the reality of the moment can be extremely helpful in making a choice in what to do in the next moment.

John Rudisill, a mentor of mine who wrote a book about organizational consultation with me,[1] told me that one of the best compliments he ever received as a consultant was, "You ask very good questions." In consultation and psychotherapy work, clearly defining the problem often allows clients to find solutions from within themselves.

But what about ethical behavior? Can mindfulness become a tool for evil? Whether or not you believe in any kind of cosmic retribution, when you pay attention, you will notice more and more how interconnected we are with the world and everyone in it. If I treat someone badly, I have just made more disharmony in the world in which I live. I would much prefer to live in a world full of happy people. Likewise, if I throw litter on the ground, I just made my own home dirtier.

Of course, you may subscribe to or be inspired by the moral codes of a specific spiritual tradition, but anyone who does comparative religion studies will notice strong similarities between traditions. How to act in any given moment becomes clear when you pay close attention.

Problems can arise when we take ourselves too seriously, and when we expect others to share our zeal in spite of having different life experiences. Very likely, at some point in this book so far, you read something and thought, "Oh, my friend really needs to read this!" As my mentor Stephen K. Hayes said, if you give unsolicited advice, it is called meddling. If someone becomes interested in asking you about how to deal with a specific problem, then you can say, "I'm so glad you asked." If you find mindfulness to be helpful, it is best to show by example, not by talking.

Don't become a "militant for mindfulness," either for yourself or others. Even experienced mindfulness practitioners get caught up in the tyranny of the "shoulds."

The famous Zen master Seung Sahn was known to often tell his students, "When eating, just eat. When walking, just walk." His message was to simply practice being present in whatever activity you were doing in the moment. However, one morning a Zen student came in and found the Zen master sitting and reading the newspaper while he was eating his breakfast. The student stopped and said, "Great Zen master, you have always told us, 'when eating, just eat,' yet here you are, eating and reading the newspaper!" Without skipping a beat, the Zen master casually responded, "When eating and reading the newspaper, just eat and read the newspaper."

We may get the idea that since mindfulness is about paying attention, we "should" pay attention all the time – as if your teacher will be spying on you, or the Mindfulness Police will give you a citation for mindlessness.

When I check in with people after leading them through a mindfulness exercise, I sometimes hear, "I did terribly! My mind was wandering all over the place!" After normalizing that experience, I might ask, "What percentage of the time were you able to stay present in the moment?," to which the person might respond with something like "50 percent of the time." For most of us, a 50 percent was an F in school, so we feel like failures. I emphatically state that consciously recognizing that one's mind has wandered and consciously bringing it back half the time is an amazing accomplishment! If they continue practicing, they may bring it up to 55 or 60 percent.

Remember that there is an arousal, or "waking up" component to mindfulness, which requires energy. No one ever said the goal is to be mindful 100 percent of the time. If you are fully present in your life about 5 percent of the time right now, imagine how much richer it would be if you showed up 10 percent of the time. Perfectionists tend to have a hard time with this concept, but that too can become an important part of their mindfulness practice.

Mindfulness is also not a race, and not something to be forced. When I was 15 years old, I really wanted to become a ninja, so I decided to train myself to become more aware, inspired by novels that were not at all based in reality. I decided to place caltrops, twisted bits of metal that always landed with a sharp point up, on the floor of my bedroom. I also placed a few semi-sharp knives pointing outward on a couple of shelves just inside my door. I was proud of myself for how well I noticed and avoided these objects for the first week or two. After a while, however, I became accustomed to them being there, and I should have put them away the day one of the spikes cut a hole in my sneaker, barely missing my foot. However, I felt spurred to carry on with even more diligence.

After about another week, I came walking into my room barefoot. In a scene that looked like it could have been rehearsed for a slapstick comedy movie, I stepped on a spike, jumped up and scraped my back against a knife, fell over as I tried to avoid stepping on more spikes, slammed my hand into a mirror and shattered it, and dripped blood all over the floor. I still have a scar on my hand from the cut.

It is impossible to "force" a natural process, and we usually only confuse ourselves or wear ourselves out when we try.

There is a classic Zen story of a student walking with his teacher in the mountains. As they paused to rest, they gazed out at all the beauty around them. The student said, "The hills are the body of the divine, the wind is the breath of the divine, the sound of the bird is the voice of the divine. Is that not so?"

"Yes," said the teacher. "But it's a pity to say so."

This student would be said to "stink of Zen." He is making something artificial, putting legs on a snake, putting frost on top of snow, gilding the lily. The mountain beauty can be much more directly experienced without all that talk.

Mark Muesse[2] relates an interesting modern analogy. He once rented a movie he had never seen before and was excited to watch it. As the credits were rolling, he could hear commentary from the director and the producer. He tried turning off the commentary, but was unsuccessful. He was hoping it would stop when the movie began, but it continued. Even when the actors began their dialogue, the voices continued to comment on what was happening. "The actor actually was supposed to say something else, but this was so funny we decided to leave it in the final cut." Dr. Muesse became more and more annoyed as the continuous commentary interfered with his ability to hear and experience the actual movie.

It then dawned on him that this defective movie was similar to how we live our lives. We are often so busy thinking about and commenting on our experiences that we are not fully engaged in them. This layer of thinking between us and reality is not usually perfectly transparent. It distorts our perceptions. As we are talking to a friend, we may be thinking about how she is dressed, and miss something she says. If we are telling ourselves we need to do well on the test we are taking, we will get in our own way.

Many mindfulness teachers suggest using words or thoughts as a scaffold for strengthening attention. They may suggest saying, "I am breathing in," as you inhale, and "I am breathing out," as you exhale. This is useful as a learning tool, but it is not technically mindfulness, as it is adding a filter, a layer of thoughts and words, between reality and our experience of it. Ironically, even telling yourself, "I am being mindful right now," means you are thinking, and not fully in your experiences. Of course in those moments the words are part of your experience too, but you may confuse the words with the experience. Eventually, you don't need to rely on the words.

It's a pity that I'm writing so much. I sincerely apologize that this book "stinks of mindfulness." Words are very limiting. As you read through this book, you will find many inconsistencies, judgments, and contradictions. Once you have your own experience of mindfulness, you are likely to find much better ways of expressing many of these concepts.

Eventually, or maybe in an instant, there comes a point when you "get" all this. We are using words as tools, but when you have a deep experience of it, you don't need the words anymore. You will embody it. It is so rewarding to me when I see that shift taking place toward the end of my mindfulness groups. The individuals no longer have to ask me questions to get the "right"

Flower. © Jeremy Rogers.

answers. We can share things, and learn new perspectives from others, but there is no "thing" to "get." You just become a more fully human being. This is the real meaning of transmission that is often used in meditative traditions.

Once, when he was asked to give a teaching, Siddhartha Gautama only held up a flower. Of the hundreds of people gathered, only Mahakasyapa smiled. Siddhartha said, "I transmit my true teaching to you."

What was transmitted? What did Mahakasyapa get?

I am smiling as I write this, hoping that you are too.

Mindfulness as "Getting Something"

And yet, it is so hard to let go of the idea that we need to "get something," because we have been conditioned to feel that we are not complete in this moment. Even throughout this book, I have been saying things like "mindfulness is a tool," which implies that you are to "use it" to "get something." But what else can you truly get outside of this very moment?

Of course, you may well have picked up this book because you are really suffering in this moment, and aren't interested in any "philosophy." In the next two chapters, I will give you very concrete principles for working with difficulties, based on psychological science. For now, just consider some of the ideas in this chapter lightly.

Understandably, people initially want to learn mindfulness to get something or to get rid of something. Even mindfulness teachers will sometimes say "Let's use mindfulness to _____ (relax, be positive, change our thoughts, etc.)." Originally, the publisher suggested "Using this Moment to Enhance Your Life" for the subtitle of this book. But how could you possibly "use" this moment? Mindfulness is simply stepping into the moment with conscious awareness. In the space of this moment, you can choose what you want to do, with more clarity, compassion, and wisdom.

Have you ever had the experience of wanting something really badly, and finally getting it, then discovering that the feeling wore off rather quickly? Maybe the thing you were chasing after just wasn't really the thing you wanted.

What do we really want, fundamentally?

Stephen K. Hayes taught me a profound exercise, and I had the privilege of having him do this with me as a demonstration at a couple of his seminars, the first one as a late adolescent. I was asked to sit down in a stable posture with my eyes closed. The exercise began with a very simple question.

"What do you want?"

My first answer came fairly quickly. "I'd like to own my own 4-seater airplane."

"Good," responded Mr. Hayes in a calm, encouraging voice, as he would do for the rest of the exercise. "And if you had your own 4-seater airplane, what even more important thing would that give you?"

It took me a few moments to ponder the question. I had just thought it would be "cool" to own an airplane – I hadn't thought much about what it would give me. "The ability to fly around the country with family and friends."

"Good. And if you had the ability to fly around the country with family and friends, what even more important thing would that give you?"

I paused longer as my answer came to me. "Rich experiences with people I care about."

"Good. And if you had rich experiences with people you cared about, what even more important thing would that give you?"

Even though I knew the questions would be coming, it was as if they were unexpectedly shifting me to something deeper. "The enjoyment of loving and being loved."

"Good. And if you had the enjoyment of loving and being loved, what even more important thing would that give you?"

You get the idea. My thinking mind became more frustrated to keep searching for answers, but the questions kept patiently coming. My answers took longer to bubble up, and got shorter and shorter, until they became one word answers, like "love," "freedom," "peace," and "oneness." My mind gradually entered a deeper, more expansive state of being.

I suggest you try this exercise for yourself. For some, it only takes a few minutes to reach a deep, open state. For others, it may take 30 minutes, or may take a few weeks of practice. It is not a race. Though you can try it on your own, we find that it works best to have a supportive partner there to ask you the questions.

Exercises like this can help us shift into our more natural "being" mode. We can get so caught up in "getting" and "doing" that we forget the big picture. We focus on acquiring money, and may forget that it is a tool that we exchange for things in the real world. We confuse the map with the territory. We collect menus but forget how to enjoy the dinners.

Compulsive doing and getting can be a form of avoidance. If I am not comfortable with who I am, I may chase after someone that makes me feel good about myself. If I am feeling a lack of meaning in my life, I can work hard to get some nice material object to help me feel better.

Of course we want deep intimate relationships, and to enjoy comfortable, interesting lives. But if we are not coming from a place of being, we will never feel content. If I still don't feel good about myself, the new relationship wears off after a while. If I still haven't created meaning in my life, I will get bored with the fancy toys I purchase.

Practicing mindfulness helps us to come back to "being." Whatever our initial motivations for learning it, we learn to let go of the habitual desire to get something "out" of life, and learn to be in it and enjoy it.

When I was young, I explored many different systems of self-development, always hoping to "get" that "secret something" that would make my life clear and easy. I spent years searching through and translating ancient texts. I would often find elaborate philosophical ideas and practices, designed to keep thinking minds like mine engaged, but they all seemed to come back to "just this moment." As an example, I once engaged in a complicated practice that took several hours, but left me feeling amazingly open, in the moment, peaceful, and patient for several days. When I later read over an excerpt from a private commentary that was passed along with the practice, it read:

> Although these categories are created to explain things, ultimately, all individual categories are false. The six great elements, the four mandalas, the three secrets, and so forth, do not really exist. Those categories are aids. They are devices used for the sake of practice. In the secret teachings, the practice itself is the end. This is the same idea as in mindfulness practice. Therefore, the accomplished practitioner is able to discard these categories and the devices they contain, and simply be awake in each moment.

So, all that complicated philosophy and those sophisticated practices were really just tricks, "skillful means," of helping me rediscover this moment.

I know people who shop around for secrets all their lives. This month they are studying some system, and next month they are just as excited about another system they just discovered. The problem with this approach is that they are constantly distracted from the moment they are in, and change when things get difficult for them, and therefore never get into any real depth of understanding.

Some people do this with their relationships. They find someone new, and think, "This is the one!" But the strong feelings fade over time, as feelings do if you don't actively work to maintain a relationship, and they are no longer distracted from their low sense of self-esteem. They become restless, look for someone else, and feel better for a little while, but get stuck in an unending cycle.

Don't misunderstand me. If you are suffering, of course you don't want to suffer any more. Of course you want to find and move toward those things that bring meaning and value to your life, like relationships, family, career, and spirituality, as we will discuss in Chapter 6. You are the one who chooses your direction in life, and you can have very active "doing" within your "being." The important thing to remember is that you are always starting your journey from right here, right now. Mindfulness is just noticing in the moment. In that moment, you can set a course toward what you value.

If you are continuously, compulsively trying to avoid this moment, or thinking about getting something in the future as a way to not feel bad now, you won't have much practice at being. How could you possibly enjoy that future when it finally does come, if you have only practiced thinking of other moments?

Practicing mindfulness does not mean you throw out common sense. Of course we still desire and try to get things out of life. It's nice to look forward to a weekend of fun, a new movie coming out, or buying the latest technological gadget. But by learning to pay attention, you might just find that the moments of your daily life are already far richer than you ever noticed they were.

Practice and Daily Life

In the mindfulness groups I lead, we do an exercise in which we have people write down the activities they do on a typical day. For most, it is very eye opening. What you are doing on a daily basis IS your life. Sometimes we get the idea that our daily lives are just something we go through to get to the weekend, or to some special practice retreat in the future.

I was once hooked by a question about practice and daily life. When I first began learning to give Zen *kōan* interviews to students, my teacher Paul Wonji Lynch would sit quietly and observe, giving me feedback afterward, and sometimes rescuing me when I got stuck. A Zen interview requires one to fully participate in the moment through dialogue and interactions. Students come to a teacher and are asked questions that hook their thinking, like, "Before your father and mother conceived you, what was your original nature?" However, the student is also free to challenge the teacher, or to ask any question about practice. A student once asked me, "I am feeling inspired now, and have been practicing regularly for several years, but I have this fear in the back of my mind that after I leave this retreat, I will slack off and not keep up the practice. How do I avoid slacking off?" As a new teacher in training, I was aware of at least three streams of thought going through my mind. I wanted to say something clever from a Zen perspective without falling into psychotherapist mode. I also wanted to say something that would actually help this person in front of me, because I had also shared that struggle in the past, and he was asking his question with sincerity. Simultaneously, I was aware of my teacher observing me, and wanted to impress him, or at least not say something stupid.

"So, you're concerned right now about slacking off in the future?" I asked, feeling a bit clever with what I thought was a Zen-like response.

"What would happen if you slacked off?" I was hoping the question would stop his thinking for a moment, but he simply said his cushion would sit unused, and he went on about how many times in his life he had stopped practicing.

Eventually, I began talking about how surrounding yourself with like-minded individuals can keep you inspired. My teacher suddenly slammed his stick on the ground and yelled in a loud voice, "Teacher – you've been hooked!" and we all laughed. "He turned the tables on you!"

He then turned to the student, "You ask me that question."

"How do I avoid slacking off in my practice?"

My teacher looked at him carefully. "So, you are making your practice separate. What is correct practice?"

The student thought for a moment, then hesitatingly said, "moment to moment … "

My teacher leaned closer to him. "How you keep your mind moment to moment. How can you slack off from your life? So, when you sit on your cushion, you are saying, 'This is my practice, and this is my life.' And you are saying that slacking off can't also be practice."

The silence in the room was palpable, effectively cutting off our thinking.

"Why can't you keep moment-to-moment mind while slacking off? What's preventing you from doing that?"

The student smiled. "Absolutely nothing!"

A moment of clarity burst through, and we all laughed out loud.

Having a regular formal practice is important for building our mindfulness muscles, as we will discuss in Chapter 7. But if you are only "present" during formal practice, what is the point? Why make formal practice different from daily life? There is only this moment! Are you not practicing right now? What do you see, hear, feel, taste, and smell?

It is certainly inspiring to practice in a meaningful place with inspiring friends, but we don't need to always seek out new, exciting experiences. We can bring more awareness into any moment.

It is easy to attend to novel things. The real practice is to cultivate wonder for daily things. We can begin by noticing how many "gaps" there are in the moments of even the busiest day. Instead of thinking and worrying about all the things you have to do while you are showering, and then standing there for a moment trying to remember whether or not you washed your hair after you turn off the water, you can actually experience the shower. Feeling the knob turn, watching the sparkles of light reflect off the water, hearing the patter of drops hitting the floor, feeling all the sensations on your skin as you wash your body, and smelling the soap. How could that be any less significant than formal practice?

One of the challenges is to stay fresh in each moment. A student of mine once said he had an amazing experience when he chose to pay attention during his shower. But then the next day, he felt like, "Oh, I did that already, no big deal." Can you imagine coming home to your friend or partner, and thinking, "Oh, seen her already." Or eating food, and thinking, "I've had chicken before, I'll zone out now." Unfortunately, these sentiments are all too common, and we don't realize we contribute to our own experience of life being dull. If we pay more attention, we will find that each moment, each experience is fresh and new, despite what our thinking tell us.

People also often express that they "don't have time" to practice mindfulness. Why can't you be in the moment when you are busy? Why would you want to wait for another moment to be in the moment? If you are busy right now, you can still be in this moment. In fact, you may even begin to let go of the stress of "feeling busy" when you are just doing what you are doing right now. As a side effect, you may even find yourself less stressed, more focused, and able to get more done.

In the Moment versus For the Moment

"Okay," you may be thinking, "just this moment. But what about paying my bills, finishing my college degree, or dealing with all of the awful things that happened to me in my past?"

Since most of the people I work with or who attend my classes are very busy, and are often living for the past or for the future, I tend to emphasize the importance of coming into the present moment. But choosing to more often be in the moment does not mean you neglect to plan for the future, or fail to learn from the past. It does not mean that you become forgetful, or fail to keep appointments. Individuals that I have met who are very good at being in the present, like the Dalai Lama, often have and keep many commitments, and reflect on and cherish their histories.

I am sometimes asked, "What about people who are 'too in the moment'?," meaning those who only live "for the moment" and neglect their responsibilities. When some people get money in their hands, they may spend it immediately, even though they need it for their rent. In part, this occurs when society does not truly provide equal opportunities. When you live in poverty, you often choose to do what you can for some relief from your distress in the moment, because you don't ever expect things to get better. If I will always feel stress about whether or not I can pay the rent, at least if I buy a big screen television, I will have something with which I can distract myself.

For others, living for the moment is often a symptom of avoidance. Such individuals may be afraid of what it would be like to be responsible or to take care of another person, or they have anxiety about being able to follow through on their commitments. This is in part fostered by our "wanting things now" culture, which delivers instant food and instant communication.

Just as we can only feel things in the present moment, we can also only avoid things in the present moment. Someone who doesn't like how they feel in this moment may even use other people for distraction. Rather than creating a deep, intimate relationship in which two people share their joys and sorrows, it becomes a vicious cycle of mutual distraction and hurt. At the extreme, someone may even turn to illicit drugs to avoid feeling bad in this moment, despite the long-term legal and health consequences.

Choosing to more often be in the moment should also not be confused with getting lost in the moment. You can be present in what you are doing without forgetting to go to work, or to feed your children. Choosing not to constantly think of all the things you have to do does not mean that you forget everything. You can write things down, set alarms, or use other forms of reminders. Memory works best when you are less stressed, exercising, eating well, and getting enough quality sleep.

Sometimes we are afraid to be more fully in the moment, worried that we will forget something. And you know what, honestly, maybe you will forget once in a while. But what's the other option? Are you just going to be so constantly vigilant that you can't enjoy your life because you're afraid you might forget something? How's that working for you?

How do you develop the capacity to be more fully in the moment? By engaging in mindfulness practices. How do you keep from becoming lost in the moment? By practicing discipline. There are a myriad of practices to develop your mind.

How Mindfulness Is Different from Other Methods

There are many methods for developing and working with the mind, and many of them are very useful and well-researched. In order to more fully understand how mindfulness works, it is important to highlight how these other methods are used and why they are different.

Clinical hypnosis

Hypnosis is a method of using induction techniques to put the conscious mind into a deep state of trance, facilitating the reprogramming of the subconscious mind. In this state, past traumas can be processed, important material can be explored, and suggestions can be made to influence a person's future perceptions and behaviors.

Clinical hypnosis should not to be confused with the drama of stage hypnosis, in which the most suggestible people in the crowd are carefully selected to provide entertainment by clucking like chickens and jumping like kangaroos. Clinical hypnosis has a fairly long history of success for a variety of therapeutic goals. Of note, there are significant differences among individuals as to how "hypnotizable" they are, or how susceptible they are to suggestion. It is also important to note that unlike in movies and television, you cannot be made to do anything that you would not deep down be okay doing, as your conscious mind would otherwise take over.

While I have used hypnosis clinically with some success, I have also had clients come to me and ask for hypnosis as a way of avoiding dealing with something difficult. "I want to just lay here while you make all these feelings go away," I was once asked. As you might guess, when hypnosis is used for avoidance, it doesn't work.

Sometimes mindfulness recordings sound hypnotic, but rather than putting the conscious mind aside, the goal is to become more conscious of your current experience, which allows you to make more deliberate choices in each moment. The gentle, easy tone often used by those leading mindfulness practices is meant to model and foster an attitude of openness and acceptance in the listener, not to induce a trance.

Relaxation methods

Unfortunately, there are still some who claim to teach mindfulness, but are actually teaching relaxation methods. This is not necessarily a bad thing, but this can create confusion. Mindfulness is about noticing what is happening right now. Relaxation often comes about as a "side effect," because when we accept what is happening in this moment, we let go of our own internal struggles. But if we try to "make" ourselves relax we can get ourselves into trouble, much like when we "try hard" to fall asleep, because those are things that only occur when we let go of effort and tension.

Relaxation methods are very useful and important, but like so many things we need to use them wisely. Ironically, researchers such as my colleague Tina Luberto have done studies showing that relaxation techniques can actually make you feel more stressed. How do we make sense of this?

We can think of relaxation methods as mini-vacations or mini-retreats. A retreat can be a wonderful thing when done in the right way. Going on vacation, assuming you can forget about your troubles while you are gone, and assuming you don't constantly check your phone and emails, provides a nice opportunity to relax and refresh yourself. The problem can be the shock to your system when you come back. All the work that you were not doing while you were gone is often waiting for you, in addition to all the work you usually need to do on any given day. The vacation might give you renewed energy, but you probably won't be able to take all the vacations you would like to take.

Likewise, a relaxation method which involves something like closing your eyes and imagining you are on vacation at a beach can help refresh your body and mind, but when you open your eyes, the work you have to do, or the difficult person you have to face, will still be there. Though you may have a little more energy, you will not have changed much about your relationship to your stressors.

Although mindfulness exercises often lead to relaxed states, this is not the purpose of the practice. If relaxation comes, it is due to our acceptance of things as they are in this moment. Mindfulness is about moving into our experiences, about riding the waves of our feelings, and becoming more comfortable in whatever moment we find ourselves in. Through practice, the distinction between work and vacation diminishes, and we are able to flow more often with less struggle throughout all of the activities of our lives. Instead of living for the weekends, we learn to engage all of our moments, and our lives therefore become much richer and more fulfilling.

Of course, relaxation methods are not bad things. We definitely need that relaxation response in our bodies on a regular basis. You must simply be conscious of how and when you wish to use these methods. If you rely on them as your only option when you are feeling bad, you will only set up a cycle of avoidance, which tends to make things worse in the long term. Of course you can choose to escape once in a while, but you are less likely to get caught in a downward spiral if you respond consciously rather than automatically reacting to unpleasant emotions.

Relaxation methods include such techniques as progressive muscle relaxation, visual imagery, biofeedback, and breathing techniques.

Progressive muscle relaxation
In this method, one moves through the body systematically, tensing muscle groups so that one can relax them more fully by recognizing the contrast between tension and relaxation. In the body scan, we are not attempting to change anything, but are fostering our ability to identify the way things are in this moment. By doing this, we can more easily let go of the tension we may be unconsciously holding in our bodies, or we can choose to employ a muscle relaxation technique after we notice the tension is there.

Visual imagery
Another commonly used relaxation method is visual imagery, in which you find a quiet place (or use noise canceling headphones) and close your eyes. By forgetting the stressful situation you are in, and imagining a safe, calm place in your mind, you can trigger the parasympathetic response, which counters the stress response and leads to relaxation.

Just as imagining a tiger or thinking about work sparks a stress response, imagining a peaceful, serene place, such as a beach, can evoke a relaxation response. However, if you are running away from (trying to escape) a tiger, and find your way to the beach, you'll still be afraid of the tiger, and won't be able to sit down and relax. If the only method you have for dealing with stress is running away in your mind to a peaceful scene, you will only be putting off dealing with the tigers of your mind.

Biofeedback

We now have remarkable technologies available to us to monitor our own heartbeat, brain waves, breathing rate, finger temperature (when you are stressed, blood flow to the extremities is restricted), and galvanic skin response (how much we sweat). These wonderful tools are often even available as portable electronic devices that we can carry with us. It is a fascinating experience to control your own unconscious bodily responses without even knowing how you are doing it. People often have amazing results using biofeedback.

One of the problems with biofeedback is generalizability, that is, being able to evoke the relaxation responses when you are not hooked up to the equipment.

Breathing techniques

Breathing can be a wonderful tool for coming into the moment, and for relaxing. It is physiologically linked to your stress response system. Breathing deeply from your diaphragm, or belly, rather than shallowly from your chest, helps kick in your body's relaxation response.

Feeling your breath is a wonderful mindfulness exercise, as you take it with you everywhere you go, and you are always breathing in any given moment. As with other relaxation methods, if you are focusing on your breath as an attempt to not feel how bad you are feeling, you will have limited success at best.

Other forms of meditation

Although various other forms of meditation are frequently used in conjunction with mindfulness, they have different goals and should not be confused with one another. We will discuss the various forms of meditation in more detail in Chapter 8.

Absorption

As mentioned in Chapter 2, absorption meditation states (such as Transcendental Meditation) are quite blissful. Many studies have confirmed concrete health benefits through its ability to lower the body's stress response.

This experience feels like stepping out of present moment reality, and entering an expanded sense of self, space, and time. When the meditation is completed, people often appear a bit dazed while adjusting again to daily reality. Of course, you cannot stay in this state continuously if you want to interact with the world.

When I lead mindfulness exercises, people with experience in absorption meditations sometimes tell me that they automatically "went off" into this deep state, and don't remember anything about what we did. I tell them that it is a wonderful skill to be able to achieve such a state so easily, but it is important to maintain conscious choice about doing it. Your relationships, for example, will not last very long if you slip off to another realm when conflict erupts.

Compassion and loving-kindness meditations
As we mentioned in Chapter 2, self-compassion is a key component of what makes mindfulness work. Compassion and loving-kindness meditations are often included in groups teaching mindfulness. Although mindfulness is about being with whatever is present, compassion and loving-kindness meditations work to consciously foster these positive emotions, because so many of us may have to overcome a history of being mistreated, being held to unrealistic expectations, having low self-esteem, and so forth. Self-compassion goes hand in hand with letting go of our compulsive negative judgments about ourselves. When we learn to be kinder to ourselves, our hearts become more open to a sense of deeper compassion for others.

Goal-directed meditations
There is a broad array of different kinds of meditation that fall under this category, some of which we will discuss in Chapter 8. They all share in common the purpose of achieving a specific goal, of changing how things are now into what you want them to be. Most of these meditations utilize thoughts, images, words, and gestures to reprogram the mind.

In mindfulness, rather than creating thoughts and images about goals, we simply watch the activity of the mind as it changes from moment to moment. This allows us to make clear choices about how best to act in whatever situation we are in. Then, when we do choose our goals, we are more clear about why we are choosing them and how to make them happen.

Moving toward values and goals is a very important part of living a fulfilling life. However, if we are not careful, we may be choosing our goals for the wrong reasons, such as trying to impress others.

Building Up of Ego

In ancient China, there was a story told of a monk who was so holy, the birds used to bring him offerings of flowers. One day, as he was walking with his friend, a tiger jumped out across their path. The friend jumped out of fear, and the tiger ran away. The holy monk said, "I see it is still with you," meaning that his friend was still at the mercy of his emotions.

Later, when no one was looking, the friend wrote the word for "divinity" on the seat where the monk was accustomed to sit. When the monk came to sit, he saw the sacred writing and hesitated. The friend said, "I see it is still with you!" At that remark, the monk was said to have become fully enlightened, and the birds never brought any more flowers.

Mindfulness is about becoming more natural, not making yourself more special than everyone else. An experienced practitioner is more in touch with feelings, not less. If a tiger jumps out in front of you, and you feel nothing, you likely have brain damage. If you feel it, it will pass more quickly.

Perhaps because many teachers have been able to struggle with themselves less, they appear very calm. New students might mistakenly think the goal is to feel nothing. In their crusade to avoid their feelings, they may use mindfulness practice as a way to avoid looking honestly at themselves, or they may distract themselves by pointing out the mistakes others are making. More insidiously, they may use their practice as a way to impress others, or may become teachers as an attempt to raise their own self-esteem.

Ironically, I have seen intense competition among so-called self-development teachers. As the late Alan Watts observed,[3] there is no greater ego game than the one in which teachers are trying to feel important by teaching others to get rid of their egos. "I have less ego than you do!" "I am more humble than you are!" "I am more compassionate than you are, you son of a bitch!" Though it sounds funny, such attitudes are frighteningly common and lead to tragic consequences.

Another form of this attitude is "that's the way we've always done it." Tradition can be important, and we shouldn't be quick to throw something out before we understand why it has been passed on. But just because you have always done something a certain way doesn't mean it's the best way. Hundreds of years ago, Europeans thought bathing was bad, which contributed to the loss of half its population to the Black Death.

In Zen, if you want to be a teacher, it's suspicious. If you are paying attention, you realize how little you know, so don't really want the responsibility of being a teacher. You also see that mindfulness is a natural process that everyone already has. Zen teachers often make fun of themselves, saying that all they are doing is "selling water by the river."

Why do you want to learn mindfulness? It's okay to want to feel important, but it helps to be aware of that, and not fool yourself.

Although ostensibly being willing to protect someone else's life with your own is the supreme demonstration of humility, protecting the Dalai Lama was actually quite an ego trip. It was hard to pretend to be humble when I walked out next to the Dalai Lama onto a stage lit with bright lights, with a crowd of thousands cheering and standing up. I most certainly felt alive in those moments.

Though our job as protectors was to be invisible, I have to confess that I greatly enjoyed the spotlight. We watched ourselves on the Chicago evening news, and felt like kids as each of the four members of our ninja team pointed and said "That's me! There I am! There you are, David!" We spent time with celebrities, who in fact sometimes just became ordinary people who also wanted to get near His Holiness.

Despite the significant expansion of my own ego, I was so impressed by the humility of many of those around me. The three Tibetan bodyguards who always traveled with the Dalai Lama at that time were always smiling and appreciative toward us. I never sensed any attitude of "We're the real bodyguards here."

At one point, as we were making security preparations at a theatre in Chicago before His Holiness arrived, a woman approached us and said, "Mr. Gere is about to arrive. Can I have one of you secret agents come out with me to meet him?" Doing my best to maintain my professional composure, I calmly volunteered. There was a light rain as we walked outside, so the woman gave me a large umbrella. Richard Gere soon pulled up in a limousine. He leaned forward and spoke to his driver in a kind tone about when he would like to be picked up, then opened his door. I held up the large umbrella for him as the woman introduced herself as one of the event coordinators.

When we turned around to reenter the building, there was a flood of camera flashes in our eyes, with reporters asking questions that he calmly answered. We moved into the crowded building, and the first thing Mr. Gere did was shake hands with the volunteers who were working the tables. As I escorted Mr. Gere backstage, I saw those women holding their hands over their hearts, looking at each other in disbelief. Later, Mr. Gere gave a very moving, personal account on stage about the tragedies he witnessed when he traveled to Tibet.

At another venue, after completing our security sweep of the theatre, I sat down and chatted for quite a while with a very nice man named Philip Glass. I had no idea he was a famous composer until a friend of mine at the Indianapolis Symphony Orchestra, Ryan Singer, made a comment about him. Even my daughter has heard of him.

Of course, it was wonderful to have a chance to spend time with His Holiness, both "on stage" and "off stage." The Dalai Lama has always described himself as "a simple monk." He did not make himself special, and often seemed mildly annoyed with all the hoo-ha being made over him. He found specialness in each moment, in each person that he greeted.

What I really enjoyed, especially in light of the fact that he is often called "His Holiness," was his wonderful sense of humor. At one point, after wrestling our way through a noisy crowd, we were enjoying the silence of the elevator ride up to the stage level. Knowing that we were all ninja, the Dalai Lama gently placed his fist against the chin of one of my friends and softly pushed it through. My friend jokingly wobbled his head back and forth while making cartoon-like sound effects. The Dalai Lama laughed playfully with his full being.

I have certainly gotten a lot of mileage out of telling my Dalai Lama stories. And as I read back over what I have written about my past experiences in this book, I sometimes feel pretty awesome. But I also have a sense of humor about it. I have close friends that keep me humble, and are quick to point out my shortcomings and lack of holiness in a humorous way when necessary.

I believe it is important to have a sense of humor, and not take yourself too seriously. Humor has a way of loosening our attachment to our ideas. Of course, humor can easily be overused, or used as a defense mechanism. Sometimes humor can hurt, so it is important to pay attention and balance humor with respect.

How do we prevent getting too caught up in our own ego? Teachers, mentors, and close friends can call us out on things with both humor and respect to keep us both inspired and grounded. I have found the best "teachers" to be the ones who are always learning. In truth, the more you learn, the less you know you know, but you become more comfortable with that.

Teachers can be valuable to give inspiration and guidance. But true teachers do not want or need you to make them feel important, and do not want you to become dependent on them. They are catalysts for your own internal growth processes.

It is good to have role models. This can certainly be helpful in the beginning, if your goal is to try out a new way of being in the world. However, the goal is not to imitate someone else. It is to be more fully yourself. I've been around some schools where everyone tries way too hard to imitate the teacher, to the point of adopting that teacher's dress, mannerisms, and broken English. I find this rather creepy. The last thing I would want is to live in a world where everyone looked and acted like me. Variety is the spice of life.

What do you want? What do you value? What is important to you? How do you want to live? I am certainly not a guru. In this book, I am sharing my own style, my own perspectives, along with my interpretations of mentors who have inspired me. I'm sure I add an occasional pinch of ego here and there, but my viewpoints are not anything "official," or something you should memorize. I do not possess, and would certainly not withhold, any "advanced secrets."

The Myth of "Advanced" Mindfulness

In ancient China a Zen student approached the teacher and asked, "What is the secret teaching of Zen?"

The teacher smiled and whispered, "Wait till there's no one around, and then I'll tell you."

Later, the student accosted the teacher, saying, "There's no one around now, what is the secret teaching of Zen?"

The teacher motioned for the student to follow him, and they went out into the garden. The teacher pointed to the bamboo plants.

"I don't understand," said the student.

"What a tall one that is. What a short one that is," said the teacher.

In that moment, the student recognized the absurdity of the question, and experienced a deep sense of clarity.

We all want that ultimate secret, that certain something that would make everything easy, that thing that is kept hidden but accessible. The title of one of my Zen teacher's books came from a saying he found in a fortune cookie: "You think it is a secret, but it never has been one."

There are no secrets. How could you be in the moment "advancedly"? Seeking something "advanced" can be yet another way of avoiding things we don't like. If only I had the secret, then I wouldn't be pushed around by my feelings anymore. Many of us also feel like we need to work very hard to feel worthy of anything, even of being alive. If it comes too easily, it must not be very valuable, or I must not deserve it.

Learning mindfulness is not like learning calculus, where the information builds up over time, and you are lost if you miss one of the concepts. In this book, we are simply looking at this natural process from many perspectives. The goal is to find a centered, balanced life. There are many ways to get there, and many analogies to express the concepts. Instead of taking on something new, mindfulness is about un-learning, letting go of old, unhelpful, inefficient habits.

It takes conscious effort to drop old patterns to allow our natural state to come through. When I was a teenager training in the martial arts, I worked hard to imitate forms and techniques. When I began training in the arts of the ninja, I wanted to add on more "advanced" stuff, when I actually spent a lot of time letting go of old habits.

When I wanted to learn the secret of punching, it turned out that the key was getting out of my own way. Robert Johnson would have me stand in front of him in a natural, neutral posture with my hands relaxed at my sides. We often practiced from this position, since if you are attacked, you may not have a chance to say, "Pardon me, would you mind halting your attack while I assume a cool fighting pose?" From this neutral position, he instructed me to punch him with either hand as fast I could, not telling him which one was coming. He was also standing relaxed in a neutral posture fairly close to me, so I had no idea how he was going to figure out which hand I was coming with, much less have time to respond. I had already been teaching another martial art for a couple of years, so I thought I was pretty fast.

The moment I decided in my mind to punch with my left hand, Mr. Johnson calmly said, "Left." My jaw dropped. Was he able to read my mind? Maybe he just got lucky. I reset myself. Again, as soon as I had the thought of hitting again with the left, he said, "Left." He did this consistently, every time. I was never able to even try to punch him.

"How are you doing that?" I finally asked in exasperation.

Mr. Johnson smiled. "Just stand in front of the mirror and watch yourself."

I spent many hours over many years standing in front of a mirror. Even though my fist appeared to move at lightning speed, because it was attached to my body, it was preceded by hundreds of small yet noticeable movements, such as a slight leaning of the body, a flexing of one knee, a shoulder shift, a small bit of tension growing in any of a dozen muscles. Once I noticed all these things in myself, I could practice letting them go, developing direct, smooth, efficient movements. I discovered that even the slightest muscle tension slowed me down, and that bone alignment and body weight provided the most solid power. Practicing this, and teaching others, also helped me to notice all these things when someone was about to attack. With a clear, open mind, I could see not only when an attack was coming, but follow its development with plenty of time to respond.

The ninja art of To-Shin Do is about letting go of extraneous movements and efforts. I'll never forget an experience I had with Stephen K. Hayes, head of the system, at a black belt workshop.

Black belts from all over the world had gathered to train with Mr. Hayes. He strapped on some padded gloves and called me up to be his training partner. We both stood in somewhat traditional defensive postures, bodies sideways with leading arms pointing forward. This made it very difficult for anyone to make it past the arm to land a strike. Our heads were about eight feet apart.

Mr. Hayes looked at the crowd of teachers, and said, "Up to now, this is how I've taught you to punch." He then turned back to me and said, "Don't let me hit you." Unlike some teachers I've worked with, Mr. Hayes always wants you to do your best to really defend against him or hit him. He finds it useless to practice working with people who only let the teacher look good.

Mr. Hayes launched a high-speed punch from his rear hand toward my head. At that time, I was a third degree black belt, and even from that distance, even with my arm already out in front of me, I barely had time to flinch out of the way as his glove grazed the side of my head.

Mr. Hayes looked back at the crowd of teachers, and said, "Now that you are black belts, this is how you should punch." He turned to me again and said, "Don't let me hit you."

I felt like I was in a movie with frames removed. Mr. Hayes was standing far away, then his fist hit my face. Even knowing it was coming, knowing all I had to do was shift my head a couple of inches in the time it took his fist to travel eight feet, there was nothing I could do to avoid being hit. He repeated what he did several more times to show that it hadn't been a fluke. Even more amazing, Mr. Hayes did not appear to be straining or working hard. He explained how he was letting each part of his body move in its own natural way, and the effect was synergistic. We all fumbled around with jaws agape as we attempted to imitate the movements, without much success.

Any "advanced" person makes things look easy, because they have learned to get out of their own way. An experienced therapist can say just the right thing at the right moment, because they are not busy thinking of what they "should" say, and have no need to impress anyone. An artist can just draw a few curving lines, letting go of judging what they are doing as they are doing it.

In martial arts, just as in life itself, there is no "secret technique" for winning every encounter. The most important thing is to be present from moment to moment. Beginners want to impress others by performing a fancy, flying, spinning, backwards, upside-down kick. But the most "advanced" technique is simply not being in the same place at the same time as the attacker's weapons, or better yet, not setting up your life in such a way that anyone would want to harm you.

Even mindfulness students and teachers can be seduced by the idea of finding something "advanced." Despite the title of one of my professional mindfulness workshops having "an introduction and overview" in it, I often see "didn't get much out of it" in the evaluations from people with a little experience, but often see "learned a great deal" from those with lots of mindfulness experience. Can you imagine if you wanted to get in shape, and said, "Oh, push-ups and sit-ups, I've done those already – I don't need to do those anymore." Or your partner wants a kiss, "We've kissed already, what else ya got? I want something more advanced!" If what you are doing seems boring to you, you are probably filtering your current experience with memories or expectations of other times. Each moment is fresh, rich, and new.

All we have is this moment. What else could possibly exist? Where else will you find the "secret?" Even if you had the "secret," what would you be doing right now? How would your life be different if you were "advanced"?

It all lies in how you are in this moment. Yes, an artist is only drawing a line. Very simple, very direct, in the moment. But how those lines come together can produce amazing images of feeling and beauty.

Now that you are learning to be in the moment, what will your canvas look like?

Of course, if you are feeling terrible suffering in this moment, these words likely make no sense to you, and may even feel dismissive of how bad things can truly get. So, before we move into how to enrich all the moments of your life, let's explore how we can work with the pain and suffering in your life right now.

4

When Things Go Wrong
Responding to Challenges

The very things that we do to try to get rid of problems often make them worse.

While an admittedly extreme practice that I would not recommend to most, years ago I was exploring the way of Shugendo, a traditional Japanese discipline of seeking enlightenment through nature (see Chapter 8). It taught me a valuable lesson for dealing with challenges, and helped me understand the importance of moving into unpleasant feelings rather than avoiding them, in a very memorable way.

I was very excited when my friend and mentor Don Myochiriki Siclari told me he would be able to meet with me for waterfall training in the Green Mountains of Vermont. Don had trained in that area with a traditional Japanese teacher for years.

We drove into the area as evening began to fall. At first glance, the waterfall didn't look like much, but as we approached it, I saw that it was much larger than it had first appeared. Peering down from a cliff, I could see that a vast amount of water was flowing through this waterfall, which had been carving away solid rock over the centuries. A curtain of water spread perhaps 30 feet wide, and the waterfall itself was about 20 feet high. We made our way down a dark, rocky trail with flashlights in hand. There was no easy way to reach the waterfall directly, so we would have to go downstream in order to

Mindfulness: Living through Challenges and Enriching Your Life in This Moment, First Edition. Richard W. Sears.
© 2014 John Wiley & Sons, Ltd. Published 2014 by John Wiley & Sons, Ltd.

swim and climb our way toward the waterfall. Getting down to the water in the dark was a bit challenging, and a couple of times one of my feet slid from the dirt on the slippery rocks. Don turned around and asked me if I was okay after one particular slip, and then immediately said, "Oh yeah, I forgot who I am talking to." I was nine years older than Don, had been training in the martial arts perhaps a decade longer, and was ordained in the *mikkyo* "secret teachings" tradition years before he was, so he assumed that I didn't need looking after. However, Don was very much my senior in Shugendo training, and practicing in the mountains, and doing waterfall practice. He had probably done this waterfall practice hundreds of times. I had previous experiences in the mountains of North Carolina, with a very special waterfall, but the waterfall we were approaching appeared to be 10 times the size and power. I had been under a few other waterfalls in the Western United States and on the island of Jamaica, but they had been mere trickles compared to this one.

When we got down to the water's edge, Don opened up a small bag I had not noticed he was carrying. He stepped into the water and spent a few minutes performing a traditional ceremony to give respect to the area and to put us in the proper mindset. He then placed the ceremonial items back on the shore and began walking out into the water. Don walked out barefoot, but I chose to wear rubber shoes to protect my feet against the

Vermont waterfall. Note people in upper left for scale. © Richard Sears.

sharp rocks on the bottom of the river. As I stepped out into the water, I was stunned by how cold it was. Had I been alone, I probably would have turned around, thinking it ridiculous to willingly subject myself to such icy cold. Don marched unhesitatingly toward the center of the river where the water was deeper. Moving upstream toward the waterfall, the muscles of my ankles and the surface of my skin became tightened by the cold. I was reminded of times as a child that I would go very slowly to let my body adjust if I ever went into a cold swimming pool, but Don was moving ahead so quickly that I was falling behind. As the water came up to his waist, he turned to me and said, "The water feels quite good tonight, don't you think?"

"Uuh, yeah," was my response. I couldn't tell if he was being facetious, but he marched forward very determinedly. I was supposed to be a senior practitioner in these types of arts, so I was partially pushed forward by ego. Though my mind was screaming that this was a bad idea, the coldness of this water, now almost up to my waist as well, was not at all like what I imagined as I sat in a comfortable, warm house reading about Shugendo. I could not turn around now, after being so motivated and making such an effort for Don to bring me to this place.

Don gave a shout, then submerged himself completely in the cold water. Intellectually, I knew that it would probably be best to do the same, and allow my body to acclimate, but my feet and legs were still freezing cold, and my mind was rebelling. I knew I needed time to adjust to the cold, but Don began swimming and moving forward even faster.

I felt I had little choice, so I engaged my will, and despite my misgivings, gave my own shout as I submerged into the water. The water was so cold that it literally took my breath away. Looking back now, I realize that most likely all the muscles of my ribs and diaphragm tightened, making it difficult to breathe. At the time it felt as though the water was simply stealing away my breath. I began swimming, hoping that the movement of my body would help, but it did nothing to take away the cold.

The water soon became too deep to touch the bottom, having been carved away by the rushing waters of the stream and waterfall, so we moved to one side of the stream and pulled ourselves along by the rocks on the cliff wall. I did my best to breathe deeply and remain calm, but it was difficult to be aware of anything but the coldness of the water. There were very few finger holds, and closer to the waterfall, the rocks were covered with moss and were very slippery. At one point, Don pulled himself up out of the water and onto a rock ledge along the cliff wall. It was difficult to get up there because of how slippery the rocks were, but the current of the stream was far too strong to swim into. As I crawled along, many times I began to slip, but was able to lower my body weight and find some other grip to hold onto. A couple of times I began slipping with nothing to grab, and felt myself helplessly sliding down in slow motion back toward deep water. All I could do was to wait until my momentum was somehow slowed, and crawl back up to a position where I could find a hand hold. Once I fell all the way back in, and simply laughed at myself after making my way back to the rock wall again.

Finally we made it to the roaring cataract. The sound of the water was deafening. Don asked me if I wanted to do the standing waterfall or the sitting waterfall first. When I shrugged my shoulders, he said the sitting waterfall was easier to start with. As I looked out and saw the rush of the torrent and the turbid waters around the area where we would need to stand, I could see his point.

To get to the place where we could sit, on the other side where the water hit a ledge that was up above the stream, would require us to walk behind the flow of the water in a small cave. As we carefully walked over the moss covered rocks to get behind the water, the noise pierced my ears as the sounds of the water echoed off the cave walls. Halfway behind the curtain of water, Don stopped in front of me and prepared himself mentally. He then quickly walked over to the other side of the waterfall, climbed up on some boulders, and disappeared into the water. All I could do was immediately try to follow him. A part of my brain was concerned about how cold the water was as it sprayed and splashed all around, but my more immediate concern was not slipping and getting pounded onto the rocks by hundreds of pounds of rushing water. I took a deep breath and stepped in.

As soon as I got beneath the torrent, I was a bit stunned by the power and the weight of the water. Through the spray, I could see Don sitting on a ledge, and I crawled to a spot next to him where I could sit. I tried to concentrate and experience the rush of the water. It was quite overwhelming, and even breathing became difficult with the massive amounts of water washing down over me. Because of the volume flowing down, it was not a steady current, and I was strongly buffeted by the water. Through much effort, I was able to cross my legs into a meditative position, but my legs were constantly being pushed up and down in the wake of the crushing current. It was also challenging to keep my back and head erect under the weight of the water. I raised my arms and put my hands together, but the current kept breaking them apart and forcing my arms down. It was such an overpowering physical experience that after a few moments, it felt as if my thoughts, my ordinary sense of who I was, and even the very boundaries of my physical body, were being washed away. I increasingly felt a sense of connection to the water that I was sitting under, to the rocks that held me up, to the air that I breathed, and to the mountains all around me.

Amazingly, after a few minutes, I found myself able to relax into the water. It became easier to let go of my thinking mind, even though it was still present at some level. My muscles felt massaged by the powerful changing torrent, and I no longer felt any resistance or discomfort from the water. The experience began to feel quite blissful and pleasant. When I peeked out of the water and saw that Don was ready to be finished also, I crawled away and felt a twinge of sadness. I felt invigorated, like I had supercharged my being. As I stepped out of the water, I felt radiant, as if the inner heat of my body had been kicked into high gear, as if all of my senses had been cleansed so that I could more purely experience the world around me. I felt physically lighter and more free.

Next, we attempted to stand up under the main part of the deluge. It was challenging to get to, again, because it was so rocky in the space behind the waterfall. Getting there required sliding on my buttocks until I found a place right at the edge of the waterfall where the water had cut the rock down, creating a place to stand. I got one leg down into the water, the other still up on the rock, as the torrent began to hit my body. Again, the cold was awakening as it struck my body, but my thinking brain was focused on finding a place to stand under the torrent. When my foot hit the bottom, it was very sandy, and not a very stable place to stand. I eased my way in, and immediately felt an even stronger torrent than what I'd felt while sitting. As I struggled to stand up against the weight of the water, my feet slipped in the sand beneath me. I was unable to dig in, and in an instant, the heavy cascade pushed my head under the water, spit me out, and I floated downstream.

The current was very strong, so I did my best to swim to the side and pull myself out of the water to try to make my way back up to the waterfall. I was ejected from the waterfall a couple more times, until I found a way to keep my knees bent, my posture solid, and my feet dug into the sand for stability. The weight of the waterfall was extremely intense. I finally found myself, in good balance, embodying a sense of the power of this water. At that point, I was no longer concerned about the cold, becoming more relaxed and free to experience the weight, power, and rush of the water. After a few minutes, the rush of the water pushed so hard that once again I could not resist and I was shoved under the water and pushed downstream.

It was fairly dark by that point, and as I looked back at the waterfall, I could not see Don. The water pushed down so hard into bedrock of the stream that it was a very real danger that someone could be pinned under the current and drowned. As I made my way back, Don's head surfaced, and we decided to head back.

We made our way back down the stream, sometimes swimming, sometimes pulling ourselves along the rocks and the cliff walls. It had been such an amazing experience, and I was glad that I hadn't turned back.

As I stepped out of the water, I felt no coldness. I felt peaceful and calm, yet had a sense of being energized, awake, and alive. We toweled off and made our way back up to the road. Every step seemed magical, and I knew that this was a special time that I would always remember.

Though this is a very dramatic example, such experiences have taught me that I can have all kinds of thoughts and feelings, and still choose my behavior, however difficult it may be at times. Thoughts and emotions should inform our choices, but always living according to their dictates makes life an unpredictable roller-coaster ride. Unpleasant emotions, like the feeling of cold in that water, often rise and fall by themselves if we are able to let go of the habitual reactions that make them worse.

Moving into our difficulties does not mean there will always a happy ending. I'll spare you the details, but I did not have such a magical experience when we went back to the waterfall the next morning. Because the water upstream was coming down from the mountains, some of it tended to freeze overnight. When we stepped into the water, even Don said it was really cold. I tried to grab on to the experience I had the night before, but my body never adjusted to the bitter cold. I sat under the freezing waterfall for quite a while, and the entire time, it felt like an army of demons was attempting to pound me into submission. It was not pleasant at all. It never got "better." However, this was an even more important lesson. I was willing to sit with the experience anyway, without making it worse by struggling with myself or my thoughts and feelings. I paid attention, I allowed myself to feel miserable, and I made conscious choices about what to do. I wanted to run screaming the moment my foot touched the water, but I valued the opportunity to push my boundaries under the guidance of a trusted friend. I chose to stay with it for a while to see what might happen, and then I chose to get the hell out of there afterwards.

Of course, the average person would say that jumping into a mountain waterfall was an unnecessary, dangerous thing to do, and that is certainly what my feelings told me. I would definitely not recommend it to most, and I would not have done it without an experienced guide, who had himself had an experienced guide when he learned how to do it.

When we are facing difficulties, it can be very helpful to have a mentor to help us navigate the dangerous waters, until we can learn to stay present with intense feelings and develop more trust in our own inner wisdom. In this chapter, I will share the timeless strategies that have been scientifically shown to be helpful in moving through life challenges, both big and small.

Friends have asked me why I am writing so much in this book about stress, anxiety, pain, and other problems. Shouldn't I focus on the positive? Shouldn't I talk more about enriching our lives?

While mindfulness can definitely be a tool for enriching your life, which we will discuss in a later chapter, in my professional experience, people are not ready to hear that when they are suffering a lot. It will sound as if I am giving them pie-in-the-sky platitudes, and not being realistic, or not understanding where they are coming from. Just a few days ago, I was reflecting with a client how amazing his life had become, how he was living the life he had wanted since childhood. However, he told me that he wouldn't have gotten to that point had we not dealt with the negative stuff first. Sometimes, trying too much to focus on the positive is a subtle way of avoiding the negative. Very often, challenges need to be addressed directly to break through them.

On the other hand, I have never met a human being who didn't experience at least some suffering, so you don't want to spend your life waiting for all the problems to go away. Even if it were possible to eliminate all your life problems, what would be important to you? What direction would your life take? Would it be worth being with the difficulties to bring those values to life?

Would you want to accumulate a lot of debt, give up most of your leisure time, spend hours reading dense scholarly writing, give up a huge part of your social life, put a significant strain on your family, live hand to mouth for five years, and work with the most challenging and stressed out individuals imaginable for almost no pay? It is hard to imagine anyone willingly choosing to do that. But that is what my classmates and I did to get a doctoral degree in clinical psychology. We were willing to do that because we value having a meaningful career, and the chance to make a difference in the world. We even did it for family – even though it was stressful those five years, our families can now live much more comfortably. Of course, we also enjoyed those years, moment to moment, as best we could, but we were willing to experience the suffering that came along with it because we were moving toward something we valued.

In this chapter, we will explore some general considerations for responding to challenges, and talk about the most common underlying factor, stress. In the next chapter, we will look at more serious challenges.

Resilience is the ability to bounce back after you get knocked off your feet. But before we look at how we can learn to be more resilient, let's look at our common reactions that keep us stuck.

Our Usual Ways of Relating to Our Experiences

In general, there are three ways we tend to react to things. We want to grab on tightly to pleasant things, we try to push unpleasant things far away, or we simply don't pay attention or actively ignore things. These automatic reactions can get us into trouble if we do them without awareness. This is true for material objects, situations, relationships, and most importantly, for our own thoughts, feelings, and sensations.

Grabbing

We all want to obtain and hold on to the things we desire. Many cultures impress upon us from a very young age that all the magical goodies are "out there" waiting to be grabbed. We internalize a sense that we are not complete as we are now, and we hope that something out there somewhere will complete us, make us feel happy and whole. As Alan Watts noted, instead of experiencing our lives, we constantly try to get something "out of life," as if it were a bank to be robbed.

Worse yet, some people still hold on to a scarcity model of resources. If the things I want are in limited supply, and surely everyone else wants them as badly as I do, I better do whatever I can to get as much as I can, as quickly as I can. With such a mentality, if someone else gets it first, I may feel jealous, or try to figure out how to get it from them, or even work to destroy it so I don't have to feel bad by seeing what I don't have.

Once we get what we desire, we want to hold on tightly to it. We can't just enjoy an experience, we want to take pictures and capture it, and announce it to all of our friends. As Alan Watts observed, not content with feeling happy, we want to feel ourselves feeling happy, so as not to miss anything.

But how satisfied are we when we finally get what we want? Most people are shocked when they hear that famous celebrities or wealthy business people commit suicide. On the surface, they have everything we think will make us happy, yet they felt so miserable they believed their only option was to escape into nothingness.

Recently, I heard two songs on the radio back to back, with the lyrics, "I still haven't found what I'm looking for," and "Though I keep searching for an answer, I never seem to find what I'm looking for." So many of us can relate to this, but ironically, the looking itself can be what keeps us feeling this way. By definition, "desire" is wanting something we don't have. When we finally get that something, we don't "desire" it any longer. And if we don't feel happy in that moment, or when the joy fades away, we search for something else.

We live in a world of words. Because words represent something else, we get confused, and think that things represent something else too. While we are continuously trying to find that "something else," we miss what is right in front of us.

Chasing after and grabbing onto things, if done compulsively, becomes a distraction from the uncertainty, ambiguity, and suffering that is a natural part of the world. But the chasing is only a temporary distraction, and the longing remains unfulfilled. Mindfulness can help us see that in this moment, everything "is what it is," and we are okay as we are. It is wonderful to pursue our values in life, but if we are only doing that to avoid how we are feeling in this moment, we get mixed up.

When I was in college, I was trying to take a class on everything, and was either studying, working, or training 14 hours a day. My ninja teacher Robert Johnson sat me down one day, and told me that life is like a buffet, with so many wonderful dishes and tastes spread out before me. I was trying to eat everything. The fact is that I can only eat one thing at a time. Appreciating that one thing is better than compulsively chasing after other tastes. This really had an impact on me. My pursuit of the next new thing to learn was my attempt to "get something" out of life, and a side effect was that I wasn't dealing with other important issues in my life, such as my relationships.

Perhaps most common, most subtle, and potentially most troublesome is our tendency to hold on tightly to our thoughts. While this is usually harmless, thoughts can sometimes put us in serious danger. When I was a young, newly licensed pilot, I very much enjoyed taking friends up for a ride. On a particularly warm day, I was eager to take off, and didn't feel it necessary to go all the way down to the end of the runway and turn around. After all, with all the practicing I had been doing, the plane always lifted off less than halfway down the runway.

So that day, my thought was that I didn't want to waste time going all the way down the runway. I was a little farther than halfway, so figured I had plenty of room. What I hadn't taken into serious enough consideration was the fact that in hot weather, the air is less dense, and that I had a passenger, adding weight to the aircraft (and in a plane that only has two seats, I was doubling the cargo weight). As we picked up speed, we were running out of runway faster than I anticipated. To make matters worse, there was a river flowing around this particular airport, so at the end of the runway was a 20 foot high levy of earth. As the grass wall loomed before us, I realized I only had two options now. I could kill the engine, slam the brakes, run into the wall and damage the plane, and perhaps sink it in the river, but probably keep us alive. With that thought, I had a flash of an image of myself embarrassingly telling the airport operators what a dumb mistake I had made. Or, I could just push forward and pick up even more speed, hoping to use "ground effect" (having more lift from the air pushing against the ground) to at least get over the hill, and hopefully pick up enough speed to keep flying. Of course, this plan also had a higher risk of injury due to the increased speed with which we would hit the wall if we didn't get airborne.

I felt my muscles tense as I reached the decision point. I was ready to slam the brakes and cut the engine, but I chose to go full speed ahead. My heart began pounding as I carefully watched the airspeed indicator. If I tried to take off before picking up enough speed, I would actually slow the airplane down by making the wings drag more air when the nose of the plane came up. As the wall of earth grew bigger before us, I was worried that my friend would start panicking. A couple of years before that I had taken a martial art friend up with me who kept grabbing my knee because the air was bumpy. Thankfully my current passenger remained calm and quiet, so I didn't have to add her anxiety to my own.

Like an action movie where the miss is so close that it thrills the audience, I managed to just barely lift the plane over the hill. I then leveled the plane off for a minute to pick up speed before climbing higher. It was a very low view of the river and of a waste treatment plant that I had not seen before or since. I'm sure my friend saw that I was visibly shaking as I apologized for what had just happened. She said she was a little worried, but figured that screaming wouldn't help. I thanked her for that. I decided against the fancy aerobatic moves I had thought of doing, and we enjoyed a safe, smooth flight.

Since that time, whenever a thought appears that I'm in a hurry to take off, I set it aside, and go all the way to the end of the runway, no matter how long it is.

Even when we know we are holding on too tightly, it can be hard to let go. Some cultures make use of an interesting trap to catch a monkey. They put fruit into a heavy jar, and the opening is just big enough for monkeys to put their hands into it. When a monkey grabs the fruit, the widened grip of the hand prevents it from being pulled back out of the jar. They hold on tightly to the fruit, wear themselves out trying to pull their hands out, and are captured.

It is the grabbing that creates the problem. If they only knew to let go, they could be free, and they could even tip the jar over and let the fruit roll out.

Letting go is hard to do. While we are searching, struggling, and holding on, it is a nice distraction. It takes an initial leap of faith to realize that things will not fall apart when we let go of our internal sense of grabbing on.

Many of us strongly experience a tendency to grab on in our intimate relationships. When we connect with someone we deeply care about, we naturally want to hold on to the relationship. But relationships are dynamic, changing processes, which is what can make them both exciting and scary. If we hold on too tightly, we can choke the life out of the relationship.

If someone's feelings change for you, you are probably not going to grasp them back into loving you. It will not likely be helpful to throw the romantic cards they sent you back at them in anger. They will probably not respond well to "Remember when you said 'I want to keep you in my life forever'? You used to hug me all the time, why don't you even look at me now? Were you just lying when you said you loved me?" You might be able to guilt them into changing temporarily, but saying these things will likely only push them away further.

The best relationships evolve when the individuals involved simply learn to enjoy being with each other, rather than "getting something" from the relationship. Their commonalities develop through spending time and sharing experiences together. If you are using someone solely for your own benefit, or you are allowing yourself to be used just to feel wanted, it will not be a very fulfilling relationship. Although balance, or reciprocity, is generally important, if you have a strict accounting system demanding an equal exchange, that is more of a business relationship.

Letting go does not mean you stop caring, stop loving, or stop desiring to be close to someone. It means letting go of the unnecessary mental grasping, which we are likely doing out of fear. We don't want to lose someone or something important, we don't want to be alone, and we don't want to suffer. But grasping only makes it worse.

The big joke in all of this is that you really can't permanently grasp anything anyway. You do not, you cannot, possess even yourself – how can you hope to possess anyone or anything else? Material things fall apart eventually, relationships are always evolving, and feelings come and go. When we grasp, all we are doing is creating a sense of mental tension that gives us the illusion that we are holding on to something. Everything, including ourselves, is changing every moment.

This is what the ancient wisdom traditions meant when they warned against getting too attached. It doesn't necessarily mean you live a life of poverty and chastity. It means recognizing that we are part of the flow of life, and the act of desperately grabbing interferes with that flow. Of course we want and need material comforts. What causes us difficulty is trying to hold on to emotions, which by their nature are transient.

Practicing letting go also doesn't mean that we pretend we don't feel anything. We can learn to enjoy and appreciate our moments more fully in the good times, and we can allow ourselves to feel sad and cry more fully in the hard times. We can enjoy our desires, and even learn to appreciate the bittersweet sorrow and longing of unfulfilled desires. When we get out of our own way, we can flow through life more freely as our moments unfold.

When I was a teenager working in a cornfield, I saw a beautiful morning glory flower. I plucked it so I could carry it with me, and I watched it whither in my hands in just a couple of minutes. The next time I saw a live one, I paused for a moment, enjoyed its beauty, and moved into my next moments.

Pushing away

We are also programmed to push away the things we find unpleasant. This is a very important survival skill. Things that taste bad are likely to be poisonous, so we learn not to eat them. A bite from a poisonous snake can kill, so we learn to avoid them, or push them away if they approach our families.

What gets us into trouble is when we confuse our emotions with the experiences that evoke them. We end up pushing away the feelings instead of recognizing them as important sources of information. Because we don't like the message, we kill the messenger. We end up struggling with our own feelings, instead of dealing more directly with the problems. We can become so afraid to feel anything that we start to avoid actual experiences and relationships in our lives. When word gets out that messengers get killed or imprisoned, they stop showing up to give messages. Our feelings become flat, or they become very confusing, or they get locked up in a vicious cycle instead of flowing freely.

Wouldn't it be great if everyone in the world treated me nicely? Wouldn't it be wonderful if our economy was always prosperous? Wouldn't it be awesome if I never got sick? Meanwhile, back in reality, awful things will happen throughout our lives. Whether you've so far lived a charmed life, or had more than your fair share of suffering already, unpleasant experiences are an inevitable part of the human experience.

While we can definitely work to structure our lives to prevent or minimize many potential future problems, it is important to learn to relate skillfully to our problems when they do arise. Oftentimes, the more we push away, the more the struggle builds up. It is a like a Chinese finger trap – the harder you pull to get away, the more trapped you become. Paradoxically, if you move into it, it loosens up, and becomes much easier to deal with.

In our mindfulness groups, we tell the story of a king who had three sons.[1] The first two sons were handsome and popular, so the king had nice castles built for them close by. The third son was neither handsome nor popular, so the king's advisors suggested that the king build a castle for that son outside the city walls. However, outside the city, the prince was frequently attacked by bandits, so the advisors suggest building a bigger castle, even farther away. Unfortunately, that castle too was attacked, this time by nomadic tribes. Eventually, after building a massive castle far, far away, and fortifying it with 500 troops, the prince sent word that armies from a neighboring kingdom were attacking, and that he feared for his life and for the lives of the troops. Finally the king said, "Let him come home and stay with me.

For it is better that I learn to live with my own son than to spend all the resources of my kingdom keeping him at a distance."

We can spend so much time and energy pushing away our own feelings. Because we often operate on automatic pilot, we can sometimes spend more of our resources struggling or avoiding than it would take to just deal with the problem directly. When you get in the habit of cowering away from something that seems very overwhelming, it grows into a hideous monster. When you finally get the courage to turn and face it, it may turn out to be just a little tiny thing that was projecting a big shadow on the wall. In any case, you will deal with it most effectively if you are looking directly at it.

Our mindfulness practice can help us learn to accept things as we find them in this moment, as bad as they may be, as strongly as we may want them to change. We can then respond from a place of wisdom.

Ignorance

Sometimes we deal with difficulties by doing our best to remain blissfully unaware. Like an ostrich thrusting its head into the sand, for a short while we can pretend everything is the way we want it to be, but it is not usually the best way to handle challenges. You can't ignore things forever. In the back of your mind, and sometimes screaming in the front of your mind, is the knowledge of what is really there. You can pretend for a while, and fool others, maybe even yourself temporarily, but that doesn't make the situation change.

Other times, we are so hypnotized by our habitual patterns that we simply have no conscious awareness of what we are doing. How often do we find ourselves, literally or metaphorically, looking for the glasses on our own face?

Years ago, I was at a Zen retreat, engaging in intensive *kōan* work with my teacher Paul Wonji Lynch. *Kōans* are questions designed to show us how our thinking traps us, causing us to miss the obvious, simple truth in the moment. When I became stuck on a certain question for several days, I was repeatedly told things like, "The answer is so obvious! You already know it! You're dancing all around it!" I was even told a story about an emperor in ancient China who dreamed that he had been beheaded. When he woke up, he ran around looking for his head. "My head! My head! I can't find my head!"

As the days went on, and I was still missing the obvious, my teacher would compassionately shout, "My head! My head! I can't find my head!" so loudly that all the other meditators in the next room could hear, and even though they were practicing silent meditation, we could not help laughing when I returned to sit.

Of course, I eventually found my head. It was right in front of my face. I was so busy thinking about it that I couldn't see it.

Mindfulness is about increasing awareness. It can help us more consciously recognize the patterns we develop and get stuck in.

When I worked at a veteran's administration hospital, I did group and individual drug counseling and psychotherapy for veterans who were homeless. Frank had lived on the streets for years, addicted to crack cocaine. He told me that simply finding a half-consumed bottle of soda on the sidewalk would make his day. I sat with him one day as the nurse had to give him the news that he was HIV positive. His response was simply, "I'm not surprised. I'm really just lucky to have survived living on the streets."

Frank began to find a deep appreciation for the new direction his life was taking, and took the program seriously. Because he could appreciate where they were coming from, he was always the first to welcome someone new to the program and show them around. Yet, when you first met him, he struck you as someone who could bite your head off. I was still a psychology student at the time, and I was worried that maybe he didn't like me, or that he resented coming to individual psychotherapy. Once I developed a relationship with him I brought this up directly. "Frank, having worked with you for a little while now, you strike me as a really nice guy. I've seen how much you help everyone else here on the unit. But right now, the expression on your face makes it look like you want to kill me!"

Frank looked sincerely surprised. "Huh? What are you talking about? I enjoy working with you."

I let the topic go, but when I saw him the following week, he said, "You know, you were right! I looked at myself in the mirror – I look mean! I never realized that!"

It was no accident that Frank had become really good at subconsciously looking mean all the time. It was crucial to his survival when he lived on the streets. If he looked angry and tough, people left him alone. Had he looked too soft, compassionate, and nice, people would have taken advantage of him or hurt him. The "don't mess with me" look on his face kept him alive. However, in his current circumstances, trying to get a job and trying to make more friends, it wasn't a very helpful pattern to continue. It created fear and mistrust in others. Once he became aware of that, he could change his own behavior, and stop blaming others for why he wasn't getting called back after job interviews, or for why he was having trouble making friends.

It's scary to ask for feedback, but what is the price of ignorance? You certainly don't want to become overly self-conscious, and try to notice everything, but are you satisfied when you ask yourself the question, "How's this working for me?"

I recently had a very bright young surgeon come to me for counseling. She said she had gotten into a series of passionate, yet destructive relationships.

"I could easily blame these men for how badly things went," she said with a wry smile, "yet I realize that I am the common denominator in each of these relationships." With the courage to look into herself instead of ignoring her own contributions, she began a proactive path of conscious choices to break out of the old patterns.

A more subtle form of ignorance is boredom. One of my colleagues received an email from a student who was trying to find out what was going on in an online course. The student's message simply said, "Not much going on here. Please advise." However, it turned out that she had been looking in the wrong place.

If you are feeling bored, it is very likely that you are looking in the wrong place. You are probably seeking something outside of the moment you are in, likely as a way to ignore a deeper feeling like loneliness. How could you possibly be bored with the present moment? No matter where you are, if you can set aside your thoughts for a moment, and pay attention, you will find an incredible richness, even within the strongest of unpleasant emotions. Attention counters ignorance.

Of course, we don't know what we don't know. We are all ignorant of the vast majority of things in our lives and in the universe, and even a lifetime of study and effort will barely scratch the surface. When I meet people who are famous for how expert they have become at something, I am often amazed at how humble they are. The more we know, the more we know we don't know.

Though you can't possibly know everything, you can learn to recognize that when things go wrong, it may be a sign that you were unaware of some of the causes and conditions contributing to the situation. When you begin noticing patterns of unpleasant things happening to you, it's easy to put all the blame on others, or to think you are just unlucky. But if you let go of those thoughts temporarily, and pay attention in the moment, you may just find that you are missing something important going on in the present.

Staying Present

It is only natural to grab onto things, to push things away, and to remain ignorant of things. But if we don't get the answer we want from the "How's this working for me?" question, another option is to stay present with our experiences as they are. Through paying attention, we can learn to relate to our thoughts, emotions, and sensations in a more flexible way, and can then be more flexible in how we act.

If we want to be resilient, if we want to let things roll off us more often without knocking us down, we need to be flexible. Civil engineers know that large structures need to have some give in them. An inflexible bridge will crack up and break from the weight of the vehicles crossing over it. Skyscrapers are designed to move a little in the wind. An old, stiff tree will fall over in a storm, but a green, flexible tree bends in the wind, and comes back up.

This is even more true for our thoughts and feelings. If we are too rigid, we may "break down" emotionally. By staying present, we can discover a larger sense of spaciousness in our moments, giving us more room for our emotions, and more flexibility in how we respond. Instead of always pushing something away, we might choose to move toward it and explore what it is. Instead of habitually grabbing onto something, we can learn to hold on loosely. Instead of ignoring, we can stop to see if we are missing something important.

Staying present helps us loosen our compulsion to try to control everything. By its nature, the world is full of uncertainty and ambiguity. We cling to old habits and patterns, often even when we know they are maladaptive, out of longing for the comfort of the familiar.

After a lifetime of trying to hold onto, fix, or deny strong thoughts and feelings, it takes a lot of practice to make the shift to see them as important sources of information. Mindfulness practice can help us take notice of these thoughts and feelings in a more open way. For example, if you notice yourself ruminating about work, instead of engaging in long-running, imaginary battles in your head, you can pause, and say to yourself, "I can't stop thinking about work right now, I must be feeling anxious." You can then choose to keep thinking about work, stay with the anxiety and watch it change, or do something to take care of yourself. By first staying present, you retain executive powers over your life, instead of "jumping" at every whimsical suggestion from your advisors.

Of course, strong thoughts, emotions, and body sensations can cause us a great deal of suffering, so let's get a little more concrete and practical. This will provide a good foundation for the specific, particularly serious challenges we will explore later.

What can I do when strong, unpleasant thoughts arise?

We have all experienced having thoughts stuck in our heads. What can you do with them? What happens when you try to stop them with willpower?

Therapists were once taught a technique called, "thought stopping," and it works sometimes, but the research found that it often makes them worse. Try this right now – put this book down and try really hard not to think of a pink elephant.

How successful were you? There may have been moments when you weren't thinking of a pink elephant, but you were put into a double bind.

In order not to think of it, you had to remember what it was you weren't supposed to be thinking about. You can't force yourself to stop thinking – that would be like trying to smooth out waves with a flat iron.

Even if you really wanted to, you won't be able to stop the flow of thoughts for very long, as that's what minds do. Instead of getting rid of strong thoughts, we can learn to relate to them differently. What makes a thought "strong" is its emotional component. As we discussed earlier in the book, strong thoughts are usually fueled by underlying emotions, so you can choose to shift your attention to what is going on in your body. We will discuss emotions and sensations in the next two sections.

There are also techniques for working directly with thoughts, though these can take a lot of practice. As mentioned previously, we are often "fused" with our thinking, or see our thoughts as the center of who we are. Defusion, or decentering, helps us loosen the grip our thoughts have on us. We see that we have thoughts, but our thoughts don't define us. You cannot be what you are able to notice. If you notice a thought, that thought is not you.

When we are sitting in the front row of a movie theatre, we can literally feel like we are in the movie. We can feel our hearts pound with excitement, our eyes fill with tears, our fists clench with anger, and our bellies burst with laughter. In reality, all these reactions were triggered by flashes of light on a screen. The images may have been captured from the physical world, or a computer, but the people and places depicted on the screen are not really there.

Likewise, we are often drawn into the theatre of our minds. A memory of a past experience can evoke deep sadness. A worry that something bad might happen in the future can create fear in this moment. An image of a loved one mistreating you can make you feel very angry. In reality, thoughts are only events in the mind. They may correlate with something in reality, but they themselves are not the reality they represent.

If you sit in the back of the movie theatre, it is easier to see the context of the pictures on the screen. If you are able to "step back" from your own thoughts, you can see them in the broader context of who you are. You are having thoughts that come and go, but you are not your thoughts. Of course, the movies can be very engaging, so they will continually pull you in. It takes practice to remember that you can choose to step back when you want to.

You can also practice setting the thoughts "off to the side," letting them play more in the background rather than always taking center stage. The brain is a thinking machine, so instead of fighting with your thoughts, you can just let them be there. This is different than trying to push them away, as you hold an attitude of acceptance, allowing them to do what they do, but still making a conscious choice of where you want to place your attention in this moment.

In a seminar, Stephen K. Hayes once shared an exercise that I found very useful for loosening up the stranglehold our thoughts often have on us. We paired up with a partner, and were asked to tell a short story about a time in our lives when we were treated unfairly by people or circumstances. What immediately came to mind for me was how someone took advantage of me, damaged my life and my family irreparably, and broke many promises, all to satisfy her own selfish needs. The negative impact of this relationship was still strongly affecting my life.

Mr. Hayes then asked us to tell our partners the same story again, but this time, to pretend that we meant for it to happen that way, that we made it happen. For purposes of the exercise, we could even imagine that we had some kind of magical insight or powers about why we chose to make this happen. I had some trouble wrapping my head around this, as I was very attached to the story I just told as being the "truth," even years after it happened. I took a deep breath and "played along," though I was surprised by the effect it gradually had on me. It was such an odd perspective. I said that I felt trapped in a relationship and didn't know how to make it better, so I allowed someone to take advantage of me to help me escape. I struggled a lot with how to be more direct, more assertive, and how to set boundaries, and needed to be forced to practice doing this. I had lived a relatively sheltered life, and needed to break out of my naiveté. I needed to have this experience to inspire me to become a psychologist, allowing me to help thousands of other people.

Next, we were asked to tell a short story about a time in our lives when we got very lucky – when a number of things just happened to come together, and we were in the right place at the right time. For me, the opportunity to be a bodyguard for the Dalai Lama for a couple of weekends came to mind. I talked about how lucky I was that he was going to be within driving distance of where I lived, and that my teacher Mr. Hayes was going to be protecting him. Luckily, my friend David Piser was already working with Mr. Hayes, and he suggested I show up at one of the public events wearing a suit and ask if I could help. Fortunately, Mr. Hayes said yes. It was such an amazing experience, and I had the opportunity to spend time with His Holiness, and I even met half a dozen celebrities.

Mr. Hayes then asked us to tell the same story again, but this time, to pretend that we meant for it to happen that way, that we made it happen, imagining special powers if necessary. Again, I found taking the opposite perspective quite challenging at first. Most of us had some trouble with this, as it made us feel like we were bragging or being arrogant, but we certainly learned a lot about how thoughts shape our perceptions. I stated that I had read the books of Mr. Hayes and realized that I wanted to become a ninja, and wanted to spend time around others who were on a path of self-development. I made a conscious effort to put in years of training so that I would be ready for greater service. I learned about the Dalai Lama so that I would be ready when the time came, and I took advantage of the networks and connections I had to become his bodyguard. Because family was important to me, I chose to only do this for a couple of weekends.

The point of an exercise like this is not to find the ultimate "truth," and not necessarily to convince ourselves of a better story. It illustrates the power of thoughts. If I see my whole life as due to luck, whether good or bad, I can waste a lot of time complaining or worrying that my luck will run out. If I can more often recognize all the choice points in my life, I am empowered to more consistently move toward the things I value.

Talking out loud to someone, as in the above exercise, or writing down your thoughts, helps you get some distance and some perspective on them. You can also ask yourself some questions about your thoughts. Did these thoughts arise automatically? How would I be thinking about this if I was in a different mood right now? Am I making things worse than they really are? Am I thinking in all or nothing terms? The important thing is to maintain a sense of curiosity about what you discover, to prevent getting too hooked into the content of the thoughts.

Acceptance and commitment therapy uses a wide variety of scientifically researched techniques to help us relate differently to strong thoughts. Even something as simple as repeating a thought over and over again can change it. When you say the word "milk," that sound has a strong association with the white liquid it represents. But try this – close your eyes and say "milk, milk, milk ... " over and over for about a minute. You will find the word loses the strength of its association. Now try this – pick a strong thought that you are having, or that you might often have, like, "I can't do anything right," and say it over and over for about a minute. What did you notice?

You might fear that repeating a strong negative thought will only make it stronger. But in fact, it is avoiding it that creates the problem, as above when I asked you not to think of a pink elephant. Repeating it to yourself activates the exposure effect, like jumping into the swimming pool and letting the feelings pass.

When we drop the need to battle strong thoughts, we can choose to mindfully investigate them. Pay particular attention to thoughts like, "Things are really bad," or "I hate my life." Those thoughts feel very true for those who say them, but it can be helpful to look deeply within those feelings. What things are bad? What makes them bad? What do you mean by bad? What parts of your life do you hate? What about those things do you hate? How do you experience that emotion? Where do you feel that hate in your body?

It takes a lot of practice, but you can also learn to just watch thoughts come and go. All thoughts arise, linger for a moment, then pass away. When I ask the participants in my mindfulness groups to purposefully sit with a strong, unpleasant thought, they are often surprised that when they try to focus on that thought, it tends to dissolve. They find it difficult to keep in mind the thought they were trying not to think about. The challenge is that your brain wants to keep coming up with other things to worry about, in its attempt to help distract you from the current difficult thought, and each new thought sparks a new set of reactions. Staying present with the thought as it is will reveal its transient nature.

There are many more ways to relate to thoughts, but the people I work with tend to get better results in the beginning by remembering that strong thoughts are often trying to distract them from strong emotions. When we allow ourselves to feel the underlying emotions more directly, the thoughts often lose their fuel.

What can I do when strong, unpleasant emotions arise?

Despite all the things we learn in our schools, we don't get much education about emotions. We are often taught to minimize or deny our feelings, or that we need to "do something" about them. This sets up a love/hate relationship with our own emotions.

Though a bit of an oversimplification, we can divide the brain into three separate regions to help us understand emotions and how we experience them. The brain stem controls our body's regulatory systems, like heartbeat, breathing, and sleep. Raw emotions come from a set of structures known as the limbic system. The outermost regions of the brain are known as the cortex, which is where our thinking takes place.

Though we can view these regions as separate areas of the brain, they are all thoroughly interconnected with brain fibers. A perceived threat causes an increase in heartbeat, a basic emotion like anger arises, and thoughts interpret the experience to create complex emotions like jealousy. Because we tend to identify our sense of who we are with our thoughts, we often feel pushed around by our emotions. But we can learn how our thoughts often contribute to our perceptions of threat and safety, and how our cortex can modulate our limbic system responses.

To make this more practical, let's explore the "ABCs" of emotion as taught by cognitive-behavioral therapy. "A" stands for antecedent, or activating event, the thing that happens first. "B" stands for belief, or our thoughts about the event. "C" stands for consequence, the resulting situation.

Many of us are unaware of that middle part, the belief. Someone calls you a name (A, the activating event), then you get angry and perhaps yell at them (C, the consequence). It almost seems instantaneous, but we can learn to notice and expand the gap between A and C. There could be numerous thoughts and beliefs lingering there. For example, you could discover that you believe you are "less than" other people, so you need to strike out at others to feel better about yourself. Perhaps there is a history of this person trying to strike you down, so you believe they are doing it to purposefully hurt you. However, if a complete stranger calls you a name (A), and you feel good about yourself, you may have thoughts of pity for the poor individual who has such little happiness in his life that he has resorted to calling people names in his desperate attempt to feel better (B), and you choose to walk away (C).

Our thoughts and beliefs affect our emotions, which affect what we feel in our bodies, and vice versa. Mindfully noticing our thoughts, emotions, and sensations give us much more information to work with challenging situations.

Imagine you are making dinner for your significant other. A promise was made to be home by 6pm, and now it is 7pm, and you haven't heard anything. You call and there is no answer. What thoughts or feelings might come up for you? An exercise like this is interesting to do in a room full of people, as everyone will have a different answer. "I would think he didn't respect me!" "I would wonder if she had an accident." "I would think he was having an affair." "I would guess she was stuck in traffic." "I would be glad to have some extra time to myself." Obviously, each of these thoughts would likely lead to a different emotion.

Not only do thoughts influence our feelings, but our feelings and moods can influence what thoughts we have. Imagine the above scenario again, in which you are working to get dinner ready, but earlier that day, your best friend said they don't like you anymore. When you got home, you found three bills that were past due. You worked very hard to have dinner ready on time, despite the fact that your phone kept ringing with more things to deal with, and you ended up burning the main dish. Chances are, your thoughts and feelings about your partner being late will be more negative.

Now imagine the same scenario, but earlier in the day, you received lots of praise from people you respect. When you got home, you discovered that you received a large sum of money that you weren't expecting. While you are making dinner, an old, dear friend calls to catch up with you, and you have a very pleasant conversation. Chances are, your thoughts and feelings about your partner being late will not be so negative.

When our close friends are being uncharacteristically unpleasant, we assume they are having a bad day, and try to be patient with them. However, it can be harder for us to see that maybe the way we are acting toward someone else is influenced by our own mood and beliefs.

When we become more mindful of our thoughts and feelings, we can pause to stay present with them before deciding what to do next, if anything. As with thoughts, when strong feelings arise, we can express them, investigate them, or watch them rise and fall.

There are many ways to express strong emotions, and paying attention helps us make a conscious choice about how to do it in a healthy way. You can use anger to energize you to take thoughtful action to correct an injustice. You could choose to express an emotion directly to the person that sparked it, letting them know how you feel in a way that doesn't damage the relationship or cause them to shut down. You could also choose to write down your feelings, or express them to an understanding friend. For me, playing guitar allows me to fully feel and express my strong emotions. In the flow of music, I can almost savor the bittersweet qualities of feelings as they pass through me, knowing that hurting deeply is only possible when you are able to love deeply.

As we will discuss in the section on anger in the next chapter, freely expressing every feeling that arises is not always helpful. Shouting at someone doesn't usually make them like you more. Using passive-aggressive moves, like completely avoiding a person who once said something you didn't like, usually backfires, and contributes to the continuation of the unpleasant feeling.

Again, though it takes some practice to make the shift, you can begin to experience strong feelings as important sources of information, and you can investigate them. What are your feelings trying to tell you? How much do they relate to the current situation? Is there something about what is going on that is bringing up old, unprocessed emotions?

It is important to know that your brain tends to connect memories to feeling states. In other words, when you are sad, you will more easily remember all the other times you were sad, so be careful about chasing after every sad thought that arises and giving it too much significance. When you practice staying present with your feelings, you will often find they get worse at first, which is why we want to distract ourselves with more thinking or some other behavior. But if we stay with the sensations in our bodies, they always top off eventually, and they gradually come back down again.

Emotions are body sensations that are labeled by thoughts. If you get more directly in touch with the sensations in your body, the emotions will flow through you more freely.

What can I do when strong, unpleasant physical sensations arise?

As with thoughts and feelings, we often end up doing battle with our physical sensations, despite the fact that they are coming from our own bodies. We sometimes go to great lengths to avoid unpleasant physical sensations. While, of course, you should do what you can to relieve yourself of discomfort, there are times when distractions and pain relievers don't work, or set up a vicious cycle of avoidance. As an alternative, we can learn to experience the sensations with less resistance.

As with thoughts and feelings (are you noticing a pattern here?), we can choose to take some action, investigate the sensations, or just wait for them to rise and fall. If you notice that there is a churning sensation in your stomach, you could choose to get some rest, drink some fluids, or make a doctor's appointment.

You could also choose to investigate them. What are the qualities of these sensations? Are there thoughts and feelings connected with them? What foods did I just eat? What are these sensations telling me?

If you choose to just stay present with the sensations, you will likely notice that they change from moment to moment, and you can begin to let go of any unhelpful thoughts or emotions that may be making things worse. If the sensations are very strong, you could choose to use something like your breath as an anchor for grounding yourself, and then "dip your toe" into the water of the sensations as a way to begin befriending them instead of always pushing them away.

Although not necessarily easy to do, these same principles can be helpful for things like chronic pain and panic attacks, which we will discuss in the next chapter. I find it easier to start with less overwhelming sensations like itches. In fact, if you close your eyes and tune into the physical sensations present in your body right now, you may notice an itch or two. You can choose to scratch anytime you wish, but experiment with waiting a bit first, and observing the nature of the changing sensations. When you feel the urge to scratch, you might decide to wait five more seconds, and see what you notice. Over time, you can choose to wait 10 seconds, then 30 seconds before scratching. Eventually, you will find that itches often come and go by themselves.

If you are allergic to poison ivy, scratching the itch gives immediate relief, but makes it worse in the long run. If you can separate out your thoughts and emotions, apply the proper medicated ointment, and allow the sensations to rise and fall, the rash will pass more quickly on its own. This is an important lesson.

The above suggestions can be challenging to implement after a lifetime of grabbing, pushing away, and ignoring. But if you want different results than what you are currently getting, you have to be willing to try something different.

Willingness

Why in the world would you want to move into difficulties and unpleasant feelings? Shouldn't you just always do your best to avoid them?

It all depends. What is important to you? If being healthy is important, you will need to exercise, even though it will be strenuous, tiring, sometimes painful, and can make you stinky. Are you willing to accept those things in your life in order to be healthy?

Sometimes we are so afraid we might do something wrong that we end up doing nothing. Or we are so busy trying to decide what to do that time passes and the decision is made for us. Or we can't accept the reality as it is in this moment. Or we think we have to fix all our problems first, and then we can start living. To move toward the things we value, we have to be willing to move from where we are, even if we are feeling overwhelmed, afraid, or depressed.

When I began my martial arts training in middle school, I was teased by the bullies once they found out. One day, I was walking through the halls with a friend, who was also training with me, and I was jumped from behind and placed in a headlock. The intensity of the attack was of course not how we practiced in the system I then trained in, so at first I was confused about what was happening. I was frozen for a few seconds, though it felt like a few minutes. Once I accepted the situation, a technique we had practiced in training popped into my mind, and I had to commit myself fully to executing it. To the surprise of my attacker, as well as myself, it worked perfectly, and the attacker fell to the ground. By that time, a crowd had gathered, and my friend and I walked away as the attacker stared up from the floor with mouth agape.

Later, I asked my friend why he didn't help me. He said he felt completely paralyzed, and that he couldn't believe it was really happening.

When we have had many challenges in our lives, we can fall into a state known as "learned helplessness." In a classic, though somewhat cruel, experiment, dogs were given electric shocks that they could either control or not control. Later, when they were placed in a cage and given shocks, the dogs that had been able to escape the shocks before jumped over the low partition in the cage and got away. However, the dogs that had been unable to control the shocks before merely lay down and whined, enduring the shocks, even though they could have escaped. They had learned to be helpless.

To break out of this cycle, we need to be willing to jump, no matter how bad things feel to us in this moment. Jumping takes a commitment. You cannot "try" to jump. Try to close this book right now. If you just closed it, you did not follow my directions of "trying" to close it. You either closed it or you didn't. You either jump or you don't. It doesn't matter if you jump an inch or six feet, but you must jump to move in a new direction.

My first ninja teacher, Robert Johnson, again used a rather dramatic method to teach me about willingness. He would have me face him, standing up in a natural posture. He would then raise a practice sword over his head, ready to strike down onto the top of my head. I had to wait perfectly still, sometimes a few seconds, sometimes a few minutes, knowing the sword was about to come down at lightning speed. In the beginning, I got nailed every time, unable to move. I could see it coming, but I was frozen in place, which we referred to as having "lead *tabi*" (*tabi* is a type of Japanese split-toed shoe that we wore in formal classes). If I flinched, or telegraphed any movement, I also got nailed as I tried to come back to a balanced position.

Of course, Mr. Johnson was very clear about how not to get hit. All I had to do is take one step forward. The tip of the sword is what was flying so fast. Stepping toward him, into the eye of the hurricane, was the safest place.

It was hard to be willing to do that at first. The sword was flying down so fast it made a whizzing sound in the air, and it really stung when it hit (catching the ear was the worst). I instinctively wanted to get away from it, to back up, but he could move forward with the sword faster than I could move backwards. Ironically, the more I tried to move out of the way, even flinching to the side, the more I got hit.

Of course, trusting my teacher, I tried to move forward, but the harder I tried, the more I got hit. "Trying" meant I was exerting muscle effort, which actually slowed my movement down.

At some point, perhaps out of sheer desperation, I just stepped forward like I was talking a walk in the park. It was an amazing yet strange experience. Despite the frightening, lightning fast sword tip slicing through the air, underneath, there was a lot of time and space, if I was willing to move into what I feared.

Are you willing to do something different to break through some of the patterns that are no longer working in your life? Are you willing to stay present with some unpleasant feelings to move toward a richer, more fulfilling life?

Now that we have explored what mindfulness is, what it is not, and some general principles for working with challenges, let's get more specific and concrete on how these principles can help with real life challenges, starting with something that relates to all problems.

Stress

If you are alive, you are no stranger to stress. It is an integral part of life. Given enough chronic stress, anyone can develop a significant health or mental health problem. For some it might come out as anxiety, for others it might turn into depression, and for others it might manifest with physical symptoms. Relating skillfully to stress is essential to our health.

Most people think that stress is always a bad thing. While we all know that too much stress lowers your performance, not many of us consider that too little stress also lowers performance. Moderate levels of stress arouse you to pay attention, and give you energy to get out of bed and accomplish things. Our goal is not to completely eliminate stress, as if that were even possible, but to find more balance in our lives. (Though I'm sure some of you might be thinking you'd like to try that no-stress life for a little while to see what it's like.)

In the short term, the stress response is a very good thing. It gives us the ability to fight, run, or freeze to survive a life-threatening situation. If you suddenly see a tiger coming at you, unless you are a cold-blooded, experienced tiger killer, your sympathetic nervous system quickly activates. Chemicals like adrenaline and cortisol are released. Your heart beats more rapidly and more strongly to increase your blood pressure and get oxygen out to your major muscles. Your immune system kicks up in preparation for healing your wounds. Since there is no need to reproduce or digest food for the next few moments, you decrease blood flow to your reproductive and digestive systems. In fact, you may even evacuate your bladder and bowels to lighten your load a little.

This stress response is crucial, because if you didn't have it, and you started running, you would fall over dead after about 30 seconds, because your muscles need that increased oxygen flow from your bloodstream to function like that.

Now, if you were running from a tiger, and you managed to escape (or at least run faster than the person next to you), the tiger would soon give up, and lay down to rest. You too would then lay down to rest, you would have a sense of, "Ahh, everything is okay now," and your parasympathetic response would be activated to return your body to its normal state. Thankful to be alive, you would probably notice profound beauty all around you, and tell everyone you see how much you love them.

As our brains evolved, the power to think things through, learn from the past, and predict the future gave us an enormous survival advantage. The problem is that our stress response can't always tell the difference between a real tiger and a tiger of the mind. When you think about the presentation you have to give next week, your system gets a little squirt of stress hormones. As you drive to work, all those drivers cutting you off get your body ready to fight. We check email when we're lying in bed, or standing in line, or while we're eating in an effort to "save time." Each time we do, a small shot of cortisol hits our bloodstream, in an attempt to "help us" deal with things. All day long, we have small, and sometimes not so small, bursts of stress chemicals, and not enough of those "Ahh, everything is okay now" responses in between.

So, what was meant to be a short-term response that can save your life becomes a chronic response that creates problems. Your muscles become tight and sore. Your heart becomes strained. High blood pressure develops. You develop reproductive problems. Irritable bowel syndrome and stomach problems become more prominent. Your immune system becomes overactive and attacks your own cells, or it begins to fail from being overworked.

The amount of work we take on, the stress that accumulates, and the fatigue that overtakes us can come on so gradually, so insidiously, that we fail to notice how much it affects us. It becomes our new "normal," and we forget how alive we used to feel, how often we used to laugh, how the little things used to bring us joy. Unless we work to actively change things, we are at risk for "burnout," in which we work harder but achieve less, suffer from emotional exhaustion, and become cynical about life.

Breaking the cycle

Mindfulness has been shown to be helpful for such a wide variety of health problems because it helps us relate to our stress more consciously. It can helps us become more aware of how our thought patterns contribute to the stress response, and can help us become more conscious about taking care of ourselves.

People often come to me feeling so overwhelmed that they feel like they are drowning. In dealing with stress, it is important to take a two-pronged approach. In the short term, we can learn techniques to ride the waves. In the long term, we want to lower the water level. If we are up to our noses in stress, every little wave that comes along will be a big deal. If we lower the water level down to our knees through actively working to take care of ourselves, we can handle the little waves much more easily.

To use another metaphor, if you are being shot at, it's good to learn how to dodge the bullets, hide in safe places, and to put on a bullet-proof vest. In the long term, you want to set up your life such that no one would want to shoot at you, do your best to create a safe environment, and try to avoid places where shooting is going on (avoidance is a good thing in this case).

For handling things in the short term, we have already talked about how we can use mindfulness to relate differently to our thoughts, emotions, and body sensations. Something unique in dealing with stress is the importance of breaking up the continuous stress response, and allowing the relaxation response to bring our bodies back into balance. We can do this with two simple but powerful tools: checking into the moment, and taking a breath.

Our breathing is intimately tied to our stress systems. If you watch your pulse rate with an instantaneous heart rate monitor (which can now be purchased as tiny, portable, infrared devices), you will find that your heart rate goes up when you inhale, and goes down when you exhale. Because our pulse is usually measured as an average over time, like 80 beats per minute, many of us don't know that it is constantly changing. When most people first try an instantaneous monitor, they are a bit surprised (and often a little worried) about how jaggedly their heart rate is going up and down. After consciously taking some good breaths, the jagged lines become more of a smooth curve, moving up and down with the breath. The breath is intimately tied to the sympathetic (arousal) and parasympathetic (relaxation) responses. As an immediately useful and practical technique, if you are feeling sluggish or drowsy, place emphasis on your inhalations. If you are feeling stressed or anxious, place emphasis on your exhalations.

Your stress response wants you to breathe fast, so you can get more oxygen into your bloodstream for fighting or running away. I am always amazed by how something as simple as teaching people to breathe more slowly and deeply reduces their stress and anxiety. Doing so signals your brain that there are no physical threats in this moment, and the relaxation response is activated.

One of my meditation teachers, Stephen K. Hayes, once conducted a class on meditating on the breath. At the end, he told the class, "Your homework assignment is to breathe six times a day." There was a moment of confusion, then we laughed. What could he mean? After all, we breathe thousands of times per day. Mr. Hayes smiled and said something like, "The challenge is in remembering to stop and take a breath six times per day."

I invite you to try this yourself. The number six is somewhat arbitrary, but having a specific number helps you remember. We get so caught up in our daily lives, our thoughts and our busyness, that just remembering to stop and take a deep breath can do wonders for interrupting escalating stress responses.

I once had a conversation with a stress research team. They said that they gave the research subjects pagers, so that at random points throughout the day they could stop and write down how stressed they felt on a scale of 1 to 10. To the researchers' dismay (because they wanted everything carefully controlled), even the subjects who did not get the stress reduction intervention reported that just stopping to check in with themselves when the pagers went off helped reduce stress.

The hardest part is remembering to remember to notice, but it gets easier with practice, or by using little reminders. When I feel stressed, I can use that as a reminder to stop and ask myself, "What am I thinking?" Much of the drama I am experiencing may only be taking place in my mind. I can practice coming back to this moment. "What do I hear, what do I see, what do I feel, what do I smell, what do I taste?"

Sometimes we are afraid to take that pause. I was once working with a psychologist who was feeling overwhelmed at work. When I suggested that she try doing a 3-minute mindfulness exercise during her workday, she was very resistant. "My anxiety gives me energy and motivation to get done all the work I have to do. If I stop to relax, I might lose that drive and not get much done." Listening to her concerns, I simply invited her to experiment with it to find out for herself. To her surprise, she actually became more efficient as well as more relaxed. When she was working with a client, she was more present with that client, and not thinking of the six other clients she had to see. When she was writing a report, she focused on that report more, and less on the other 12 reports she had to finish.

A large part of why we feel stressed is because we carry so much in our minds. While we are thinking of all the things we have to do, we are not as present in what we are doing now. I often work with people who come to me and say, "You don't understand. I am too busy at work to practice mindfulness. In fact, when I leave here, there are going to be 47 texts to respond to in just the hour of being off line while I'm here with you." But the fact is, if you get so busy with busyness, you're not going to be very productive. We can practice just being in each moment and letting go of the mental ideas we have about the moment. When it's time to respond to texts, just respond to texts (and you might even stop and question the thought that you have to respond to every single one). Thinking about everything else you need to do won't help you get it done faster. Write things down on a reminder list if that helps, and return to what you are doing in this moment. Relaxation and efficiency become a convenient side effect of being in the moment, because you struggle with yourself less, and therefore have much more energy to invest in what you're doing right now.

Self-care and prevention

Many of us get so busy putting out fires that we don't invest enough time in preventing fires from breaking out in the first place. Mindfulness can be an important self-care tool that helps prevent problems. And when our overall stress levels are down, we have more reserves and resources to handle problems when they do arise.

Self-care is about being kind to ourselves. At the beginning of every jet plane flight, the flight attendants tell us that if cabin pressure is lost, oxygen masks will drop from the ceiling, and that we should put our own masks on first before assisting others. It is ingrained in most of us to not be selfish, and to help others first. But if you pass out, you will not be of any use to anyone. Yet, how often do we prioritize the needs of everyone else, only doing things for ourselves if there is time left over? Is it any wonder that we can fall into states of being overwhelmed with stress, anxiety, and depression, wherein the harder we try, the less we get done?

Typical day exercise

Here is an important exercise that we do in our mindfulness groups.[2] Right now, write down a list of activities that you engage in on a typical day, from the time you wake up until the time you go to bed. If all your days are very different, just pick a recent day. Most people write down about 10–20 items, though you are welcome to do this in more detail if you like.

Things I do on a typical day

_____	_____
_____	_____
_____	_____
_____	_____
_____	_____
_____	_____
_____	_____
_____	_____
_____	_____
_____	_____
_____	_____
_____	_____

Now, take a look back over your list, and put an "N" next to the activities in your day that are nurturing or nourishing, that is, the ones that give you energy. Write a "D" next to the activities that are draining or depleting, the ones that take energy away from you. Sometimes people feel that a given activity is both, either, or neither, so feel free to write N/D or leave it blank if you wish.

Now, take a look back over your list. What do you notice?

People are often stunned by this typical day exercise, as it forces them to compare their actual day-to-day life with their ideas about it. In a very real sense, THIS IS YOUR LIFE. What you are doing day by day, moment by moment, is the majority of your lived experience. It is important to have future goals, but what you are actually doing every day affects and even defines who you are.

What did you notice about the relative number of Ns and Ds? Once in a while, people tell me that they are surprised by how many Ns they have, as the Ds get more of their attention. However, many people notice, perhaps for the first time, that their days are full of Ds. If so, it is no wonder that they are stressed, anxious, depressed, or overwhelmed. Even if you have relaxing weekends, two days of rest cannot compensate for five days of drain, and it will take its toll over time.

Are your typical days what you want them to be right now? If not, you can develop some new routines and habits, starting today. You begin making the shift by asking yourself three questions: How can I increase my Ns? How can I decrease my Ds? How can I relate differently to my Ds?

Do you have enough Ns in your typical day? Think about what you can add into your day to nurture yourself more regularly. This could be something substantial, like adding in a meditation routine each day, or joining a yoga class. It could also be something small, like turning off your phone for 15 minutes while you are eating lunch. What is nurturing for me might be draining for you, and vice versa, so give yourself the time and flexibility to come up with some things that you find nurturing, not what you think others think you "should" do.

Is your day full of Ds? If so, are there any you can eliminate? I'm not necessarily suggesting you quit your job if that is a big D for you, but there may be some things you just never stopped to question. If checking your email before going to bed causes you stress, perhaps you could experiment with waiting till the next morning. Maybe you could even wait until you get to work the next day, instead of starting the first few moments of your morning worried about how you will reply while you are still in your underwear.

Let's face it though, some Ds you just can't get rid of. For example, if "feeding the children" is one of your daily activities that you gave a "D" to, you can't just decide to let them go hungry.

For one thing, if you are actively increasing your Ns, it will be easier to make it through the Ds. In fact, when you feel less stressed, you may not even consider some things to be Ds anymore. If you don't get enough sleep, skip lunch, and push yourself too hard at work all day, then feeding your children may be yet another stressor. But if you have been taking care of yourself, mentally, physically, emotionally, and even spiritually, staying in the moment and involving your kids in a meal could become an enjoyable experience.

If you marked any of your activities with "N and D," or "N or D," what about that activity makes if feel like both, or what factors contribute to whether or not that activity gets an N or a D on any given day? Is there anything you can do to increase the chances of it being nourishing, or to diminish the drain?

I once worked with a woman who said she keeps a bowl full of coffee beans in her office, and "plays with them," feeling them in her fingers and smelling them. She started doing that because she couldn't drink coffee (due to high blood pressure and a high pulse rate), but she found it a very good de-stress thing to do. This is a great mindfulness exercise – it gets you out of your thinking and into your senses.

I know another woman who always takes a cup of chamomile tea with her when she knows she has to go into a difficult meeting. The warmth, smell, and taste keep her grounded in the moment to help her get through the meeting.

After attending a few of my mindfulness groups, my colleague Tina Luberto had an important insight, that I don't really expect most people to get right away, so hear this now and believe me later. After doing the typical day exercise, she realized that the Ds were actually thoughts. The experiences themselves, when she is in them, are usually not that bad. She realized that maybe there are no draining moments, that the sense of drain comes mostly from our thoughts about them, our reactions to them.

Noticing *before* you get overwhelmed

If you've ever gotten to the point of feeling completely overwhelmed, whether from stress, anxiety, pain, or depression, you know you don't ever want to experience that again. Unfortunately, the way your brain works, once you've been there, your chances go up that you might fall back into those vicious, cyclic grooves again.

But the good news is that training in mindfulness has been shown to help prevent this from happening. Why would paying more attention help? Shouldn't we think positively, and not give power to how bad things are getting?

If you are sliding down a hill into a deep pit, it is much easier to climb back up the hill than it is to dig your way out of the pit. Although positive thinking can be very helpful at times, it will only distract you if you are sliding down a hill. It is best to open your eyes, acknowledge what is really happening, dig your feet in, and actively work to get yourself back up. Mindfulness strengthens new brain grooves, and the old pits will eventually fill back up with dirt.

The challenge is to recognize when we are beginning to slide down, instead of denying it. It is perfectly okay to recognize it, and tell yourself, "Yes, I'm getting stressed, but this project is very important, and it will be done by this weekend." But if you deny it, you may end up in the pit before you notice how stressed you have become.

What is your "relapse signature," the signs that you are getting overwhelmed? Everyone reacts differently to stress. Some people become more talkative, some become more quiet. Some people sleep more, some sleep less. Some of us want to be around people more, some of us want to be alone more. There is not usually one big neon sign flashing "DANGER," it is usually a pattern of small things that tends to build up gradually.

Go ahead and take a few moments to create your own list. If you have trouble coming up with things, just ask your intimate friends – they will probably be able to give you a long list of what they notice about you when you are getting stressed. If you trust them not to throw it in your face all the time, share your list with someone close to you so you can have another source of information. Just remember to thank them for the input when they say you seem to be getting overwhelmed, and try not to yell at them with, "I AM NOT GETTING STRESSED OUT!"

Proactively preventing the downward spiral

Once you notice the signs that you might be slipping down the hill, it is important to actively take care of yourself. If you are just starting to slide, it can be something small. If you are on the edge of the pit, you may need to be very active, and even seek help.

It is very hard to think of fun things to do when you are getting overwhelmed. It is therefore very important to make a list when you are not feeling too stressed out. One of my friends wrote out all the letters of the alphabet, and came up with self-care activities under each letter. If you do this as a computer document, or put it on your smartphone, you can easily add things whenever you look the list over.

Make sure your list contains lots of useless, unproductive activities. Don't make your self-care activities something you have to do to "improve" yourself. It's fine to be unmindful and distracted sometimes, as long as that's not the only thing you do when you get stressed, and as long as it isn't harmful.

There are three types of activities you can do to help pull you back up the hill: something pleasurable; something that gives you a sense of satisfaction, mastery, or control; and coming to your senses.

Pleasurable activities are what usually come to mind when we think of self-care. Again, your list will be unique to you, as each of us finds pleasure in different things. Common things in this category are things like listening to music, taking a bubble bath, going for a walk, calling a friend, and watching a comedy movie.

We can also do something that gives us a sense of mastery, satisfaction, or control. The activity itself may not be pleasurable, but we feel a little better after it is done. If your kitchen is full of dirty dishes, you will feel a little better after you wash them, instead of feeling stressed every time you walk by them. For mastery activities, it can be important to break them down. Giving yourself the task of cleaning your entire house may be overwhelming, but washing the dishes is something that is usually doable. If even that seems like too much, you can just wash 10 dishes, so that at least you are moving in the right direction.

You can also do something mindfully in the moment, that is, you can come to your senses. When you are sitting, feel the sensations from the chair. As you walk, feel the sensations on your feet. Take a look around you, and notice what you see. Close your eyes and listen to the soundscape surrounding you (you may want to keep your eyes open if you are walking, though).

Once you become aware that you are sliding down that hill, a crucial point is that you need to engage in self-care activities whether you feel like doing them or not. This is the opposite of what we normally do. If you have a thought early in the day that going out to the park would be nice, and then you feel too tired when you get home, you will probably decide not to do it. But if you are getting overwhelmed, it is important to "make" yourself take care of yourself. Otherwise, you will keep sliding down the hill. You feel down, so you skip the park. Because you ended up staying home alone, you feel a little more down. Because you feel more down, you decide not to go out again the next day. This makes you feel even more down, so you decide not to take your weekly bubble bath. Feeling a little more down, you start to tell yourself you don't deserve to do things for yourself, because you've been lazy. If the cycle continues, you can drop into getting overwhelmed, depressed, or anxious, at which point it is a lot more difficult to pull yourself up.

In our mindfulness groups,[3] we ask participants to write themselves a letter they can read when they are getting overwhelmed. Try to write things that you know will be good for you to remember, along with your self-care activity list. You might even have some fun with writing it.

Dear Richard,

If you are reading this, it probably means you are starting to feel overwhelmed. I know you don't feel like it right now, but it is very important to pick two of the following activities from the list below. Don't expect a miracle, just do it. Hang in there – you're the awesomest dude I know, and this will pass. Stay beautiful!

Okay, maybe I wouldn't really include those last couple of sentences, but it's good to be kind to yourself. Just be careful not to say something like, "Well, you screwed up again, you weakling, so you better do something fast so you don't look like a pathetic loser!"

Social supports and mentors

Social support has been shown to be one of the biggest factors in preventing and recovering from problems. How strong and reliable are your relationships right now? We can't choose our blood families, but we can choose how we relate with them. Having a number of supportive friendships can be invaluable for sharing our joys and processing our sorrows. If relationships are very difficult for you, that will be something important to address on the path to wholeness. As we will discuss in Chapter 6, relationships need to be actively maintained.

Having mentors in your life can also be very helpful and inspirational. Whether it is a family member, therapist, coach, teacher, or spiritual leader, having guides can give us hope, direction, and support.

Proactively doing things to take care of ourselves can facilitate the healing of our past hurts and help prevent a lot of future problems. However, despite our best efforts, bad things can still happen to all of us. How do we respond when things go terribly wrong?

5

When Things Go Terribly Wrong

Sometimes we become so overwhelmed that our ability to cope breaks down. We will likely need professional help when this happens, but mindfulness can be a powerful tool on the path to healing.

Several years ago, I was teaching a martial arts class, and began feeling thirsty, with a sharp headache near my left temple. As I was talking in front of the students, demonstrating a gun disarm technique, I became very light headed. This had happened occasionally when I was in graduate school after standing up too fast, and it would pass quickly if I lay down for a few moments. Because I was talking in front of everyone, I just kept going, hoping it would pass. First my vision faded to black, and then the entire right side of my body went numb and lost all muscle control. I collapsed to the ground, though somehow I curled the left side of my body to control the fall. I felt something strange under my head. Stephen Hayes, the 10th degree black belt founder of our system, just happened to be there watching. Later, he told me that I went down so smoothly that at first people thought I did it on purpose, perhaps to demonstrate how to do the technique from the ground. He told me he must have unconsciously known something was wrong, because he placed his foot under my head to catch it.

I lay on the floor as everyone looked at me, unsure of what was going on. After a few moments, I was able to say, "I think I'm having a stroke." As evidence of what a nerd I am, as I was lying there, I thought, "Interesting – my

Mindfulness: Living through Challenges and Enriching Your Life in This Moment, First Edition.
Richard W. Sears.
© 2014 John Wiley & Sons, Ltd. Published 2014 by John Wiley & Sons, Ltd.

language centers must be either in my right hemisphere or both hemispheres, because I can still speak and understand what people are saying." (Most people's language centers are in the left side of the brain, which controls the right side of the body.)

Not long after I went down, sensations gradually began to return to my right side, feeling like pins and needles. As it happened, my friend David Sink, an ER nurse, who lived several hours away and only came down to train once a month, was the person I had been demonstrating the technique on. He recognized what was happening, and did a quick assessment on me, noticing some right arm drift. Even though the event only lasted a couple of minutes, he strongly advised going to the emergency room.

I was never given any definitive diagnosis. I had every imaginable test done (CT scans, CT-angio, MRI, MRI-A, EEG, echocardiogram, carotid artery scan, transesophageal echocardiogram, cardiac monitors, a sleep study, and a multitude of blood tests) but they could not find anything definitively wrong with me. It could have just been "a syncopal episode," or fainting. I've never passed out before, but was told by a research psychologist colleague who helped test how many Gs a pilot could take that it's not unusual for one side of the brain to go before the other.

I cannot remember much about what I did on that day before that event happened, but I was definitely fully present during the experience, and still remember it well. People who heard about what happened would tell me, "I bet that was scary!" But the thing I remember the most was how peaceful and in the moment I felt on the ambulance ride to the hospital. The sunshine sparkling through the leaves of the trees out the back windows was so lovely. I also remember sitting in the hospital, telling David that if I were to die now, it would be okay. It could have been due to my training, though it also could have been due to the momentary lack of oxygen to my brain.

As I recovered from this episode, I was very fatigued and in a state of "brain fog," feeling as if I wasn't sure if I was awake or asleep, or even alive or dead. Mindfully taking one moment at a time was very helpful in getting me through these challenges, as there were many days I would have preferred to stay in bed all day rather than fulfill my responsibilities. I came to appreciate a multitude of things that I had taken for granted. I also found mindfulness helpful when I was squeezed into small tubes for my brain scans, and when I was still fairly conscious as I swallowed a probe to scan my heart from the inside.

Serious medical and mental health issues will affect all of us at some point, either directly, or through family members or friends. When we are young, many of us feel immortal, but anyone can experience a serious medical problem, or a life crisis of some kind that knocks us off our feet.

In the United States, about one quarter of the population will meet criteria for a mental health disorder in a 12 month period, and almost half will over their lifetimes. In Europe, one in ten will over a one-year period, and one quarter over a lifetime. And these numbers are considered underestimates, because many people will not admit what they are going through or will not seek help.

Although we will be talking about specific disorders in this chapter, it is important to note that these are all a part of the human experience. They are not distinct, all-or-nothing categories. All of us fall somewhere on a continuum of how anxious, depressed, or addicted we are. It is called a "disorder" if it significantly interferes with your life, but we can all benefit from learning about these issues.

There are now a wide variety of evidence-based clinical interventions that utilize mindfulness, including mindfulness-based cognitive therapy (MBCT), acceptance and commitment therapy (ACT), dialectical behavior therapy (DBT), mindfulness-based relapse prevention (MBRP), and mindfulness-based eating awareness training (MB-EAT). The principles of these and other well-researched methods will be the basis for our explorations of responding to the serious challenges below.

As mentioned earlier, mindfulness is not meant to be a cure by itself, but it can be an important tool. As with any difficulty, you should use everything available to help you. These disorders can sometimes become very serious, even life threatening. If you or someone you know is suffering from a full-blown disorder, it best to consult a professional.

Anxiety and Fear

Anxiety is the most prevalent mental health issue around the world. Patrick McGrath, an expert on anxiety, says the two words that best define it are "What if," followed by the most terrible things that could happen. No one ever worries about, "What if everything goes perfectly for me today? What will I do?" It is always anticipation of something bad for those who struggle with anxiety.

The development of brains that could ask the "what if" question was wonderful for survival, because if we can anticipate danger, we can prevent it, and live long enough to pass our genes on to the next generation. Really scary events get strongly encoded in the fear part of our brain, so we don't repeat our mistakes. We also are programmed to encode fear and anxiety vicariously – that is, from watching other people's mistakes.

Knowing that we are programmed this way, we can learn to be kind to ourselves, and not beat ourselves up for getting caught up in these cycles. The good news is that our brains are malleable, no matter how old you are. We can reprogram ourselves to shift from surviving to living. We can let go of the compulsive habit of trying to anticipate every single thing that could theoretically go wrong.

The people I know who suffer from the worst anxiety are very intelligent. The smarter you are, the more you can come up with ideas about what could possibly go wrong, including some that no human being has ever thought of before. And yes, theoretically millions of terrible things could happen, but is worrying about all those things all the time working for you? Is it interfering with the quality of your life right now?

Sensitivity, in terms of being very aware, is a gift, as is intelligence. It is our thinking that turns our sensitivity into anxiety. Fear can also be a gift. It can give important, lifesaving information. When you are able to stay with your emotions, you can learn to listen to them when they are real, separating out the old patterns of thinking from the present situation.

As with any disorder, it is very important to see a physician to rule out any underlying medical factors related to anxiety, like thyroid or sleep problems. I once worked with a woman who had significant anxiety problems, and it turned out she had a tumor on her adrenal gland. She was still thankful for our mindfulness work though, as she learned how to relate differently to her body sensations.

It is also important to monitor your intake of stimulants like caffeine. I have had a number of clients with anxiety issues tell me that they drank four pots of coffee a day, or five 2-liters of Mountain Dew, and didn't see the connection with their anxiety levels.

For serious anxiety, especially related to trauma, it is also important to work with a professional to customize the treatment to your personal situation. Though sometimes people feel guilty that they have to take something for their anxiety, medication can be an important boost to help you function, especially drugs that increase your serotonin levels.

Using fast-acting anxiety medications, like benzodiazepines (Valium, Xanax, Klonopin, Ativan, etc.), can be tricky. While they work immediately, in the long term, they tend to reinforce avoidance. When you don't like the way you feel, a medication like Xanax takes away the bad feeling and makes you feel pretty good. Hence, you don't experience that rising, cresting, and falling that extinguishes anxiety, so you are caught in that vicious cycle.

However, stopping benzodiazepine use cold turkey is dangerous, both medically, because of withdrawal effects, and psychologically, because knowing that you are going to quit the medication makes you anxious, and makes you want more medication. When my clients tell me they are ready to quit them, I suggest (in consultation with their prescribing physician) that the next time they feel like they need it, wait 30 seconds, then take it. Then they can practice waiting 45 seconds before taking it. Then a minute. Eventually, the anxiety will rise and fall before they take it, and they discover they don't need it any more.

Stress, anxiety, and fear are closely related, so many of the principles we have already described will be useful. Here we will explore some more specific concepts for working with a variety of anxiety problems, including fear and panic, phobias, social anxiety, heath anxiety, obsessive-compulsive disorder, generalized anxiety, and trauma. But first, let's explore more about how anxiety is acquired and maintained.

Anxiety as a conditioned response

Anyone who owns a dog or a cat knows that just the sound of opening a can or bag of their food brings them running. If you wanted to do so, you could even measure an increase in saliva flow in their mouths, even before they see or smell any food. Their brains basically rewire themselves to make a strong connection between the sound of a can opening and saliva flow. This can also generalize to other similar sounds. When you open a can of beans for your own dinner, they may come running with drooling mouths. You could even sing "Rumpelstiltskin" right before you give them their food, and it won't take long for them to become conditioned to salivate whenever you sing that word.

This is called "classical conditioning," and it plays a huge role in anxiety. Anything that was happening right before or during feelings of anxiety will be associated with that physiological response. If you hear your phone ring several times with bad news, your brain will start to release anxiety chemicals just from hearing that ringtone.

The good news is that these associations can also be broken. If you keep singing "Rumpelstiltskin" without giving the dogs their food, their drooling will gradually fade and stop completely. If you keep listening to your phone ring, and there is no bad news when you answer, the anxiety response will eventually stop kicking in.

The not so good news (in terms of anxiety) is that old conditioning can be retrained more quickly once you've had it, because the old brain connections don't completely go away. If you had to sing "Rumpelstiltskin" on ten different occasions to condition the dogs to drool, and then you extinguish it, the next time it might only require seven occasions to retrain them. If your phone rings with bad news only a few more times, your body will go back to having an anxiety response sooner than it did the first time.

The other type of conditioning that is important in starting and maintaining anxiety is called "operant conditioning." Basically, if I do something and get a good result, my brain wants to keep doing that thing. If I do something and get a bad result, my brain doesn't want to do that thing so much.

Avoidance becomes strong in anxiety disorders, because when I feel anxious, I want to do something to not feel it, and anything that takes my anxiety down (a good result) makes me want to keep doing it. If I run away from something that makes me anxious, or distract myself, or drink alcohol, my anxiety goes down, and my brain urges me to keep doing it.

Put these two types of conditioning together in the right way, and it becomes a difficult trap to escape from. If I hear my phone ring after getting several calls with bad news, just hearing my phone ring activates my body's anxiety response. If I then walk away from the phone, my anxiety drops, so I get in the habit of avoiding my phone. The only way I can extinguish the classical conditioning anxiety response that started the whole thing is to keep hearing the ring without anything bad happening. But because I always walk away, that can't happen.

So, to break through anxiety, we have to feel it, and wait for it to pass. Anything we do to avoid it, even by distracting ourselves from it by thinking, will keep it there longer. What makes this even more difficult is the phenomenon known as an "extinction burst," which simply means it usually gets worse before it starts to come down.

Consistency is the best way to extinguish a behavior. Intermittent reinforcement, which means getting a good result randomly, makes it harder to extinguish. If your young child asks for candy at the checkout line, and you consistently say no, they are not likely to push you for it very hard. But if, every once in a while, you say yes after they cry really loudly, you reinforce the loud crying (the child got a good result from crying). The next time they ask, and you say no, they might just up their asking even more (since it worked last time, they'll just do more this time), maybe even rolling on the floor and kicking things over. The worst thing you can do at that point is give in to their extinction burst. You have to firmly stay with your boundaries, and wait for their tantrum to subside.

When your own anxiety throws a tantrum, as challenging as it may be, stay with it, and wait for it to subside.

This extinction burst phenomenon is what keeps us trapped in anxiety patterns. Extinguishing your anxiety is like exorcizing a demon. In the movie The Exorcist, the possessed little girl was pretty creepy, but she got really mad when they were attempting to purge the demon. When you decide not to avoid your anxiety, your mind may tell you that all hell is breaking loose. In the short term, we may prefer to live with the creepy little girl than face our demons, but she will eat away at our souls.

We can also learn our anxiety responses from others. Monkeys raised in captivity are not afraid of snakes. But if they watch a video of a wild monkey getting anxious in the presence of a snake, domesticated monkeys will acquire a fear of snakes. Hence, not only do we get some genetic loading toward anxiety if we have anxious parents, but we learn from their examples as we are growing up. The good news is we can also extinguish fear and anxiety vicariously, that is, by watching others do something that we are afraid to do. However it's done, it all comes down to letting the anxiety rise and fall.

Fear and panic

A 30-year-old man once came to me seeking help for anxiety. He said it was something he had suffered from all his life. When asked what life would be like without the anxiety, he could not even imagine it.

In fact, just coming there to my downtown office, talking about difficult things with a stranger, sparked a panic attack right there in the first session. Obviously that wasn't the time to educate him about the principles of mindfulness, so I simply did it with him.

"Describe to me what you are experiencing right now," I said.

"I feel like I'm going to die!" he said immediately.

"So you're noticing a strong thought that you're going to die." I said in a calm voice. "If it helps to know, I used to be an emergency medical technician, and I'll call 911 if necessary. But since you have told me you suffer from panic attacks, I'd like to help you experience this in a different way."

His eyes were closed, and his body was clenched, but he agreed. I gave him some information to settle his thoughts down, but modeled a mindfulness approach. "The sensations in your body will pass. All you can do is ride them out. What are you feeling in your body right now?"

"I feel like I'm going to throw up!" I immediately placed a trash can next to him just in case. Incidentally, I later found out that he hadn't thrown up in seven years, and that was after he had eaten something bad, but the fear of throwing up in front of someone else was very strong in his mind.

"What else are you noticing in your body?" I inquired.

"I feel like I'm going crazy," he replied.

"So you noticed a thought about going crazy – your thinking is trying to help by distracting you, but it ends up keeping the panic going longer. Can you come back to noticing what you feel in your body right now?"

"There's a churning sensation in my stomach … my fingertips are tingling … my heart is beating fast … I'm feeling lightheaded … "

"Well done," I said encouragingly. "What you are going to notice is that when you stay with it, it will get a little worse, then it will top off, then it will slowly come back down all by itself. Stay with the sensations as best you can."

Of course, the panic did pass, and he learned he had more choices than just trying to fight it off. We talked more about the concept of feeling it, knowing it's going to get worse, and waiting for it to pass.

Once he got this concept, he became a new person. A few weeks later, he told me he approached an attractive woman at a party, something he normally would have avoided. He said he felt the anxiety rise as he got closer, waited for it to pass, then asked her out on a date (and she said yes!). He began trying more and more new things. In just a couple of months, his life was transformed. The energy he had been wasting on worry and anxiety became channeled into new things. I believe he even tried skydiving.

Anxiety is a natural human feeling designed to help us pay attention and help us plan for the future. As we've been discussing, when you begin to make anxiety itself the problem, and do everything you can to avoid it, it gets worse. It's like having an important message to tell your best friend, and every time you try, they keep running away from you. You just run faster to try to catch up to them and give them the message. You may end up tackling them, but they still won't listen, because they are covering their ears and shouting "I'm not listening to you!" So out of desperation, you grab their face and shout your message to them.

A panic attack is anxiety shouting its message. Your heart pounds as if it is going to explode. It becomes difficult to breath. Your stomach churns, and your chest tightens. Your muscles clench and you want to jump up and run, or try to curl up in a ball and hide. You feel dizzy or lightheaded, and strong waves of panic wash over your entire body. It is the fight, flight, or freeze response at full strength, without any external tigers to use it for.

If you've ever had a panic attack, it is very frightening. You don't ever want to experience it again, but ironically, all the efforts you make to avoid feeling the anxiety is what makes it worse, like trying to escape from that persistent messenger. Also, paradoxically, your worry about having another one, which is called anticipatory anxiety, makes it more likely that it will come again.

When fear and anxiety begin to build, mindfulness practice reminds us to come back to the moment we are in. It's your own body! Why fight yourself? The enemies here are usually in your own mind. Stay with the sensations as best you can, like waiting out the sensations of cold when you are in a swimming pool. Don't try to talk yourself out of it, don't think of a peaceful scene, don't berate yourself with judgments. Every thought you have is a way of avoiding the feelings of anxiety, which is like jumping out of the pool. You probably won't be able to stop the thoughts, so just notice them, and keep getting back into the pool of sensations in your body. They will rise, level off, and pass.

It is crucial to stay with the sensations until they begin to come back down. If you try to avoid them when they rise, you reinforce avoidance, and stay stuck in the cycle.

After my psychology internship ended, one of my previous supervisors asked me to take him for a flight over his house. When we arrived at the airport, I think he was surprised to see that we were about to get into such a tiny aircraft. As we strapped in and closed the doors, squeezed in shoulder-to-shoulder, he looked a little nervous. As we taxied down the runway to prepare for takeoff, he asked, "If I get scared, will you take me back down right away?"

I smiled and said, "Only after your anxiety starts to go down a bit first."

He didn't really laugh at the time either, but then, few people get jokes about extinguishing anxiety responses.

Of course, nobody wants to feel anxiety. It is unpleasant by definition. If it felt good, you would call it excitement. On a program called "Phobias," cameras followed a woman named Jacqueline who struggled with an intense fear of birds and feathers her entire life. It became obvious that all of the "treatments" she was trying did not help, because they were all attempts to avoid feeling the anxiety. Even recovering a memory that the phobia started when she was a little girl, being terrified when a bird was trapped in her house, did not help alleviate it. Finally, she worked with a clinical psychologist named Paul Salkovskis. He asks if she is ready to face the fear, which is not really of birds and feathers, but of dying, and that she needs to learn that if she stays with it she will not die. "I wish you could just wave a magic wand and make it go away," Jacqueline says. "I do have a magic wand," Dr. Salkovskis replies, "but it has feathery bits on it."

Dr. Salkovskis brings out a feather, and the client has a full-blown panic attack, screaming and crying that she feels like she is going to die. But in just a few minutes, the anxiety drops significantly. The feather comes closer, up goes the anxiety, and they wait for it to pass again. In just one session, after a couple of hours, Jacqueline is able to hold a feather in her hands without anxiety for the first time in her life.

Because we don't want to feel anxiety, we get very clever about how to avoid feeling it. Not only will thoughts jump around, attention will too. It is important to stay with each experience, watching it rise, crest, and fall, before moving to the next one. If I jump from my stomach, to my heart, to my fingers, to my eyes, I never let any of the unpleasant feelings extinguish. Each jump to a new sensation, or a new worry, might just be an attempt to avoid the one you were just feeling.

I once worked with a young woman named Chastity, who came to me saying, "I've been struggling with anxiety for years, I am a professional counselor myself, and I've worked with a dozen other therapists. No one has been able to help me, so I'm hoping you can."

In fact, she knew so much intellectually about anxiety that thinking about all those theories actually served to help her avoid feeling it.

Because she expressed an interest in learning mindfulness, I described how to approach anxiety in a new way. I talked about feeling it in her body as a way to undercut the thoughts. When I asked if she would be willing to try an exercise in session with me, she hesitatingly agreed – hopeful that a new approach would help, but worried about what might happen.

"I would like you to try to get more in touch with the actual physical sensations in your body," I suggested. "Try to set aside the thoughts and images in your mind, and actually feel whatever you are feeling in your body right now."

After a few moments of silence, she said, "I have a thing about noticing my body."

I lightheartedly said, "That doesn't surprise me at all." She smiled, so I gently encouraged her to just begin to let herself explore a little, to begin to notice something in her physical sensations.

"This is embarrassing," she said, "but the first thing I notice is my underwear." She laughed nervously.

"Very good," I said. "I want you to stay with that sensation."

"I don't know why that is. It's like I'm usually trying not to think about it," she said apologetically.

"Even those thoughts you're having right now are trying to help you, to protect you from feeling the unpleasant sensation. So thank your mind, and try to just feel it as best you can, separating the actual sensations from your thoughts about them."

"I'm also feeling a tightness in my shoulders," Chastity reported.

"Good to notice that. Right now though, your mind is probably trying to avoid the feeling in your underwear. I'd like you to stay with the sensations there a little longer. As we talked about, your anxiety is going to rise, level off, and eventually start to come down if you can stay with it."

How is your underwear feeling right now? Is it in the right place? Is it bunched up, or uncomfortable? Do you get a little feeling of anxiety that makes you try to forget it, and the more you try, the more you feel it? Isn't it amazing the struggles we can create with our own minds?

There are many things in our lives that spark a little anxiety, but after it delivers its message, it usually passes on its own. If we don't feel comfortable allowing it to flow, however, we attribute the problem to something outside of us and then try to avoid that something.

I was once working with a middle-aged professional woman named Daisy who gradually developed a fear of driving. As her fear and anxiety increased, she tried her best to avoid it more. She stopped driving on highways, and tried to never drive alone. The more she tried to avoid the anxiety, the worse it got. She began having thoughts that she might have an accident, or hurt someone, or accidentally run over someone. The thought of running over someone made her more anxious, so she started turning around to check the road after she felt a bump, to make sure it wasn't a person, as a way of temporarily easing the anxiety. As this vicious cycle grew, she became more embarrassed at the trouble this was causing her family. Daisy knew these thoughts were irrational, but she could not stop thinking about running over someone, despite all her efforts. Her inability to stop her thoughts made her more anxious, and the anxiety sparked more obsessive thinking.

After some education about the nature of anxiety, and how thoughts attempt to distract us from unpleasant feelings, Daisy agreed to do some exposure therapy. I hooked her up to a monitor so she could see what her heart was doing. We began with having her imagine that she was walking up to her car. Her heart rate seemed fine, so we continued, having her get inside and start the engine. When she imagined pulling onto the road, she reported a high level of anxiety.

"Where do you feel the anxiety?" I asked.

"My heart – it's pounding like crazy. I'm worried that it's going to get damaged," she said, doing her best to sound calm.

"Go ahead and look at the heart monitor," I suggested.

When Daisy opened her eyes to see her pulse rate, it was 85. I explained to her that the resting heart rate for a lot of people is higher than that, and that her heart would even be fine over 200 for a little while. She was very surprised that her heart rate was so low. She appeared to have an "aha" moment, realizing that much of her anxiety was created by her own mind, by her interpretations of what she thought she felt, instead of the sensations themselves.

After a few sessions, we tackled her biggest concern, the thought of running people over. After imagining herself driving no longer produced much anxiety, I asked her to imagine running over someone. Her heart rate jumped up a bit, then came back down. To make it realistic for her brain, I asked her to imagine as much detail as she could, in slow motion. First a man, not paying attention, steps out into the street. She realizes he is moving right in front of her car, and she slams her brakes, but knows she won't stop in time. The look of terror on the man's face. Her bumper hitting the man's knees. His body bouncing on the hood. His face pressing into the cracking windshield. Each time, her anxiety went up a little, leveled off, and came back down. Each time, it went less high, and passed more quickly.

In addition to thinking I must be a sadist, you might also be thinking, "But wait – wouldn't having her imagine running over people encourage her subconsciously to drive dangerously?" In this case, no. The problem she had was that she was trying not to think about driving over someone, but she couldn't stop worrying about it. Exposing her directly to the thoughts allowed her to pass through her fear, and the thoughts went away after being robbed of their fuel. Are there some instances when doing this would be a bad idea? Yes – for a person who lacks the capacity to feel empathy for others. Of course, this underscores the importance of seeking competent professional help when necessary.

Having an expert guide you through serious anxiety can help you get an objective perspective on the countless subtle avoidance strategies we can come up with. A colleague of mine was once working with a man named Rush who also had a fear of driving, and after feeling stuck for a while, my colleague called me in to consult. I even had to drive to his office, because Rush was not willing to drive all the way to my office. Not surprisingly, he was very intelligent, and had read all the books and theories on anxiety. He quickly grasped the swimming pool analogy, and understood how avoidance made things worse. Imagining driving didn't have much effect on him, so I encouraged him to keep taking more actual trips. His biggest fear was a stretch of road with the river on one side, and a retaining wall on the other, because it offered him no escapes once he got on it.

Rush came back the next week and said he was able to drive that most feared stretch of road, but didn't feel better yet. When I asked him to say more about his experience, he described "white knuckling" it, grabbing tightly onto the wheel, full of thoughts, rushing to get through the stretch of highway as fast as he could, then turning around and coming back as fast as he could.

I told him that he never gave himself a chance to experience the leveling off and falling of the anxiety. It was as if he jumped into a cold swimming pool, swam as fast as he could to the other side, and climbed back out. He needed to stay in the water longer. He needed to feel his body more.

Health anxiety

So, if moving through anxiety is about feeling your body more, what about those who suffer from anxiety related to their own health? People who come to me for these kinds of issues, known as hypochondriasis, somatic symptom disorder, or illness anxiety disorder, are very surprised when I tell them they need to pay *more* attention to their bodies. It's not the noticing, it's how we relate to our bodies that creates problems.

We all experience this to various degrees. Have you ever noticed something like a bump on your hand, gotten a little worried about it, then realized that there was one just like it on the other hand? You had just never noticed it before. If you decide to look up "bump on hand" on the internet, you may find thousands of opinions about what it might be, ranging from "nothing at all" to "rapidly spreading deadly cancer." If we allow our anxieties alone to drive us, we may not make the best decisions about how to proceed.

People who suffer from the more serious forms of this disorder may have started worrying for a very legitimate reason. Maybe you have suffered from cancer or some other disease, and are paying attention to the possibility of relapse. Perhaps your parents had serious health problems, and died when you were very young.

Sensitivity to your own body is actually a good thing. Years ago, I noticed some odd bumps on my neck, asked someone to look at them, and decided to go to my local urgent care. It turned out to be shingles, and had I not gotten the necessary medication within the first 72 hours, it could have become much more serious.

Rather than sensitivity, it is our emotional reactions, how we relate to what we notice, that tend to create problems. We feel fear that we might get sick, and to avoid feeling the fear, we look for something to focus on to reduce our sense of helplessness. As we have discussed, the more you avoid anxiety, the worse it gets, and the more you want to keep doing what you were doing to avoid it. In this case, you keep noticing your own body sensations and interpreting them in a way that creates further anxiety.

I once worked with a young man named Arnold who was a college weightlifter. One day, as he was squatting to lift a large amount of weight, he felt something pull in his rectum, causing a great deal of pain. The pain passed, but it still didn't quite feel right, so he went to his doctor. The doctor didn't see anything wrong, but referred him to a specialist. Arnold ended up seeing two specialists, and they both told him everything was normal down there. Yet, he was convinced that it just didn't feel right.

Ask yourself right now, does your rectum feel right? What's it supposed to feel like? We often don't notice it's there, so when we become hyper-aware of it, we can attach all kinds of thoughts and reactions to the sensations, which creates anxiety. It takes practice to be able to consciously separate out our sensations from our thoughts and feelings about them.

Awareness of our bodies, and control of things like blinking, is both conscious and subconscious. This is a good thing, because it would take a lot of work to make sure you were always blinking enough, but it's nice to be able to blink on purpose when something gets in our eyes. Of course, even just reading this may now make you aware of your blinking, perhaps with a tiny feeling of anxiety, but it will return to its normal rate by itself if you don't interfere.

Breathing is also something we can consciously control, but also happens by itself, which makes it a wonderful thing to use for practicing mindful awareness. At first, people often get in their own way, trying to control their breath rather than allowing it to happen naturally. If you have suffered from asthma, and have experienced some serious losses of breath, you may have developed a desire to hold on to your breath more tightly so you don't lose it. Unfortunately, breathing shallowly from the chest, and more rapidly, triggers the sympathetic system (stress) response, ironically creating a higher chance of triggering another attack. The breath is definitely something you will lose if you hold onto it too tightly.

In practicing mindfulness, we learn to watch our sensations, emotions, and thoughts more objectively. If an odd sensation arises in our body, we can notice it, and separate out our thoughts and emotions about it. We can then decide to stay with it and investigate it, let it go, or take some considered action to deal with it.

Obsessive-compulsive disorder

Sometimes we get caught up in using thoughts (obsessions) and/or behaviors (compulsions) to control our anxieties. Again, we all do this to some degree, but a full-blown obsessive-compulsive disorder (OCD) can become debilitating.

Eileen came to me for therapy because she could not stop doing ritual behaviors. Before she could leave her house, she had to go around and check each door to make sure it was locked. Then she would have a thought flash up that maybe she missed one. With that thought came a tiny bit of anxiety, because she wouldn't want to leave a door unlocked when she was gone all day, so she would go back around and check all the doors again. As she was checking, her anxiety went down, because she was making sure. But then as she went to leave again, the thought would pop up, "What if the button on one of them didn't quite go in all the way, and it wasn't fully locked?" Again, a little anxiety, so back she would go to check them all again, temporarily dropping the anxiety created by that thought. Then she would think, "What if one of the windows is not secured?" Off to check all the windows.

Eventually Eileen would make it out to her car. A thought would pop up, "What if my tire pressure is too low?" So she walked around the car and checked all the tires, and felt a little better. "But what about the oil?" So she checked that. "What if the back doors are not closed all the way?" After a few more things, she might just have to start over again to make sure a tire hadn't lost air or something in all the time that had passed.

When things were going well for Eileen, she could get through these routines in 10 or 15 minutes. When her stress levels increased, it could take her 2 or 3 hours to be able to leave for work.

We all can relate to questioning ourselves and going back to check something, but it can grow out of control if we don't pay attention. Have you ever had the experience of leaving your home, then wondering if you locked the door, or turned off the light, or turned off the stove? In that moment, you get a small spark of anxiety. If you go back to the house and check, it lowers your anxiety in that moment. Most of the time that will satisfy you, so you go on your way. But if you are already feeling stressed or anxious, you might question yourself as you are leaving. Did I really check it? Was I distracted or thinking of something else at the time? Maybe I'm remembering that I checked it yesterday, and not today? Another tiny bit of anxiety. Since you just experienced that checking it lowered your anxiety in that moment, you might choose to check again. The more you check, the more you feel silly, and the more you doubt yourself, and the more anxious you get. You can slip into a vicious cycle very gradually.

When Eileen's anxiety got worse, she even hallucinated seeing eyes looking in through her windows. When we explored this, it turned out that her anxiety had started when she was much younger, after someone had broken into her house. Her checking had begun as a way of trying to gain some sense of control after the helpless feeling of having her home invaded. However, this insight alone was not enough to stop the cycle, because it had become self-perpetuating.

OCD is a serious anxiety disorder. People who suffer from it know that logically what they are doing does not make sense, but they think it is the only way they can reduce their anxiety, which is what keeps them stuck.

In OCD, one can have obsessions, compulsions, or both. Compulsions are behaviors one feels compelled to do. If I am doing something physically, I am distracted from my anxiety. When I stop the behavior, the anxiety comes back, so I keep doing the behavior. Sometimes the behaviors are done to one's own body, like hair pulling, skin picking, or nail biting.

Obsessions are also an attempt to control anxiety. Random thoughts come and go in our minds, but most of the time we don't take them too seriously, or we aren't aware of them. Those who have practiced remembering their dreams by keeping a dream journal quickly discover what a bizarre place the mind is. If a thought pops up that you would like to have sex with your mother, it will likely spark a feeling of anxiety or guilt, even though it probably wasn't a thought you consciously wanted to have. Because it sparked an unpleasant feeling, you try to push it away. The more you try not to think about a thought, the stronger it tends to become, fueled by anxiety.

Unfortunately, sometimes OCD is rewarded by society, especially in its mild form. If I feel the urge to clean my home when I'm anxious, as a way to distract myself with a sense of organization and control, my roommates may not mind that at all. If I am a perfectionist at my job, and take charge of a lot of projects to gain a sense of control, my laid-back coworkers may not have to work as hard.

One of the best, most researched treatments for OCD is called exposure and response prevention (ERP), and mindfulness fits well with this model. Expose yourself to the anxiety, and don't escape from it with thoughts or behaviors, and you will find that the anxiety rises then falls. If trying not to think about a thought is the problem, you can say it to yourself over and over, or you can record it and listen to it in headphones over and over, until the thoughts lose their meaning. You will realize that nothing bad happened because you thought it, and that thinking that you'll do something doesn't mean you'll do it, and the anxiety will extinguish if you stay with it.

Social anxiety

For some of us, the thoughts that create anxiety are related to social situations. We sometimes have this unrealistic fear that everyone will remember everything embarrassing we have ever done or might ever do.

Many years ago I was at a banquet with several hundred people, celebrating the launch of a new endeavor. When it was my turn to speak, I spoke about the positive impact our organization had already had on many lives, and the inspiring vision of the potential impact to come on thousands more. I thanked all the members of the management team, each in turn. I then said something like, "I would also say something nice about Joe, but he's the lawyer." There was a laugh from the crowd, though I don't think Joe laughed. I then continued with presenting a memento to the CEO. After I sat down, I realized I forgot to go back and say something nice about Joe.

I thought of what I would say the next chance I had to speak, but the chance never came. I felt badly about not thanking him, because he had laid the crucial legal foundations for the creation of the organization, and I felt even worse that the only comment I had made was a put down. I was worried that I might have damaged our professional relationship.

I didn't see Joe again until our next organizational retreat several months later. The first thing I did was apologize to him about my comment at the banquet, and how much I actually appreciated having him on the team. He stared at me blankly for a moment, and said, "I have no idea what you're talking about." After I gave a little more detail about what had happened, he said, "I have no memory of that whatsoever," and we both laughed.

Social anxiety is a funny thing. We are worried that we are not important enough, that we will be judged and belittled. Yet, we think we are so important that other people will pay attention to every little thing we do or say, and spend lots of their time talking about us later!

I learned a valuable lesson when I was in my early 20s, when I had a weekly public access cable television show called *The Modern Ninja*. In my head, I knew I wasn't sure about everything I wanted to do and say, and knew I felt nervous in front of the camera. But when I watched myself later, I looked like I knew what I was doing. No one can see my inner thoughts and feelings unless I say them or show them. The more people I have met and gotten to know, the more I have found that everyone has doubts about themselves, and that even celebrities are just people.

As with other forms of anxiety, our thinking is what creates problems, and our reactions to our anxiety. What if I say something stupid? What if I get so nervous I throw up in front of everyone? What if I pass gas and it smells really bad?

Yep, those things could happen. Ironically, the more you worry about them, the more anxious you will get, and the more likely they are to actually happen. But if someone else says something "stupid," you might not even notice, or you'll probably forget about it later. We can learn to be just as kind to ourselves. If you do something you regret, just apologize and move on. The anxiety and embarrassment will pass. If they don't forgive you, it's probably due to their own issues.

I once took a drink in front of a crowd of 200 mental health professionals during a mindfulness presentation, and spilled water all over the front of my shirt. I could have pretended it didn't happen, or run out of the room, but it was pretty obvious – I now looked like a contestant in a wet T-shirt contest. I paused, felt my cheeks turn red, then said, "Okay, I'm going to feel the embarrassment, wait for it to level off, then watch it fade away," which brought a nice laugh. By staying present, my accident actually made the presentation better.

As you may have guessed, social anxiety begins with avoidance, and resolves with exposure. Of course, there is no need to do something dramatic to move through the anxiety, like becoming a standup comedian, or shouting embarrassing things over and over in public. Just gradually put yourself around more people and give yourself permission to feel anxious.

Generalized anxiety

Sometimes anxiety becomes generalized to a wide variety of things in your life. You worry about things like work, money, love, and friends so much that it significantly interferes with your life. This constant worry makes you irritable, tense, restless, scattered, and exhausted.

In this case, you can't expose yourself directly to every single thing that makes you anxious. It becomes a vicious loop of anxiety about anxiety. You work hard to avoid feeling anxious, because there are so many things to avoid, and your life becomes very constricted. In a disorder called agoraphobia, you dislike the anxiety you feel in open places, and eventually can end up never leaving the house.

In my experience, a large part of generalized anxiety is about one's own bodily feelings. When you can't stand the feelings in your body, you avoid anything that might create those feelings, and get stuck in that cycle of avoidance. Because there are so many things in the world to worry about, there are lots of distracting thoughts to choose from.

Don't misunderstand me. Terrible things can and do happen in the world. We *could* get hit by an asteroid, the economy *could* collapse, or your best friend *could* fall over dead from a heart attack. Maybe you really will get evicted from your home for not paying the bills. Maybe you will get fired from your job. Perhaps you really have lost all your money. Perhaps a parent passed away recently. But worrying about all these things constantly will not change the past or the future. Compulsive worrying only wears us down, and when terrible things do happen, you will handle it better if you are well rested and able to think clearly. When a worry arises, we can look at it, notice our emotions and body sensations, and then choose to take some action, stay with our feelings and watch them rise and fall, or do something to take care of ourselves. If the anxiety is an important message about the need to address a very real immediate problem, like how you are going to pay the bills, set aside a certain time to worry about it or plan it out, rather than worrying about it all day and all night.

A practice such as the body scan (see Chapter 7) can be helpful for learning to relate to your body sensations in a new way. However, if you have a history of trauma or abuse, you must be very careful when you explore your sensations, emotions, and thoughts more directly.

Trauma

Experiencing trauma can wreak havoc on our brains, whether it is a one-time event, or ongoing abuse. Anyone who experiences a life-threatening event will of course be affected as they recover from it. If trauma is the result of intentional mistreatment, rather than from something like a natural disaster, there is an increased risk of developing posttraumatic stress disorder (PTSD) if it is not processed in a healthy way.

If you have a terrifying experience, in which your life is threatened or you witness someone else being traumatized or killed, you naturally want to forget it. And yet, your brain is wired to immediately lay down a strong emotional memory about the event so you can learn from it. Hence, you get caught in an even more magnified version of the vicious cycle we've been talking about – you really want to avoid that awful memory, but your brain really wants to make sure you know about it. Hence, you may have nightmares, intrusive thoughts and images, and even "flashbacks" in which you feel like you are reliving the trauma.

Because of this re-experiencing of the trauma, PTSD causes the stress and anxiety response to kick up often and quickly. You become easily startled. You feel like you are on "high alert," paying very close attention to all the things that could threaten your safety, a state known as "hypervigilance."

One of my clients with PTSD often says things reminiscent of Sherlock Holmes. One session, as soon as I sat down, he said, "I see you've been doing some work around the house." He was right. He had noticed a little bit of black under my fingernails.

In a life and death situation, paying attention can save your life, so your brain is strongly activated to look for the worst and prepare for it. I've had friends and clients who went to war in the Middle East. After coming back, it is hard to for them to adjust to feeling safe. Their brains automatically scan the environment for potential snipers. A small box on the side of the road could be an improvised explosive device and sparks their stress response.

Though I have never been to war, after protecting the Dalai Lama for a few days, I could relate to developing a state of hypervigilance. Everywhere we went, I became very aware of my surroundings. I automatically scanned for potential entrances and exits, places where a shooter or bomb could be hidden, and quickly looked at each person to determine if they could be a threat.

At one venue, an elderly Tibetan man wanted to give the Dalai Lama an orange as an offering for an initiation ceremony. A local police agent would not let him get near the stage. The more adamant the man became, the more stern the officer became. The man then sighed and looked very sad. Mindful that I was protecting a religious world leader, who promoted love and peace, I stepped in front of the officer, respectfully took the orange with hands together, made a small bow, and smiled and nodded. The man looked over-joyed and thanked me. After walking backstage, I could not see any breaks in the peel into which an explosive could have been slipped, but placing it on the altar in front of the Dalai Lama seemed too great a risk in that moment. I carefully and respectfully put the orange under some concrete steps off the stage, hoping the man would believe his orange was one of the many already on the stage.

For individuals who suffer from PTSD, their survival instincts sometimes override their concern for others. Their urge to be safe can end up damaging their relationships. Because they have been hurt badly in the past by others, they put up walls to stay safe. While walls may keep them physically safe, it is very lonely in their self-made fortress, and they inadvertently alienate those who actually do care about them.

Old hurts can often greatly interfere with our current lives and relation-ships. What a horrible tragedy to be haunted by the voices of harsh parents who may be long dead. How sad to sabotage a good relationship because we cannot trust enough to be vulnerable again after we have been betrayed in the past.

It is important to know that the things we do to get through traumatic experiences represent our best efforts to survive a horrendous situation. The tragedy is that we get stuck in old patterns. If we were hurt in the past by the ones who were supposed to take care of us, we may find it hard to accept help from others. In a self-fulfilling prophecy, people stop offering to help us after a while, and we feel that no one will ever take care of us.

Very often, people think the traumas they experienced were normal, because that is all they knew. Many times I have heard clients say things like, "Growing up, I thought everyone's parents yelled at them and smacked their faces every day." One woman I was dating many years ago, who grew up in an abusive environment, got upset when I didn't engage her in shouting arguments. She actually said, "If you don't yell at me, it doesn't feel like you love me!"

Significant, ongoing childhood abuse could lead to the development of a condition known as borderline personality disorder. Individuals who suffer from this disorder feel empty inside, have chaotic relationships, and may even develop a pattern of harming themselves by cutting their skin with razors or engaging in suicidal gestures. If when you were growing up, even your body was not respected as a boundary, you learn to perform very dramatic actions in your attempts to get attention to get your needs met.

Though our brains are wired to pay attention to and remember traumatic events, we can also develop the ability to tune out during very intense trauma, such as ongoing sexual abuse. In this case, avoidance becomes necessary for survival, so we dissociate from our experiences.

In a condition known as dissociative identity disorder (DID), formerly known as multiple personality disorder, you may even create separate senses of identity to contain the traumas when they are too much for one human being to handle. Though there are still some who question the validity of this diagnosis, the research literature and my clinical experiences give me no doubts. It can sometimes be one of the only ways to get through horrible experiences. We all act differently in different situations to some degree. I am a completely different person when I'm playing with my four year old than when I am while playing guitar on open mic night at the local pub. I just don't give all my personalities different names (though sometimes my friends do). How could someone possibly be the same person at work or at school that they were while experiencing horrible abuse?

Although all of the disorders in this chapter may need professional intervention, this is especially important for PTSD. When you are ready to face serious traumas, you may well be opening up a can of worms.

A woman in her late 20s named Mary once came to see me in crisis. She told me that she had seen a flyer for a sexual abuse survivor support group being held at her church, and decided that perhaps it was time for her to face and work through her past. For years, she had been sexually molested by her stepfather. When Mary told her mother, she did not believe her. Her mother called her a liar and made threats to her welfare if she ever made such an accusation again. Eventually the stepfather went to prison for his behavior, but after he served a one year sentence, he moved back into the house as if nothing had happened. Mary had used sheer willpower to build up her life as an adult despite her abuse.

Mary mustered up her courage and went to the support group. The members had reached a point where they could comfortably share and process the details of their trauma, which can be very healing in a supportive context. Unfortunately, this support group was not run by professionals, and my client was not prepared for the details she heard. It immediately triggered all of the old feelings she had been working so hard to suppress for so long. After the group ended, these memories continued to flood her, to the point where she could no longer perform her work as a safety inspector.

In our individual work, we first focused on getting Mary stable. I then asked her a very crucial question. "Now that things are more like they were, you have an important choice. You can continue as you did, using willpower to keep your feelings contained, knowing that you will likely be triggered again in the future. As we get older, it gets harder to use willpower to hold down past hurts, as expending all that energy wears us out. Your other choice takes more courage in the short run, but you could choose to work through this now. We can process and let go of the old traumas in a more gradual, controlled way, rather than pushing them back down."

Mary was courageous enough to engage in the work, and though it was often very challenging for her, she made significant progress over the course of a few months.

Unfortunately, there are even some "professionals" who are not well-trained in the treatment of serious trauma. At a professional conference where I was teaching mindfulness, I mentioned working on a book about using mindfulness for PTSD. Someone in the audience said, "Since mindfulness is about paying more attention, won't it make things worse? I have a client with PTSD, and whenever her past traumas come up, she starts feeling bad, so we never talk about it."

Yes, paying attention makes you more aware of the bad feelings you were trying to avoid, so it does make it worse, so one has to be very careful when using mindfulness. However, if even the therapist completely avoids anything related to the trauma, healing will not be able to take place.

Mindfulness can be an important tool for trauma treatment, but awareness alone is not sufficient. In a treatment known as dialectical behavior therapy, which involves balancing the extremes, participants learn mindfulness skills, distress tolerance skills, interpersonal skills, and emotion regulation skills.

As with other forms of anxiety, the best treatment is exposure, to let go of avoidance and move into the feelings. However, this must be done in a careful, gradual way. It could take months or years to process serious traumas.

One of my former supervisors, Dr. Jeffery Allen, a clinical neuropsychologist (someone who figures out the connections between brain and behavior), helped me understand how severe trauma affects the brain, and why psychotherapy and writing in a journal helps.

On a computer, "memories" are laid down as complete files. When you pull it back up, the memory is exactly as you laid it down. When memories are created in the human brain, they are not stored like computer files. The hippocampus (meaning "seahorse," due to its shape) is a structure that coordinates how memories are laid down throughout the brain. Right now, your hippocampus is sending what you are seeing to your visual cortex to be laid down as visual memories, the sounds you are hearing to be stored in your auditory cortex, emotional memories to be stored in your limbic system, and so on. When you remember this moment later, your hippocampus retrieves all those pieces and puts them back together for you. Although this is not always an exact process (which is why things often look different than you remembered when you go back to your old elementary school, for example), it generally works pretty well.

During a highly stressful or traumatic event, however, your brain is flooded with stress chemicals, which disrupts your hippocampus (in fact, enduring a lot of stress or significant trauma can shrink the hippocampus, and create significant memory problems). Memories are still laid down in the different parts of your brain, but the hippocampus loses its code for reconnecting them all back together, though they may still have some connections with each other without your thinking brain's knowledge. For example, a Vietnam veteran may have experienced getting hurt in combat, or seeing buddies killed, and being picked up by a helicopter. Many years later, he may hear the sound of a helicopter off in the distance, which he may not even be consciously aware of, and suddenly he feels afraid, his heart starts pounding, and he feels a need to get away from people.

Talking about the traumas, or writing about them, helps the thinking brain reconnect the memories. Words can be the bridge to bring all the parts of the memory back together. Therapy can then proceed to process the emotional components of the traumas.

To process traumas, you must do more than just talk about them. The emotional pieces make you feel as if you are there again, reliving the trauma. A method like the screen technique, described in the last chapter for working with difficult thoughts, allows you to watch yourself as if on a movie screen, moving back from the images. You will of course never forget the traumas, but you can take the "sting" out of them, and become more free to live the life you choose.

Depression

Depression is the second most common mental health issue around the world. Everyone has ups and downs, but clinical depression is debilitating. People who have never experienced it often don't realize how different it is from just "feeling blue," or being sad. You can't just "cheer up," or watch a funny movie and feel better right away.

For clinical depression, you feel significantly sad for at least two weeks. Your range of emotions becomes constricted. You lose your ability to feel pleasure from the things and activities you used to enjoy. As the depression worsens, you may lose your ability to feel anything at all. Despite being exhausted, you may wake up at 3am and have trouble falling back asleep. Or you may sleep 14 hours a day but still feel tired, because depression interferes with your natural sleep cycle. Memory and concentration problems become increasingly noticeable.

Interestingly, slightly depressed people actually see reality a little more clearly. After all, "normal" people have to pretend that the world won't be destroyed by a meteor at any moment, ignore the fact that people are starving in the world, and so on. But serious depression literally changes your brain and how it perceives the world, which Beck[1] called the "cognitive triad." You develop a negative view of yourself ("I am worthless"), a negative view of the world ("No one cares about me"), and a negative view of the future ("Things will only get worse").

A negative view of the future, or a sense of foreshortening of your future, leads to a feeling of hopelessness, which can be an important indicator of how depressed you are. If you can tell me about all the plans you have for your life, the places you want to go, the people you want to see, and what you want to be doing 5, 10, or 20 years from now, you are probably not very depressed. On the other hand, if you have trouble imagining tomorrow, or even 5 minutes from now, you are probably deeply depressed.

This is why suicide starts to become an attractive option. When you feel horrible about yourself, see everything in the world as going to hell, and can't imagine a future where things are better, the idea of not feeling anything at all starts to become alluring. Sadly, this is more likely to happen as the depression just begins to lift, and you get more energy, but haven't yet let go of the cognitive triad. In deep depression, you can become immobilized, where not only moving, but even thinking can feel like it takes too much energy.

Although it is relatively rare, depression can get so bad that the brain even creates distortions of reality. As I sat with one seriously depressed woman on an inpatient psych ward, she kept staring off over my shoulder. When I asked her what she saw, she described skeletons and blood coming out of the walls.

Treatment of active depression

Active depression is definitely something you need help moving through, because you lose your motivation. Sad feelings, negative perceptions, exhaustion, and withdrawal from activities lead to a downward spiral. The more depressed I feel, the less I want to be around people, the less I want to do things that used to be fun, the less I want to do anything, the more depressed I feel, which makes me even less likely to engage with my life.

Again, it is important to have a medical workup to look at potential underlying issues like hypothyroidism, sleep apnea, vitamin D deficiency, and so on. Your physician may also recommend antidepressant medication or light therapy, which can help "awaken" your brain if you suffer more often from depression during the shorter days of winter.

There are a number of options for psychotherapy, including interpersonal therapy, cognitive-behavioral therapy, and acceptance and commitment therapy. Much of the research points to the most important factor as "behavioral activation," which basically means to get moving, both literally (as in exercising or just getting out of the house) and metaphorically speaking (as in moving toward something you value, like family, career, or spirituality). This can be challenging to do, as nothing feels very important when you are depressed. Normally, if you don't feel like doing something, you choose not to do it. But in depression, you don't feel like doing much of anything. You have to decide to do it anyway, and know that you may not feel any better after doing it. It can take a while for the feelings to catch up.

The problem of relapse

If you've only been depressed once or twice, you can usually point to some significant event that triggered it, like the breakup of an important relationship, death of a loved one, or loss of a job. After three or more episodes of depression, less significant events can pull you back down. Sometimes you may not be aware of any particular thing that started it.

If you've been depressed before, it becomes harder, and takes longer, to pull back out of even common sad moods. While you're in that dip in mood, your memories of being depressed become more easily activated. You more easily remember the sad things that have happened in your life, your failures, and the ways you have been mistreated. This perpetuates the low mood, causing you to withdraw from activities and people. This makes you feel even more lonely and worthless, increasing the depression, and you are soon stuck in a downward spiral.

Every time you get depressed, your chances go up 18 percent that you will have yet another episode of depression in the future. Once the brain pathways have been laid down, it's easier to fall back into them, and harder to pull out. If left untreated, it could eventually incapacitate you.

Knowing how bad depression feels, you don't want to acknowledge that it could be happening again. As discussed in the last chapter, it is crucial to notice when depression is starting, so you can take active steps to pull out of it before you slide down those well-worn brain grooves into a pit of despair.

As an example of breaking down overwhelming tasks like cleaning the house into smaller pieces, I once suggested to a client that cleaning out a desk drawer might be a good start to get moving. He immediately said, "The problem is, it will just get dirty again." This is very typical depressive thinking, but it is like saying, "Why bother eating, I'll just get hungry again." The point is to just get moving, despite what our thoughts and feelings may be telling us.

Chronic Pain

Chronic pain, and its resulting impact on your life, can be devastating. Pain is a nerve signal to your brain. Your brain is supposed to re-adjust to a continuous signal, re-wiring itself, somewhat like people learned to ignore the boy who cried wolf. There are a lot of reasons why this may not happen, but an important factor to consider is how we relate to our pain.

Of course you want to do everything you can to eliminate or reduce your pain. In some cases, after you have exhausted all of your medical treatment options, the only thing left is learning how to live with whatever residual pain you may still have. I find that the equation "pain times resistance equals suffering" can be helpful. If you can't reduce the pain, you can learn to change your relationship to it to reduce your suffering.

Unfortunately, the things we do to get rid of pain can sometimes perpetuate it. Of course you want to use every tool you can to work with your pain. Distraction from the pain, such as by thinking about other things or watching television, only works temporarily. Of course it does work, so don't eliminate that strategy, but expand the range of things you can do. If the only tool you have is distraction, then you can get caught in the same vicious cycle of avoidance we have been discussing.

Pain medications have differing degrees of success for different people. You may well need it to be able to function. But be careful about only using it because you "can't stand" any level of pain at all.

You probably will not be able to use willpower to get rid of your pain. In fact, the more you try, the more struggle you create, and the pain may even get worse. It may be challenging, but try to dip your toe, so to speak, into the pain, rather than pushing it away. Eventually, you may be able to observe it with a more open mind, uncoupling the physical sensations from your thoughts and emotions about them. The pain itself is not static. It will wax and wane, shift between sharp and dull, and change over time in many subtle ways. People are often surprised to discover that their pain is not what they thought it was. An attitude of curiosity and exploration, though very challenging at first, helps to let go of the struggle with the pain. You may discover that you have been tensing up around the pain as a way of "fighting" it, which ends up creating more physical discomfort. When you are increasingly able to accept the pain as it is, as painful as it is, you can begin to relax the muscles around it, which may even ease the pain a bit.

When you are living with chronic pain, you are likely to also be experiencing significant stress, anxiety, and/or depression. It really doesn't matter which one came first – perhaps your stress contributed to the development of the pain, or perhaps the intensity of the pain gave you a sense of hopelessness that led to depression. Even if mindfulness cannot do much directly for your pain, it can be helpful for taking care of yourself. Rather than retreating from life, you may discover that you have more options than simply curling up and feeling hopeless.

Living with chronic pain is not easy. Mindfulness is not a miracle cure. It may not be realistic to expect that your pain will go away, or that you can quit all your pain medications, or that you will suddenly become indifferent to your pain. The point is to live a valued life as best you can, even with pain in it. Research studies have shown that mindfulness often leads to a reduction in the use of pain medicines, which at least means your mind can be clearer for engaging with your life and relationships.

Anger

Anger is a natural human emotion, one that we all feel. A friend of mine once told me that he was at a self-development workshop where the presenter was talking about how we all get angry sometimes. A woman raised her hand and said, "Actually, I never get angry."

Her partner, sitting next to her, helpfully said, "But what about that time yesterday when we were waiting in line so long?"

The woman scowled, gritted her teeth, and said harshly, "I WAS NOT ANGRY."

Pretending you don't get angry can be dangerous. It is much better to notice it, feel it, and then choose whether or not to act on it. If you act impulsively and do something you later regret, it is better to notice the anger, and try to make amends later, than to pretend it never happened.

Anger is not a feeling that tends to go away when we continually suppress it. Of course, that doesn't mean you express it directly all the time. Anger, like other emotions, is designed to give you information and motivate you to take action. The important thing is to acknowledge it is there, and plan a conscious response for that moment and that situation. If you get pulled over for speeding by a police officer, it is probably a good idea to suppress your anger for a few minutes.

Anger is designed to motivate us to take action. By noticing it, we can more consciously choose what to do with that energy. My martial arts instructor Stephen K. Hayes is one of the kindest people I have ever met. Years ago, we were preparing for an important ceremony to be presided over by a very important guest. In was the middle of August, and the air conditioning unit of the building had gone out. We were having a pleasant conversation as he was trying unsuccessfully to get his contractor to repair the A/C unit. Finally he called them up with a tone of anger. "Look – this is very urgent! My boss is going to fire me if you don't get someone out here right away! My children are going to starve!" He then returned to his calm conversation with me, and the A/C was soon repaired.

When I was a college student attending a martial arts school in an office building, our classes began with all of us sitting in silent meditation for a few minutes. I'll never forget the first time that complete silence was suddenly broken with someone screaming, "G@D D@MN SON OF A B@TCH!!! I HATE YOU! YOU MOTHER F@#$ING @SSH@LE!!!!" along with the sound of a physical beating going on. A couple of us sprang to our feet to go and help whomever was being attacked, but our instructor just laughed and motioned for us to sit back down. He told us that there was a counselor conducting therapy in one of the offices next door, and he was using a therapy technique.

I found it ironic that the martial artists were calming their minds, while a mind specialist was evoking anger. There was a time when therapists thought that screaming and hitting things was good to let anger out. I even shared an office once with another therapist who kept boxing gloves, sticks, and heavy bags in the office, which made my clients a little nervous.

As it turned out, the research on this method is not very supportive. Yes, it can feel good to express anger physically, but what you end up doing is training your brain to get physical when you get mad.

Anger can often be a pushing away of feelings we don't want. In many cultures, men are expected to be tough, to feel nothing. Men are led to believe that perhaps only anger is acceptable, as it fits with the idea of being tough. But anger is usually only the tip of the iceberg. There are often many other unacknowledged feelings underneath. The first step in learning to relate differently to anger is to tune in to all of those other feelings, such as fear and loneliness.

Sometimes people think their anger is completely unpredictable, saying "I just explode without warning." What they actually discover is that the warnings were there, but went unnoticed. Practicing mindfulness can help us learn to watch the ups and downs of our feelings throughout the day to prevent our stress from building up. When you are less stressed, you are less prone to random bouts of anger.

As we discussed in the last chapter, understanding the ABC model can be very helpful. I would often hear stories about someone being called a name (A), and then immediately punching that person in the nose (C). Somewhat tongue in cheek, I talk about how much power that gives me over the person.

All I have to do is call you a name, and I can send you to jail? By becoming more mindful of the B, the thoughts and beliefs in the space between A and C, we can find much more freedom to consciously choose our actions.

I was once teaching an anger management group with my supervisor when I was a psychology trainee at a VA hospital. One of the vets said, "What about after I've been drinking? How do I control my anger then?" As I was hooked into the question, and began thinking of possible suggestions, my supervisor said, "Oh, well, if you've been drinking, all these principles go out the window. If you know you have a problem with anger and alcohol, you need to stay away from situations like being in bars."

Alcohol reduces your inhibitions, making it even harder to control your emotions. It is usually better to prevent a bad situation rather than dealing with its aftermath. It reminds me of the silly questions I would be asked when I was a martial arts instructor. "What if you're tied up, hanging upside down, and someone is pointing a gun at your head, and pulls the trigger?" Although there may be something you can do, the most important question is, "What have you done that caused someone to hate you so much that they would do that to you?" In fact, the highest ideal of the warrior is to be invisible – to not be noticed, to not make a target of yourself.

Sometimes, when underlying issues such as stress and addiction are addressed first, anger becomes much less of a problem.

Addictions

We all have addictions, whether it's our morning coffee to lift our spirits, our favorite television show, or our bedtime routine. We are all vulnerable to becoming attached to certain habits, feeling unsettled when we are blocked from them. Most addictions start off as a conscious choice, seeking pleasure and excitement, or as a means for self-medicating something like chronic pain. Our habits are certainly not always bad things, but over time, if we don't pay attention, we can end up becoming trapped by them.

We may not even become aware of some addictions until we need to quit them for some reason. When we practice mindfulness, we become more aware of our patterns, and ask "How's this working for me?" By definition, an addiction is the inability to cut back on a habit despite negative consequences. With something like heroin, the devastating legal, social, and health consequences are obvious. Some research suggests that a morning cup of coffee has some health benefits, but if you develop a serious health problem, your physician may ask you to quit drinking caffeine.

One of the reasons it is easy to fall into addiction is that in the short term, certain behaviors or substances actually do have an almost magical ability to make us feel better right away. This is one of the reasons the "just say no" campaign, while well intentioned, backfired. Youth who tried drugs discovered that they made you feel really good. "Why didn't they tell us how great they make me feel? Maybe they are also lying about how bad they are!"

The negative consequences of some of our addictions, like watching our favorite television show, may be fairly harmless. Other addictions can become debilitating, but creep up so slowly that they are overshadowed by the immediate pleasure of engaging in it. I was once doing chemical dependency counseling in two settings at the same time, working with teenagers at one site and older adults at the other. Most of the young people still had their minds intact. Many of the older people had terrible health problems and serious brain damage. I was once asked by a local sheriff to come to the jail and do IQ testing on a woman in her 50s who had been drinking 1–2 cases (24–48 cans) of beer every day for 20 years. She had done irreparable damage to her brain, and was having a hard time functioning even in the structured setting of the jail.

Everyone knows illicit drugs are bad for you. Everyone knows that cigarettes will give you cancer. Everyone knows that alcohol impairs your judgment and damages your liver. The old approach to drug treatment was to beat people over the head with this until they quit. The problem with doing it this way is that it makes them feel bad, and so they need more of the substance to escape the bad feelings.

If you haven't struggled with addiction, it's hard to understand why people don't quit. After all, for something like smoking, there is a 100 percent guaranteed way to quit. You know that rolled up paper with tobacco in it, that you light on one end? Don't touch it to your lips!

People know how to quit. As Mark Twain said, "It's easy to quit smoking. I've done it hundreds of times." Why can't they stop for good? What interferes? It comes down to motivation. We use substances to try to change the way we are feeling. We may want to avoid unpleasant thoughts (such as "Everyone already hates me anyway"), feelings (such as loneliness), or body sensations (such as pain or withdrawal symptoms). We may even seek distractions to avoid our responsibilities, and to escape the big questions about meaning in our lives.

You won't quit doing something if you see it as having more benefits than costs. You have to be able to acknowledge the benefits. I am not a smoker, but I am told it has a lot of benefits. If you are feeling stressed or tired, having a cigarette allows nicotine to enter into your bloodstream quickly through the lungs. Smokers also have sort of a "secret club" where they can congregate outside and talk about everyone else as they share their guilty pleasure. For most smokers, the thought of lung cancer is far-off, with only a small chance of it happening on any given day, but the hit from a cigarette gives immediate pleasure. (And of course you always hear stories about the uncle who smoked five packs a day and lived to be 120, rather than the cousin who died at 27 from cancer.)

Clients have told me that it is harder to quit smoking than it is to quit crack cocaine. Cigarettes are freely available everywhere, family members may continue to smoke around them, and glamorous actors are often smoking in film and television.

So, the real issue is learning how to manage our own feelings, to tolerate the strong cravings, to allow the loneliness, the sadness, or the despair to fill you up and pass through you. If you rely too much on unhealthy habits to avoid unpleasant feelings, mindfulness can become a way of learning to relate to the feelings differently, allowing them to rise and fall on their own.

Urge surfing

Mindfulness-based relapse prevention (MBRP),[2] developed by Alan Marlatt, Sarah Bowen, and their colleagues, teaches a technique called "urge surfing," which involves staying with the strong urges to use, and "riding them," waiting for the cravings to build, crest, and subside. It is very similar to how mindfulness can be used for anxiety. Typically, when a strong urge develops, it is so unpleasant that we want it to go away immediately. When we decide not to engage in the addiction, the urges get even stronger. If we give in, we remain stuck in the cycle. But if we ride out the cravings, explore the sensations in our bodies, notice the emotions and thoughts coming and going, and stay present, we will notice that they rise and fall on their own. It is not easy, and it will feel like it takes forever, but they will pass. The more you practice, the less strong the urges become, and the more quickly they pass.

As with anxiety or chronic pain, you may sometimes choose to distract yourself to get through a particularly tough time, but over the long term, it creates problems. We can get very clever with how we avoid. I was once working with a young man named Kurt who was struggling from strong withdrawal symptoms right in front of me. He kept pacing around the room, looking for something to do, something to distract him. He was willing to do an experiment with me. I explained how all those things were ways of avoiding, and that he needed to experience that the feelings will pass more quickly if he stayed with them. Kurt sat down beside me and closed his eyes, describing what he felt in his body. Several times, he realized he was confusing a thought with a feeling. His mind created images of the traumatic situation that drove him to start using heroin. Noting to him that processing that trauma would be important for his overall recovery, I told him that in this moment, even that image was his mind's attempt to avoid feeling his

Hawaii waves. © Olivia Ossege.

body. To his amazement, the feelings began to fall on their own, even without him doing anything. This was a major turning point for Kurt.

Even substances like caffeine can be tough to quit, because they not only immediately change your brain chemistry when you consume them, they eventually change your brain structure. Basically, your brain says, "There's so much of this chemical in my brain, I don't need as many receptors anymore," and the receptors die off. Or, your brain makes less of its own version of the chemical. This is why we often develop tolerance for a substance, meaning that it loses its effect over time, or that we need more and more of it to get the effect we used to get. Even if you choose to quit drinking caffeine, it takes time for your brain to change its circuitry to reestablish a new chemical balance. This is why professional support is important for serious addictions. If you drink alcohol every day, you can actually die from withdrawal if it is not done in a carefully controlled way.

Falling off the wagon

Unfortunately, up to 90 percent of people trying to quit a substance will relapse. Feelings of guilt and failure can lead to what MBRP calls the "abstinence violation effect," colloquially known as the "f**k it" effect. If you have been struggling to stop an addiction, and then end up using again, the resulting guilty feelings make you want to use even more. Your brain will question why you even tried to quit, enduring such suffering, when using the substance feels so good. Thoughts arise like, "Ah, forget it. What's the point? I might as well go back to using it."

Mindfulness helps in paying attention to this cycle, separating out thoughts, emotions, and body sensations, and taking each moment as a new beginning. One way to help continue progress is to carefully go back over what led to the slip, and add it to the relapse prevention plan.

Tracing back the chain of events

I once worked with a man named Frank who was trying to quit using crack, and he had an experience that is not uncommon. After helping his friend move, he received a $10 bill. He slipped it into his pocket and decided to take a walk. It was such a nice day, he thought he would just keep walking. He saw some familiar streets, and decided to go down them. Then he thought he'd walk by the houses of some old friends, just to see how they looked. He saw a house he used crack in before, and thought about just walking up to say hello to his old friends. They invited him in, and he decided he would just sit and visit for a few minutes. Then they said they were going to smoke, and asked if he wanted any. He said no at first, but eventually went ahead and smoked crack with them.

Frank fell victim to unconscious patterns of responding. When did he actually slip? Was it when the pipe touched his lips? Tracing back the chain of events can help to develop awareness of all the choice points he did not notice at the time.

In this case, the entire process began when he had $10 in cash in his hand. By noticing the thought that it was enough for a hit, he could have chosen to put the money in the bank or have a friend hold it for him. As he was walking down the street, he could have noticed the lingering thoughts and emotions about using arising and turned back around. Feeling the cravings grip his body upon seeing his old friend's house, he could have called his recovery sponsor.

Of course, all of those choices are very hard to make under those circumstances, which is why it seems so hard to break out of the cycle. In the short term, using a drug will take away the bad feelings quickly. But if you always make your choices based on how you are feeling in the moment, your life will be very unpredictable, and you will not move consistently toward what you value.

If you wait till the choice is easy, you may be waiting a lifetime. Though difficult, a choice can be made despite strong negative feelings. You can feel sad and still choose to exercise. You can feel cravings and still choose to go spend time with supportive friends. You could still choose to "freak out" when you are craving, or even to use, but you can no longer fool yourself into thinking that is the only option available to you.

Mindless Eating

For some of us, the pleasure we get from eating, and the cycle we develop from avoiding other feelings by distracting ourselves with food, can become a type of addiction. What makes it different from other types of addiction is the fact that we all need to eat every day. We can't become completely abstinent when it comes to food. Therefore, psychologists like Susan Albers[3] and Jean Kristeller[4] talk about the need to develop a healthier relationship to eating.

Society gives us double messages. Advertisements show very slim, attractive models, making us feel bad if we don't look like that. Yet the next ad we see may be for juicy, scrumptious food that actually contains double the amount of calories we need for an entire day. We fear people might make fun of us or find us unattractive if we gain weight, but we have scripts in our heads from childhood, like "Finish your plate, there are children starving in the world!" No wonder we develop a love/hate relationship with eating.

Eating delicious food is, and should be, a truly delightful experience. Because it can immediately make us feel good, we have to be careful not to rely on it as a way to modulate our emotions, because food is not a very good long-term solution. If we feel sad, lonely, or upset, food can be a nice lift. If we eat too much, then we feel guilty, and fall victim to the abstinence violation effect. After eating four donuts, what will one more hurt? We'll start our diet tomorrow.

Most diets fail. If you feel like you are depriving yourself, you will become anxious, and you may end up thinking about food or eating more to try to feel better. You then feel guilty, and decide to deprive yourself more, keeping the cycle going.

It is easy to fall into automatic patterns of eating. Often we're watching TV or talking to someone, mindlessly shoveling down our food, and then we look down and all the food is gone. We think we're still hungry because we didn't taste it, and since it takes about 15 minutes before our brain signals that we are full, we go get some more.

Mindful eating is something we practice on the first day of every eight-week mindfulness group. We take about 10 minutes to eat one raisin. We feel its texture, notice how the light shines on the different surfaces, smell its fragrance, and chew it very slowly. People are often amazed by how much taste there is in just one little raisin, and how rich the experience of eating it can be.

In her mindfulness-based eating awareness training (MB-EAT) workshops,[5] Jean Kristeller highlights the important concept of sensory specific satiety. Eighty percent of the pleasure of the food we eat comes from the first three bites. People who have episodes of eating uncontrollably, known as binging, are only remembering the taste, and chasing after the flavor. If we can remember to slow down and really enjoy our food, we can appreciate the quality rather than feel a compulsive need for quantity.

One of Dr. Kristeller's MB-EAT participants shared an experience that is not uncommon. She said that if someone brought donuts to the office, she would take one, and then go get a second, which was socially acceptable. Then, when no one was looking, she would sneak a third, then sneak a fourth. When taking the course, she decided to sit down and really enjoy and taste the donut. She said the first bite was delicious. Then the second bite was okay. Paying close attention to the third bite, she found that it now had a greasy quality to it, and the richness of the sugar made her stomach a little queasy. She said that for the first time in her life, she didn't feel like finishing the donut, and threw it away.

Because many of us use food for comfort, or because we just get into automatic eating patterns, we tend to lose touch with our own body cues of hunger and fullness. Some cultures make fun of those of us who need a clock to tell us when to eat, rather than paying attention to our body signals. In the MB-EAT group, participants learn to pause and ask themselves two questions: On a scale of 1–10, how full am I right now? On a scale of 1–10, how hungry am I right now?

We often confuse hunger and fullness with each other, or with any of a multitude of other feelings. The next time you sit down to eat, check in with how you are feeling. If you decide you truly are hungry, consciously choose what you want to eat, and savor each bite.

Memory Disorders

Memory problems can happen for everyone to different degrees, and can be caused by a number of different factors. We are all born with different memory capacities, and we can grow our capacity through practice, or our memory may diminish through lack of exercise or by disease processes.

Memory is a complicated system, which includes multiple stages like encoding, storage, and retrieval. When you see something, there is a very quick sensory memory, which then enters short-term memory, where you might manipulate the information in your mind, and then the information is encoded into long-term memory. Like a fancy piece of equipment, the more complicated something is, the easier it is for one thing to disrupt the system.

Memory problems can arise from a number of causes, like brain injury, depression, malnutrition, and sleep deprivation. Challenges with memory create frustration and distress, resulting in more difficulties with memory. Hence, our attitude can play a big role in how memory loss affects us.

I once did some neuropsychological testing on a middle-aged woman who had suffered from a stroke, likely due to birth control pills. She had large gaps in her life memories. While most people would be devastated to lose so much information about their identities, this woman said she felt free. "I am no longer defined by my past. From this point forward, I can be whoever I want to be!"

When it comes to memory problems, most of us think of neurocognitive disorders, commonly known as dementia, which include diseases like Alzheimer's. The older we get, the higher our chances are of getting dementia. At age 80, we are 20 times more likely to get it than we are at age 60.

Conditions like Alzheimer's disease can produce devastating problems. It begins with increasing word-finding and memory problems, and progresses from there. Relatives often don't realize how bad their loved one is getting, because the social part of the brain may still be intact. I had to be very patient when conducting dementia testing. "How old are you?" I might ask. "You know that's not polite to ask a lady. Anyway, I quit counting when I turned 30," they might reply, when in fact, they have no idea how old they are.

People also don't realize how bad it's getting because long-term memory stays intact. My mother, who is living with Alzheimer's, will ask me the same question five times in a short phone call. But she will also describe in exquisite detail the American soldier who stopped his tank to save her dog when she was a little girl in Germany. Our earliest memories are the ones we have laid down and retrieved the most over our lifetimes, and end up getting stored all over the brain, so they last the longest.

I have given lectures about mindfulness for individuals with Alzheimer's and their families, and they always seem to appreciate the concepts. Someone with Alzheimer's becomes more and more in the moment, and knowing this can be very helpful in understanding their behavior. We have all experienced walking into a room, and forgetting why we went in there, and we may just go ahead and do something with whatever is there in front of us. People with serious dementia start walking through the house, forget where they are going, and see a doorknob in front of them. Doorknobs are for opening doors, so they open the door and walk outside. This is why patients often wander off and get lost. It turns out that simply hanging long curtains on doors, hiding the doorknobs, significantly cuts down on the number of "escapes."

We all experience this "too in the moment" feeling in our dreams. I still remember an entry in a dream journal I was keeping when I was a teenager: "Was walking down the street. Started playing a harmonica, but it was really a tenderloin sandwich." When you are in dreams, they seem so real at the time. Walking down the street, pretty normal. Playing a harmonica, not very common, but not bizarre. Playing a tenderloin sandwich? My brain had me holding something in my mouth, and holding a tenderloin sandwich there to eat is pretty normal. It is only after we wake up, and regain our ability to string our moments together, that we realize how bizarre our behavior was.

Hence, it is best to "roll with it" when interacting with someone with Alzheimer's disease. If they ask you the same question five times, just answer it five times. My first encounter with this occurred while I was a security guard in a hospital emergency room. An elderly woman kept asking me the same question, obviously confused and agitated. Like Bill Murray's character in the movie Ground Hog Day, the same series of questions kept coming at me until I found the responses that she found satisfying.

My father used to get quite frustrated with my mother, but found a way to cope by being playful. While my father was driving home after taking us to a restaurant, my mother asked, for the fourth time, "Where's my purse?" My father calmly said, "It's on the roof." She laughed and playfully patted his arm, and then he told her it was in the back seat. We then put her purse in her lap, so she could see it in each moment.

Sadly, until we make a major medical breakthrough, dementia is progressive and irreversible. Medications can help you make the most of what you have left, but it can't stop the disease. As it progresses, only older memories will be left to connect to the current moment. My mother will likely begin to think I'm her brother or her father, and will probably go back to speaking primarily in German. Eventually, the rest of the brain deteriorates, resulting in loss of body function, and finally death.

If you are a caregiver for someone with Alzheimer's or some other neurocognitive disorder, don't forget to take care of yourself, too. Practicing mindfulness will help you with your own stress, and foster more in-the-moment patience.

As we ourselves grow older, practicing mindfulness is also likely to strengthen brain circuits to stave off neurocognitive problems, and will deeply ingrain habits of being in the moment and being kind to ourselves and others. Coming full circle, being born fully in each moment, and leaving this world fully in each moment.

In the next chapter, we will look at ways to enrich more of those moments in between birth and death.

6

Enriching Your Life

Imagine how rich our lives and relationships could be if we were present in them more often.

Several years ago, I had an amazing experience, one of the times in my life that I have been most present. I drove with my friend David Sink to the remote mountains of North Carolina to be with teachers and old friends for a very special martial and meditative training seminar. When we arrived, the mountains were enshrouded in the clouds, with a drizzling mist floating all around.

I spent most of the first evening just greeting people and setting up my tent. Warnings were given not to leave food out, since the 200 acres of woods that Dr. Richard Stack shared with us joined a national forest, and cougar and bear sightings were not unusual. It rained hard all night long, and much of the next day. The ground was hard, my tent leaked, my clothes were soaked and muddy most of the time, but the little boy in me had a blast.

My teacher, Stephen K. Hayes, is very down to earth, but also challenges me to be open to bigger things. He is quite an inspiration in the way he relates to others, shares his knowledge, cares about his friends and family, and brings to life the goals he sets his intentions on. He often appears wizard-like in his ability to do things, but openly shares his practical strategies. He has worked very hard over the years to become so natural and effortless in what he does.

Mindfulness: Living through Challenges and Enriching Your Life in This Moment, First Edition. Richard W. Sears.
© 2014 John Wiley & Sons, Ltd. Published 2014 by John Wiley & Sons, Ltd.

We spent several days training in a gorgeous natural setting, sharing techniques, insights, and experiences. One of the reasons I was asked to come to this particular event (aside from my charming personality) is that there are very few of us at 5th degree black belt and above, and several people were testing for high belt ranks.

A large crowd of family and well-wishers gathered one evening to show support for those who were testing for black belts. Afterwards, as the families celebrated with a feast, those few of us who were 5th degree and above climbed up to a beautiful wooden structure for a very special ceremony, a test which represents a major turning point in one's training.

The 5th degree black belt test symbolizes moving beyond conventional strategy and thinking. Mr. Hayes asks the testing candidate to stand in front of him with his or her back to him, then raises a padded sword up over his head (in Japan they use bamboo swords, but they can cause too much injury if the test is failed). He holds it there for a moment, or for a few minutes, then swings down hard and fast onto the candidate's head. If the person moves with the right timing and doesn't get hit, the test is passed. If a loud smacking sound is heard (and a sharp stinging pain is felt), the candidate fails.

It seems a strange thing to ask someone to dodge a sword coming at them full speed from behind. How could you possibly train for that? I'm a pretty scientifically minded person, and had experimented with this in my training for years. I would try to figure out how it was done. Maybe the sound of the sword moving through the air is heard? Maybe there is a change in air pressure? Maybe the body heat is felt? Sometimes I could smell deodorant as the attacker's arms were raised. Perhaps the nonverbal parts of the brain integrated a wide variety of data to signal the body to move at the right time. However it was done, it became undeniably obvious to me that verbal thinking slowed me down, as the sword came down so fast, by the time it was consciously heard, it was too late to move. One of the highest goals of this training is to learn how to get out of your own way.

Tonight's testing candidate was my friend Hardee Merritt, an amazing martial artist and human being, chief instructor at the school that organized these yearly mountain events. Mr. Hayes asked my friend Leo Pimentel, who got his 5th degree only recently, to go first, to show Hardee what to expect. Leo stood in front of Mr. Hayes with his back to him. Mr. Hayes raised the practice sword and waited. Leo seemed a bit on edge, and flinched several times as he stood there. Mr. Hayes encouraged him to take a deep breath and reset himself. He then moved with perfect timing as the sword slammed down.

Then Mr. Hayes looked at me and asked if anyone else wanted to try. He had given me my fifth degree during a very special adventure in Nepal, and I was never formally given this test, so I volunteered. In the past when I attempted to practice this test, my mind was usually racing. On this night, standing with my back to him, my mind became crystal clear in the silence of that mountain *dojo*. I let go of any concern about getting hit or what to expect. Without getting mixed up in my own thoughts, my body moved just when it needed to move, and I heard the sword whizz past my left ear.

My several other friends, who had already gone through this test years ago, could not pass up another chance for this experience. I watched all of them also move with perfect timing. The room was full of warmth, support, friendship, and mystery as Hardee moved into position for his official test. He passed beautifully on the first try.

After the testing was finished, we shared smiles and hugs before saying good night. I felt such a deep connection with my friends and with this ancient tradition. When I walked outside, the rainy weather had broken, the sky was clear, and I could see the other mountains surrounded by a glowing haze in the far-off distance. In the twilight, there was no wind, and the silence was deepened by the distant cries of unseen birds.

That extraordinary feeling of being fully alive and present lingered as I walked back down the mountain to my tent. There was enough space in those present moments for a rich variety of feelings. I felt some sadness that I wasn't able to be with some of my closest friends and family, a deep humility in knowing that I had only scratched the surface of human knowing and experience, and a profound appreciation for all the life experiences, full of laughter and tears, that came together to make me who I am.

Most of us have had the good fortune to experience being fully present in a lovely setting with special friends at least a few times in our lives. The real magic is in bringing this presence and wonder more often into our daily moments.

If you have a lot of serious problems going on right now, you might have trouble even imagining enjoying a rich life, so we first addressed how mindfulness can help with challenges. However, if you wait until your problems completely go away before living your life, you could be waiting forever. It is all too common to fall into a survival mode, always putting out fires, doing what you need to do to get through each day. It is a major shift to go from surviving to living and thriving.

Enriching your life doesn't mean it will become always happy and joyful. Life will always have some suffering in it, and learning to embrace and experience it all is what makes it rich. Jon Kabat-Zinn calls this "full catastrophe living."[1] When you chase after happiness, you end up pushing it away, because happiness can only be found in this moment. Though this is the last thing you want to hear when you are suffering, our crises are what produce the seeds necessary for profound wisdom to develop and provide the space for happiness to blossom.

On the other hand, we may sometimes feel that we don't deserve positive emotions like happiness. Perhaps guilt creeps in if we are too happy, because we know there is so much suffering in the world. But happiness is not a limited commodity. If you have it, it doesn't deprive others. If others have it, it has not been taken from you. The more we all have, the more it spreads.

This chapter will discuss how mindfulness can be used to foster more presence in our lives, work, and relationships, to find our strengths, and to move our lives in valued directions. Let's begin with taking a look at what we mean by "well-being."

Five Ways to Well-Being

Instead of only focusing on problems, scientists in disciplines such as positive psychology are increasingly looking at what contributes to well-being. The UK Government's Foresight Project on Mental Capital and Wellbeing[2] scoured the research and summarized their findings into five major ways to foster well-being: connect, be active, take notice, keep learning, and give. These will not likely surprise you, as they fit with common sense, but it is all too easy to postpone them, or to think we can only make room for them after we work harder.

We will explore these five areas in turn, and see how mindfulness can serve as a helpful tool for each one.

Connect

> With the people around you. With family, friends, colleagues and neighbors. At home, work, school or in your local community. Think of these as the cornerstones of your life and invest time in developing them. Building these connections will support and enrich you every day.[3]

Feeling a sense of connection is very important for our well-being. We often get so caught up in our personal stories and challenges that we forget our interdependence with the world and all the life around us. When we see a photograph of the planet we all live on, get out into nature, or otherwise get in touch with a larger sense of meaning, we gain a broader perspective.

Since human connections are so important, and so complicated and challenging, this section will focus on enriching our relationships. While we will never fully understand the mystery of relationships, even after a lifetime of practice, mindfulness can help us draw on our own wisdom to help navigate them.

Relationships

As human beings, we all desire to be close to other human beings at some level. Yet despite all our desires and efforts, there is always a gap. Though we are drawn to get close, we can never fully merge with another person. We can never fully understand or be fully understood, so there is always a little bit of tension, which in fact is what gives our relationships life.

In a sense, being in relationship is one of the most challenging mindfulness practices. Our relationships tend to bring out the best and the worst in us. We can fool ourselves into thinking we've got it all together, or we can have ourselves believing that we are worthless human beings, but friends and partners can give us perspective and acceptance, if we are willing to be open and vulnerable with them.

Just as we learn to notice and stay present with difficult emotions that arise within ourselves, we can learn to do so in our relationships. Rather than avoiding difficult emotions, we can practice noticing them directly. Rather than distracting ourselves, we can plunge into the heart of things. Instead of trying to fix our friends and partners, we can just be with them and listen. The self-compassion we learn for ourselves, by accepting our current moments as they are, allows us to foster compassion and acceptance for others. When we realize we can't control others, we drop the struggle of trying to do so, and a real connection becomes possible. We certainly don't have to be okay with all of their beliefs and behaviors, and setting boundaries is very important, but accepting that in this moment they are who they are prevents us from getting overly worked up or automatically shutting them out when things don't go perfectly.

Strong feelings are bound to come up eventually in every relationship, even with business acquaintances. Just as it is a major shift to realize that uncomfortable feelings are telling you something important about yourself, signaling you to pause and carefully choose your next action, strong feelings in a relationship are also important messages that something needs attention. Perhaps there is a misunderstanding, perhaps you are having an old, automatic reaction, perhaps this is not about you, or maybe you need to make your boundaries stronger or looser.

Some people feel that the emotional challenges of being in a relationship are not worth the risk and the effort. Some may grow up with no role models for what a healthy relationship can be like, and find them too confusing to figure out. Some may prefer the dull, familiar pangs of loneliness to the anxiety of becoming vulnerable.

Just as our thoughts tell us things about the world, whether or not they're true, and strongly influence the way we feel, our thoughts can strongly affect our relationships. All of our past hurts, fears, and regrets can be projected onto the person we are with in the moment. We can also project all of our hopes, expectations, and high standards. If we don't recognize our own patterns, we may end up repeating them in every new relationship, and never have the opportunity to experience real closeness.

Take the example of Eve and Wesley, who fell into a very common pattern. As they learned of each other's interests, they began spending a lot of time together, regularly eating lunch and chatting for hours at a time. As they naturally shared more and more, Eve became uneasy with the vulnerability that comes with emotional intimacy. Growing up, she had learned that she could only rely on herself, because vulnerability was dangerous. She became busier, and cut back the time she spent and the things she shared with Wesley. The less she shared, and the less time she spent with him, the less she found in common with him, and began to push him away. Wesley was stunned and hurt, but of course, played into the pattern as well. The friendship had become so important to him that he went out of his way to do things for her. The more Eve backed away, the more he chased, until he had given up a lot of his time and himself to be what he thought she needed, making him less interesting to be around. His own vulnerabilities and fears of not deserving such a friend also came into play, and Wesley was devastated when he had to rediscover who he was without Eve's friendship.

Newness can be exciting in a relationship, especially an intimate one, but chemicals wear off naturally as the brain and body restore themselves to equilibrium. Relationships then become more of a commitment, and must be actively cultivated, nurtured, and sustained. We get confused that something that starts out so easy seems to become a chore, and begin to wonder if we are with the right person.

Hence, there are those who are never in an intimate relationship very long, who jump into yet another relationship for the excitement of the new whenever things get challenging. The price paid is a lack of depth, a lack of intimacy, and a lack of growth.

I was once asked to consult for a business being developed by a group of "pick-up artists." At first, I was very concerned about an organization that might be teaching ways to manipulate people. However, it turned out to be a self-development program. If you want to attract friends and lovers, you need to be interesting and confident enough to take the risk of getting to know someone. How do you do that? By working on yourself – learning about your own patterns, realizing that chasing after relationships too strongly pushes them away, deepening and pursuing the things you find interesting, and clarifying what gives your own life value and meaning.

Relationships take effort and practice. As with mindfulness training, you are never "done." Mindful awareness can enhance all of our relationships. When we open up our hearts, we are vulnerable, which is scary. We risk the possibility of rejection, pain, and sadness. But when we learn to stay present, we no longer fear our own feelings, and can move into and embrace the wide spectrum of emotions that make our relationships truly rich.

Automatic pilot can undermine good relationships. If we take for granted the good work of our colleagues, they won't feel very appreciated. If we come home and greet our partner as casually as we might say hello to a stranger walking by on the street, there won't be as much warmth and intimacy in our home.

My 4-year-old, who still has her natural mindfulness skills, gets so excited to see me. She will come running, jump into my arms, grab my face and say, "Oh Daddy, I missed you so much!" even if I was only gone a couple of hours. Just imagine if we greeted our friends and partners that way. Most would think we were very strange if we grabbed their faces every time, but they would certainly feel more appreciated if we greeted them with a big smile and held eye contact for a few moments. Being mindful to do such simple things can be a wonderful way to deepen our connections.

One of the most intimate things you can do is look into the eyes of someone you love. Of course, different cultures have different norms for doing this, but many of us find it difficult. We may feel exposed or embarrassed. We may feel an urge to escape, or perhaps to draw the person closer. But resting in this gaze, staying present with whatever feelings may rise or fall, can be a wonderful way to connect with someone you really care about.

Conflict

Conflict is inevitable in every relationship. No two human beings could possibly agree on every single thing that ever comes up. The important question is how do you handle conflict when it does arise? Of course, no one likes conflict. But if you always avoid it, you will drift apart emotionally, and when conflict does erupt, it will be intensely expressed from building up, reinforcing the idea that it should be avoided.

The things two people argue about usually have little to do with what is actually happening in that moment. Emotions are magnified by past stuff, either from history with that person, from other relationships, or from old hurts. Again, mindfulness can help us take more notice of our patterns, before, during, and after arguments, so we can ask ourselves if what we are doing is working for us.

Perhaps you feel a strong need to connect, and are strongly drawn to finding someone to love and be loved by. Yet as you draw closer, it gets scary, as maybe in your history those who were supposed to love you the most were the ones who hurt you the most. Maybe you are accustomed to difficult relationships, in the sense that they feel "normal." If things are going well, it may feel weird, or like something bad is going to happen, so you inadvertently stir things up in a self-fulfilling prophecy.

On the other hand, perhaps you really value the relationship, and are afraid of upsetting or losing the other person, so you avoid conflict at all costs. Such a relationship loses its life, becomes boring, and you end up lonely.

Given that "opposites attract," you and your partner may be very different, and have completely different styles for handling conflict. Janis Abrams-Spring[4] calls this the "flip-flop factor." When conducting couples counseling, I might ask, "Back when you were dating, what was it about your partner that attracted you?"

"Oh, she was such an outgoing, fun person to be around, loved to do things, go places, and meet new people. I was pretty shy, so it was very exciting and fun."

"So what's the problem now?"

"Well, she always wants to get out and do things, meet with people, and go places, and I just want to stay home and rest." The very things that attract us to someone can become the very things that irritate us. Paying attention to this, noticing our irritation and sitting with it before reacting, gives us perspective, allowing us to regain some appreciation for our partner. We may even laugh at ourselves.

If you cannot tolerate disagreements, and avoid them or try to end them through "blitzkrieg" tactics (as one of my ex-military clients would do), the emotional distance between you and your friend or partner will only grow. When we are getting increasingly angry, it is likely because we are not feeling heard, so we raise our voices, which makes our partners even more defensive. Being present during our conflicts can help us choose more wisely how best to communicate. If I take my partner's feelings of being upset as an indicator that something is amiss, I can pause and be more flexible in how I respond. Perhaps I was not communicating in a way that was clear, or I was not aware of the impact of my behavior, or my mood is making me irritable, or my partner is feeling stressed.

Of course, this is very hard to do when you are feeling attacked or hurt by your partner. It can be tempting to attack back. Embarrassingly, I have heard myself angrily say that I did not like the angry tone in the way I was being spoken to, and the irony was lost on me at the time. Even if we think we are "right" about something, how we react can create significant problems.

I was once caught in a pattern like this. As an introvert, when I get tired, I get quiet. My partner would ask me, "Is everything okay?"

"Yeah," I would reply. "I'm just tired."

After a little more time passed, she would again ask, "Are you sure everything's okay? You're not mad about something?"

"Nope, everything's fine." After being asked this five or six times more, I would finally say, "I'M NOT MAD!"

It turned out that growing up, her parent would give her the "silent treatment," literally not speaking to her for days. Hence, my silence felt like anger or disappointment for something she had done. Noticing this cycle helped us both to let it go.

A misunderstood silence can produce a deep rift. A single comment can produce a deep sting. But a single hug, smile, or loving gaze can also produce a deep feeling of connection. A kind comment can go a long way. "Well, I disagree, but I love you, so let's talk more about how we can figure this out."

Humor can also be a good way to reconnect, if appropriate and well timed. The danger, of course, is in using humor as a subtle form of attack, or overusing it as a defense mechanism in a way that makes your partner feel that you don't take them seriously.

Al Franken, in a random passage in one of his books,[5] suggests always having a safe word, like "palamino," when things get out of hand. If well used, it can be like taking a mindful breath to re-center ourselves, or it could at least break things up with a smile.

It would be wonderful if we could always disagree in a civilized manner, but this is difficult to do when we are angry. We will all sometimes say things that are hurtful or that we don't really mean. In his book *After the Fight: Using Your Disagreements to Build a Better Relationship*,[6] Daniel Wile makes the point that what happens after an argument is over is crucial for the health of a relationship. What do you do to repair the bad feelings? Do you pretend it never happened? Do you over-analyze every little thing? Do you and your partner have completely different styles of doing that, perhaps recapitulating what your own families did? As challenging as it may be to process what happened after the fight is over, it can provide an opportunity to learn about yourself and your partner, and promote deeper intimacy.

Interestingly, I often have participants in my mindfulness groups tell me that their partners are becoming nicer and their relationships are improving, even though the partner is not practicing mindfulness. Since it takes two to argue, I'm sure that the person in the mindfulness group is setting up a new dynamic in the relationship. If I'm emptying the dishwasher, and my partner walks by and says, "I wish you'd have done that earlier!," my old pattern might have been to get angry and say, "Fine – I was just trying to help!" and stomp off, leaving bitter feelings the rest of the evening, that build up over time.

By practicing mindfulness, we learn to pause and respond more consciously. Perhaps I briefly notice an automatic thought or feeling arise, then say, "Sorry, I meant to do it earlier but I got distracted." My partner then says, "I just need to use the counter for a minute, can you do that later?"

I say, "Sure." Fight averted, we feel closer, we spend more time together, and our relationship improves. My partner seems "nicer" because I am less defensive, and so we have fewer arguments.

Because words and thoughts "mean" something else, we are in the habit of wondering what everything in our life "means," which takes us away from being with it as it is. If your partner is quiet, the thought may arise, "Silence means they are upset." Maybe, maybe not. Right now, there is just a quiet partner. What will you do in the next moment? Ask how they are doing? Let them know how you are feeling? Let them be quiet? Wait for a few minutes to see how things unfold? You probably have a lot more options than the first impulse that hit you.

It is important to note that none of the above may apply in situations of intimate partner violence, which is a very serious problem. Regardless of the frequency of physical or sexual violence, such unhealthy relationships are about power and control, and they are extremely complicated. They usually start out with lots of attention and affection, and may take years to build up to violence. Episodes of violence are usually followed by a "honeymoon" period of trying to make things better, until things get worse again. This cycle wears down the victim's self-esteem and creates a feeling of learned helplessness. On average, the person who decides to leave such a relationship ends up going back seven or eight times before they stay gone for good. It is very difficult to stop or escape such a cycle without professional help.

Mindful sex

Sexual intimacy is one of the most powerful experiences we can have with another human being. Ideally, a sexual encounter wakes us up to the fullness of our human existence, uniting self and other, fostering the integration of mind, body, and emotion. Partners can share a marvelous experience of openness and love, entering a space where thoughts, and even the sense of time passing, fall away.

Not everyone experiences sex in this way. I was once speaking with a group of women who all agreed that good chocolate is better than sex. My immediate thought was, "You obviously have never found the right partner!"

Now, I have traveled through Europe and indulged in my fair share of fancy chocolates, and the experience of savoring such confections was perhaps better than some of my sexual experiences, but it wasn't until later that I began to understand the point of view of these women. With a piece of chocolate, you can slow down and fully engage your sense of taste and smell, completely losing yourself in the experience. For those moments, distractions fade away, and you can be fully present moment by moment. (In fact, I encourage you to try this yourself the next time you have the opportunity.)

However, in the course of many of our sexual encounters, our minds are full of expectations, judgments, criticisms, and wandering thoughts. Chocolate is always there for you without expectation. It does not judge you, it will give you all the time you need, and it won't mind if you cry after you enjoy it.

Sex can be a deeply spiritual experience. However, depending on how we were raised, it could be seen as a source of guilt, as "dirty," or as something that "good boys and girls" don't do. Sitting with these thoughts and feelings can help you sort them out, notice what might be old programming that you no longer need, and help you decide what you value.

When we connect with a sexual partner, we are vulnerable. We want to be open and get closer, but we fear we may not like what we find, or worse, that the other person will discover our weaknesses, our frailties, and will abandon us, as others have in the past. If we stay present with these thoughts and feelings, we may be able to avoid the self-sabotage that leads to a self-fulfilling prophecy stemming from the fear that we are not worthy of love.

Sexuality provides a wonderful opportunity to practice mindful presence. Long before a sexual encounter, feelings of closeness can be nurtured throughout the day. We can attend to our partner's emotional needs and stress levels, as well as our own, and work to reduce barriers to connecting. Deep, true intimacy comes from seeing the other person as they are, learning to feel what they feel, and being a dear friend.

As with all our behaviors, sex with the same partner can fall into an automatic pilot mode over time. Some of you may have been asked the deflating question, "Are you done yet?" It becomes painfully obvious if you are performing by rote and your mind is elsewhere. When we become fully present in the moment, letting go of judgments and expectations, mindful of our partner, each encounter becomes fresh and new. Chasing after your own orgasm as the primary goal makes sex feel mechanical, and objectifies your partner. Attending to your partner's pleasure makes it a richer experience for both of you.

Remember that desire comes from not having what you want. When you get it, desire diminishes. Hence, keep a little mystery, and enjoy the chase. Then each touch, each encounter can be celebrated and savored. Of course, the price paid is the pain of separation, of longing. But this too, we can learn to savor.

Not to say you shouldn't have a wild quickie every now and then, but you can learn to savor each encounter in all of its fullness. Slow down and experience every sensation. Gaze into your lover's eyes. Hold hands. Gently move fingertips over skin. Caress and massage the muscles. Allow the encounter to unfold naturally. Notice thoughts, judgments, and expectations, and bring your attention back to your partner, moment by moment. Allow yourself to bask in the love.

When relationships end

It can be devastating when important relationships end, or when they significantly change. Whether it's a casual friend or a lover, whether it gradually fades away over time or ends abruptly, or whether it was due to someone moving away or intentionally hurting you, endings bring up a multitude of emotions.

Often, we make it even harder by how we react to the change. Perhaps we didn't have good role models for how to let go of relationships in a healthy way. Perhaps we have been badly hurt in the past, never quite processed it well, and it stirs up deep aches that never fully healed. You may not only be feeling this heartbreak, but the sadness of many past ones as well, making it even more important to make time to feel it, let it flow through you, and actively take care of yourself when you can.

Sometimes we are afraid to love fully, for fear of being hurt. Putting up walls keeps you safe, but lonely. Diving in, being vulnerable, can be scary. Perhaps you fell madly in love with someone, hanging on their every word, heart pounding when you saw their face, mind soaring when they gave you a hug. But later you discovered they did not feel the same way about you. You feel foolish for making them so central in your life when they barely seem to notice you. You can't get them out of your mind even though they don't consider you much at all. As much as your heart soared at first, it crashes in aching despair. You will not likely appreciate it at the time, but what a gift to feel so deeply. You will increasingly find moments you are thankful for the times you had, though you may sob deeply in the moment following.

Acceptance of an unwanted ending can be very difficult. Even when you know intellectually that the relationship is over, the strength of your emotions can spark all kinds of racing thoughts in the hopes of "fixing" things – going over past conversations, wondering about future encounters, and coming up with plans for drastic actions, both kind and hurtful. It can be difficult to remember that all such thoughts are ways of distracting us, of avoiding the awful feelings. Even negative thoughts like "nothing really matters anymore," or "no one can be trusted," as powerful as they seem, are mental events trying to distract you from the pain and anguish you are experiencing.

When the thoughts are very strong, perhaps as you lie awake at 3:00 a.m., it is probably not a good idea to call or send an email at that moment. Sit with what you want to say for several days. Write it down if you wish, but think carefully before you decide whether or not to send it. Read it again a few days later. Take some time to consider why you would send a message now that the relationship is over. What are you hoping to accomplish? Making them feel bad won't help – you can't guilt someone into staying with you, at least not very long.

Honestly acknowledging to yourself how badly you are hurting is an important first step in healing. Give yourself permission to feel what you are feeling. Allow yourself time to grieve, and watch for patterns that might become unhealthy, like withdrawing from all social contact, shutting your heart down, or jumping too quickly into new relationships for the wrong reasons (such as using others to help you feel better).

After the grief settles, a deeper love or sense of gratitude for what you did share can still remain. By feeling the hurt directly, it will eventually flow through you. Though you will not likely ever be happy about the loss, you can make room for the appreciation of what you did have. You will begin to find moments of hope for a new beginning, no longer defined by your old relationships. You will gradually become more free to be who you want to be and do what you want to do. You can work to rebuild your identity without the other person, integrating the best things the relationship brought out for you while letting go of the worst parts.

When a loved one passes away

When we lose someone to death, whether a pet, friend, partner, parent, or unborn child, our pain can be indescribable. Our lives may be turned upside down, and yet we are required by society to put on a happy face for our daily interactions with others.

In times of loss, people usually give us support right away, but only really good friends know that we are still hurting even years later. Our thoughts and emotions can fluctuate wildly after a loss. One moment we may miss them terribly, the next moment we may feel deep appreciation for the times we did share, and the next moment we may feel guilty if we are having fun and aren't thinking about them.

As with other feelings and experiences, practicing mindfulness can help us become more aware of our thoughts, emotions, and body sensations as we grieve. We can give ourselves permission to feel the grief as best we can, meet our daily responsibilities as best we can, and rebuild our lives as best we can, remembering to take care of ourselves throughout the process. We will never forget, but we can learn to treasure our memories even though there may always be moments of deep sorrow.

Mindful parenting

Parenting gives us an unparalleled opportunity to practice mindfulness. Our kids pay close attention to the things we do and say, even when they don't appear to be listening, which forces us to pay attention.

Our biggest tasks as parents are to provide structure, in the form of consistency, support, and boundaries, and to be emotional containers for our kids. Many kids get very confusing messages growing up. "You're not really hurt,

Father and daughter enjoying the beach. © Carrie Mason-Sears.

there's nothing to cry about." "It's not nice to be angry." "It is not okay to giggle in school."

So, if a child is crying, but told they are not really sad (or worse yet, "Stop crying or I'll give you something to cry about!"), they learn that they can't trust their own sense of what they are feeling, and that they should talk themselves out of, deny, or suppress their feelings.

Just as in our own mindfulness practice, we can demonstrate acceptance of all feelings, and the importance of making choices in each moment. If my child is crying, I can label it for her, saying "You look very sad." I can then choose to talk about it with her, give her a hug, or have her continue with a good choice of behaviors. If she is crying because she stubbed her toe, I may be more likely to give a hug, saying, "Aww, I bet that really hurt. It doesn't look too bad, so it will stop hurting soon." If she is crying because she really wants a piece of chocolate, it is probably better to say, "I know you're sad because you want chocolate right now, but we are about to eat supper, so you will have to wait."

When you pay attention, you will more often know the right response for the given situation. If I give children chocolate whenever they cry, they are reinforced, or rewarded, for their crying, and so are more likely to do it again in the future. If I give lots and lots of attention for even minor toe stubs, they will subconsciously play up every minor boo-boo.

Reinforcement is a very powerful concept for parenting. When kids are acting out a lot, what are they getting from that behavior? Sometimes it is simply attention from us. It doesn't seem logical at first that kids would want to make us upset, but what do we usually reinforce? If kids are being good, and playing on their own, we may think to ourselves, "That's great, I'll leave them alone and try to get something else done." When they act out, they get a major fireworks show from us. It would be much better to praise them when they are doing what we want, rather than only relying on punishment when something goes wrong.

Though punishment can get compliance quickly, it is not a very good long-term strategy, because it builds up negative feelings and resentments, and it can teach kids to use force to control others. In a wonderful book called "*Transforming the Difficult Child*," Howard Glasser[7] describes a way of blasting kids with praise and other forms of positive reinforcement to foster good behavior. If we continuously tell our kids things like, "Don't touch that!" "Put that away!" "Sit down!" "Stop talking!," they are always hearing negative things. It is much better to notice and praise the good behaviors so they will keep doing them. "I like how you are playing so nicely by yourself." "Thank you for picking up your trash!"

Though it may require creativity to pull off, this can be effective even with really difficult young kids in a therapy session. As the child is jumping on the furniture, I might say, "I really like how you chose not to hit your brother just now – I'm sure you really wanted to." As he looks at me with a bit of confusion, I may quickly add, "And thank you for looking at me – I like it when you pay attention." Obviously, this approach requires time and patience.

When their kids' behaviors get really bad, sometimes parents or guardians drop off their young kids in my office and want to leave, as if in 1 hour a week I can change the other 167 hours. It is much more effective if caregivers learn to create a healing atmosphere in their own homes, learn to stay present through difficult emotions, and learn to play.

Caregivers of young kids with serious temper tantrums are often very surprised when their first homework assignment is to play with their kids for at least 15 minutes per day. However, it is crucial to break the negative cycle. If your kids are difficult, you don't want to play with them, and they need even more attention. Spending quality time with them builds your relationship, and they will come to really value your attention.

The important thing for this special play time is to allow the child to lead. Don't turn it into a math quiz, or think you need to teach them their colors. Really young kids love it when you comment on what they are doing like a sports announcer, and when you join in with them. "You're making the car go up the hill. Now they stopped at the restaurant. My car is going to come up the hill, too!"

After the relationship is strengthened, caregivers practice making small requests, like "Please hand me a tissue," followed by lavish praise and smiles. It is important to state these in the form of a command. We are so accustomed to polite adult speech, that we sometimes say things like, "Honey, if you don't mind, would you please hand me a tissue when you get a chance?"

If you give a child a choice, you should not be upset if they make a choice other than the one you want.

As we discussed earlier, consistency is important, especially when the extinction burst phenomenon rears its ugly head. If a tantrum arises, stay present, don't get yourself worked up, maintain clear boundaries, and wait for it to pass.

There are now several programs that explicitly use mindfulness with kids, such as Mindfulness-Based Cognitive Therapy for Children,[8] the Hawn Foundation's MindUP program,[9] and Mindfulness-Based Childbirth and Parenting.[10] Just imagine our future if kids are routinely taught to stay present with their own emotions and notice how each moment contains countless options for making good choices.

Whether incorporated into a structured program, or interacting with a child in a casual way, modeling a sense of presence and acceptance is very powerful. I once was seeing a ten-year-old boy for psychotherapy. As we sat down, I realized I had left my phone on, so I asked him to wait a moment so I could turn it off. He looked shocked. "What if someone tries to call you?"

I smiled and said, "You are the most important person to me for the next hour." The priceless look on his face told me that he didn't hear that very often. In fact, he was living with his grandmother, because his mother was too busy for him. The sense of acceptance he experienced in that moment was probably more helpful than anything I could have said to him in the entire therapy session.

Of course, I don't always do so well. There were several occasions when my three year old said, "Daddy, stop looking at your phone, I'm over here!" She has been a great teacher.

Children definitely help with the next area of well-being – they keep us very active.

Be Active

Go for a walk or run. Step outside. Cycle. Play a game. Garden. Dance. Exercising makes you feel good. Most importantly, discover a physical activity you enjoy; one that suits your level of mobility and fitness.[11]

Being active is very important for both physical and mental health. Regular exercise keeps your body and muscles toned and your brain healthy. Ideally, you can find something that you enjoy doing, keeping you motivated to exercise regularly, such as walking with a friend, playing games with your kids, or landscaping your yard. Experimenting with different activities can keep it interesting and gives you something to look forward to.

You may choose to distract yourself with music or television while you are exercising, but mindfulness can be a helpful tool to enrich all of your active moments, and may even prevent injury. Long-distance runners tell me that if

Jumping at White Sands, New Mexico. © Carrie Mason-Sears.

they tune out with headphones, they may not notice their level of hydration, their vital signs, or any developing muscle or joint problems. Staying present becomes a wonderful mindfulness practice, connecting with the rhythm of the breath, feeling the heartbeat, and moving through the world with clarity and purpose. It also helps to ride out the fatigue and the pain. Separating out thoughts and feelings allows more conscious choice about when to push on and when it may be best to stop.

Take Notice

> Be curious. Catch sight of the beautiful. Remark on the unusual. Notice the changing seasons. Savor the moment, whether you are on a train, eating lunch or talking to friends. Be aware of the world around you and what you are feeling. Reflecting on your experiences will help you appreciate what matters to you.[12]

This is the area of well-being most closely related to mindfulness. As we've been discussing throughout this book, and will be talking more about in the next chapter, you can practice noticing more of the wonder in moments all throughout the day, not just during special times. Noticing how often we are in automatic pilot, and choosing to become more present, contributes to our sense of well-being.

We all have times when we naturally break out of automatic pilot and savor our moments. If you have been missing a dear friend, you greatly enjoy when you get to see them again, and aren't usually off thinking about other things in your mind. If you have ever traveled in a third-world country for a while, you develop a new appreciation for all the little things, like flush toilets and clean drinking water. After a while though, we tend to fall back into automatic pilot and take those things for granted again.

Because of our natural tendency to look for what might go wrong, we need to consciously practice noticing more of the other aspects of our lives. Years ago I attended a meditation class with Stephen K. Hayes, in which we were asked to think back over the day and remember some of the pleasant events that had occurred for us. Because I had worked all day, and fought rush hour traffic to just barely arrive on time, I found it quite challenging at first. Slowly, a few pleasant memories came to mind. Gradually, more and more pleasant experiences came up, and when the 20-minute session ended, I had remembered hundreds of positive things. Interestingly, I often didn't even realize the event was pleasant at the time. The cup of coffee I had drank that morning was very enjoyable, but I barely noticed it because I was probably thinking of all the things I had to do that day, as if that was going to help get them done faster.

Just as when you are depressed, your memories of sad events are more easily activated and available, the more you foster gratitude, the more you will be in touch with positive emotions. There has been research showing that if you write down five things you're appreciative of or grateful for, just once a week, your happiness will increase.

Of course, this shouldn't be forced, or used as a way to avoid bad feelings. If your cat dies, you won't feel better if you tell yourself, "Well, at least my dog didn't die." This is why affirmations, which are positive statements that you tell yourself about something you want to be true, sometimes backfire. They can highlight the gap between your present moment and an ideal that you do not have.

By taking notice, we will see that we have much to be grateful for, no matter how bad things get. We also will notice more clearly our challenges and mistakes, so that we will always be learning and growing.

Keep Learning

Try something new. Rediscover an old interest. Sign up for that course. Take on a different responsibility at work. Fix a bike. Learn to play an instrument or how to cook your favorite food. Set a challenge you will enjoy achieving. Learning new things will make you more confident, as well as being fun to do.[13]

A crucial part of mindfulness is bringing a sense of curiosity, wonder, and exploration into your experiences, ingredients that naturally foster learning. Trying new things helps to get us out of the old grooves of automatic pilot reactions, and keeps new brain connections growing. Through this process, creativity and self-awareness blossom, allowing us to develop and utilize our personal strengths throughout our lives.

Creativity

While we discussed the many ways that thinking gets us into trouble, when you develop more skill at working with your thoughts, you can actually learn to think mindfully. In his book *Wise Mind, Open Mind*, Ron Alexander[14] teaches people how to use mindfulness to foster creativity. When habitual, repetitive, meaningless thoughts begin to subside, room grows for amazingly new and creative thoughts.

Peter Matthiessen,[15] a writer and Zen practitioner, found that as he sat in meditation, he often got wonderful new ideas. He once asked his traditional Japanese teacher about this, expecting the teacher to tell him to just let the ideas go and keep staying present. To his surprise, his teacher suggested that he keep a note pad by his meditation cushion so he can write down the idea and return to his meditation. In the clarity of an established meditation practice, you will begin to notice which thoughts are potentially creative and important and which ones are simply a product of aimless mind wandering. By writing down your creative ideas, you won't be as distracted with trying to remember them later.

Of course, you can also set your intention at the beginning of your meditation to mindfully pay attention to creative ideas. Rather than trying to force creativity, you can learn to sit in a more open state of mind, patiently catching sight of new ideas or solutions to problems that burst forth from deeper parts of your mind, as you might watch an occasional fish suddenly leap above the surface of a clear, smooth lake.

Self-awareness

One of the most challenging areas of learning is that of recognizing our own patterns of thinking, reacting, and relating to others. Choosing to become more aware of these patterns takes a great deal of courage.

Self-awareness can be scary. We may be afraid of what we might discover. What if I still have biases? What if I have racist thoughts? What if deep down I really am a bad person? We may even deny what we see at first. "Wow, I didn't realize how much I act like my father!"

Even after years of training and teaching diversity and social justice issues, I am still surprised sometimes by my own lack of self-awareness. My partner and I once went to the movie theatre with a lesbian couple, and after we decided which movie to watch, we talked about where we should sit. Our friends wanted to sit in the back. I animatedly said, "But the whole point of going to the movies is to experience the big screen, and feel like you're there! If you sit in the back, it's no better than watching television!" Our friends reluctantly gave in to my fervor, and we sat near the front. It was only later that I realized how ignorant I had been. In the community where I live, many people still think it is not okay for women to hold hands or put their arms around each other. My friends wanted to sit in the back so they wouldn't have to worry about what other people thought. I embarrassingly apologized later.

These types of slights, known as microaggressions, can be very painful, whether or not the person meant them. Mindfulness helps us recognize these behaviors more consciously. We all know deep down that ignoring things about ourselves, burying our heads in the sand, is only a temporary escape, and doesn't change anything. Wouldn't you rather know if you had some lingering biases, or unhelpful habits, so you can notice when you are susceptible to them, and can respond in a better way to the current situation?

In developing self-awareness, it is important to have a supportive community of trusted friends to give you feedback. How often do people talk about or poke fun of a certain person for their habits or mannerisms, but that person doesn't seem to be aware of them? Self-awareness helps us notice both our challenges and our strengths.

Finding our strengths

Sometimes we become so focused on our weaknesses that we forget what we do well. In a book called *Mindfulness and Character Strengths,* my friend Ryan Niemiec[16] writes about how mindfulness can help us to more consciously notice and utilize our strengths. The VIA Institute on Character engaged a team of scientists to research cultures and literature around the world, culminating in a classification of 24 character strengths, which can be grouped under six virtues.[17] While you can take the detailed survey on their website www.viacharacter.org, take a look at the list below and consider which ones may best describe your personal strengths.

Wisdom and Knowledge

- Creativity
- Curiosity
- Judgment
- Love of Learning
- Perspective

Courage

- Bravery
- Perseverance
- Honesty
- Zest

Humanity

- Love
- Kindness
- Social Intelligence

Justice

- Teamwork
- Fairness
- Leadership

Temperance

- Forgiveness
- Humility
- Prudence
- Self-Regulation

Transcendence

- Appreciation of Beauty and Excellence
- Gratitude
- Hope
- Humor
- Spirituality

Once you are more aware of your specific strengths, and more mindful of your moments, you can incorporate them more consciously into your work, relationships, and self-care strategies.

Knowing both our strengths and weaknesses gives us more conscious choice about how we respond in any given moment. We can learn to recognize situations when our strengths can be weaknesses, or when our weaknesses can be strengths. For example, humor can be a wonderful thing to ease a difficult situation. But when used in the wrong context, or the wrong time, or when used to avoid dealing with something important, compulsively making jokes can get us into trouble.

Give

> Do something nice for a friend, or a stranger. Thank someone. Smile. Volunteer your time. Join a community group. Look out, as well as in. Seeing yourself, and your happiness, linked to the wider community can be incredibly rewarding and will create connections with the people around you.[18]

We have all experienced how good it feels to give. One of the biggest challenges is to let go of the expectation of getting something in return. After all, if you are only giving in order to receive praise, attention, or future favors, that is more of a business exchange, not giving. We all naturally want appreciation, so it is okay to feel disappointed if we don't get it, but be sure to stop and notice those thoughts and feelings before bashing someone for not seeing how wonderful you are.

You don't need to wait until you feel selfless to start giving. Even from a very selfish perspective, you can begin to notice that since we are all so interconnected, everything you do for others is ultimately helping you as well. After all, when you help others, you make them a little happier. When other people are happier, the people they come into contact with will then be a little happier, resulting in a world with a little more happiness in it. Wouldn't we all want to live in a happier world? Likewise, when I see how much I depend on this planet for my very survival, I am more inclined to take good care of my home, keep it clean, and carefully use its resources.

Regardless of your income level, there are many ways to give other than financially. Eye contact and a smile can brighten someone's day. A short note or email thanking someone can give a little happiness. You can even practice giving yourself more often to your present moments.

For many of us, our work is the place we give the most to others.

Mindfulness at work

Most of us will spend more of our time working than anything else besides sleeping. If you are only working to get a paycheck, and waiting for the weekends, your life will pass you by very quickly, and you won't experience much satisfaction and fulfillment in your life.

It is a gift to have a career that you enjoy doing, or would even do if you weren't being paid for it, but unfortunately that seems a rare privilege.

You may have to do the job you currently have for very practical reasons, such as paying the bills or having time to pick up the kids from school. In such a case, you may still find opportunities to notice the many ways you are helping others, to practice being more present with customers, and to foster good working relationships with your coworkers.

On the other hand, we may have more choices for what we would like to do for a living than we have been led to believe, or that we have been telling ourselves. When we are young, and are still forming our identities, our society puts a lot of pressure on us to decide what we want to be when we grow up. The average person today will switch careers three times in the course of their lives, and it is now rare for someone to do the same thing until retirement. I never made much more than minimum wage before I received my doctorate at the age of 35. Now that I teach in a clinical psychology program, we have had a number of students in their 60s who have said, "I realized that five years from now, I'll be five years older, with or without a doctoral degree, and I love learning this stuff."

We might have a grand vision of what we want to become, but are too afraid to take up the challenge, or we might not have the ability to tolerate the ambiguity of all the unknowns involved in change. Putting up with the short-term stress that we at least are very familiar with can be more comfortable than taking the risk of lots of stress for the hope that we will be happier in the long run.

Of course, there may be very real barriers, such as the "glass ceiling" (unseen but there nonetheless) for women and minorities, that need to be realistically acknowledged. You must think through drastic changes very carefully, and make sure you are doing it for the right reasons. If you jump into a new career to avoid something within yourself, you may end up repeating the same old patterns.

A man named Chuck once came to me for career consultation. He said he was unhappy in his current career and wanted to figure out what he wanted to be when he grew up. As we talked, it quickly became apparent that he had suffered from anxiety most of his life, especially social anxiety. He owned his own factory, which he had dreamed of doing since he worked in one as a kid, but now it caused him too much stress, so he wanted to try something else. He had a hard time trying to think of other things he wanted to do, however, as they would all evoke some anxiety for him. The thing that excited him most was being entrepreneurial, of getting a new idea and making it happen.

The reason he didn't like his current situation was because he felt trapped. He had a business partner who shared the profits, but didn't share the responsibilities. This partner basically only came into the factory occasionally to drink coffee and chat with the employees. Chuck was not very motivated to work hard and create new ideas or inventions when the partner would share the profits without contributing anything but frustration.

As many business owners experience, he felt the business owned him rather than the other way around. He was a good manager who led by example, but had a hard time dealing with the difficult employees.

He was also frustrated because his wife needed to keep working in a stressful job to pay a chunk of the bills, and he wanted her to have the option of working for his business, or at least to work fewer hours or get a less stressful job.

Chuck also owned a rental property, another chain around his ankle. It was an older house which needed constant maintenance. He needed to mow the grass in the summer and shovel the snow in the winter. It was only partially rented, so he was losing money, and the building needed extensive repairs to make the other rooms worth renting. Worst of all, the real estate market had tanked, so he owed more on the property than it was worth.

The frustration Chuck felt increased his anxiety, especially of being around other people, which made it even harder to be proactive. Avoiding the anxiety by getting out of the situation was what he felt strongest.

When I encouraged him to explore some of his interests, he chose to pursue golf. It was nice to see the excitement it brought to him to talk about it, and he even took lessons to help him get started. But his expectations sometimes got in the way of enjoying it, as he compared himself to Tiger Woods, and had the sense that he either needed to be great or not do it at all.

In the course of our therapy, he became aware of the way he was subconsciously carrying his parents' voices in his head. "Why are you doing that? What's the point? What's the practical value?" It felt strange to just do something for fun.

He had also learned to just avoid arguing with his parents, and do what he had to do behind the scenes with hard work. It seemed easier than dealing with the anxiety of confrontation. He even planned his day around avoiding seeing his opinionated, talkative neighbor.

All of his situations were messy, and no matter what he did, it would be messier before things got better. It was easier in the short run to avoid dealing with things, and he dreamed of inventing something that would give him financial independence. In fact, he had come up with a device he had wished for in all his years of working in a factory, and even found a company to produce a prototype. But his attorney advised him to hold off pursuing it because his partner could make a claim on it.

In exploring what he wanted to do, instead of what he wanted to avoid, he realized he enjoyed his factory, wanted to get rid of the rental property, and wanted to develop his invention. He knew he had to confront his partner, deal with his lending bank, and venture into a whole new world to make his invention a reality.

Looking at everything at once can be very overwhelming, but he broke it down one step at a time. It was hard to confront his partner, and there were a lot of hurt feelings, but they finally came up with a buy-out agreement each could live with. Upside-down mortgages were all too common at that time, so he consulted on how to work with the bank to get the property off his hands. He explored his relationship with his parents and came to a new sense of peace about it.

He also tried a medication known as a selective serotonin reuptake inhibitor (SSRI), which helped his anxiety level settle a bit. This encouraged him to be more active and take more risks, therefore moving into and working through the unpleasant feelings. This lowered his anxiety even more, allowing him to be more active and have more friends, helping him to feel even better about himself and more confident. This virtuous upward spiral continued to build on itself.

Now, years later, he is one of the happiest people I have ever met. Without all the anxiety, he has a ton of newfound energy to build his business, explore his interests, and pursue his inventions. He even developed a profit-sharing plan for his trusted managers, giving him more freedom and time with his wife and kids. The man who used to get so nervous even meeting with an attorney he hired to help him, now travels the world to make big business deals.

Of course, Chuck's life is not perfect now, but by more clearly identifying his values, and letting those guide his direction in life, he is not as driven by his anxieties, and has a life much richer than he used to think possible.

It is important to consider your values when choosing your career and how you might give to others. Doing it to impress people will quickly wear off. Prestige feels good, but there are many other ways to feel good about yourself that don't rely on the ups and downs of how others perceive you.

Committing to Your Values

However much we work to foster well-being, suffering is an inevitable part of life. If you are chasing after well-being primarily to escape from unpleasant feelings, you will feel caught in a squirrel cage.

It is important to remember that life can be worth living, even with suffering in it. The important question is: what makes your life worth living? If we get caught up in only dealing with our problems, we will begin to feel pretty hopeless. Haven't you noticed that whenever you fix one problem, something else pops up, like that game of whack-a-mole? As my friend Russ used to say, "And the hits just keep on coming … "

Bring it all with you

Acceptance and commitment therapy, known as ACT (said as one word), uses the analogy of the bus.[19] Imagine yourself as the driver of this bus, which is your life. As you drive along, you pick up passengers, which are your life experiences. Some of the passengers that have managed to get onto your bus are pretty scary, perhaps even looking like monsters. These monsters may yell at you, put you down, and metaphorically throw spit balls at your head. If you spend all your time and energy fighting with them, or if you are letting them tell you how to drive, you are likely to become lost or drive in circles. If you keep pulling the bus over to give them lectures or to argue with them, you'll end up going nowhere. If you wait for the monsters to get off the bus, you could be waiting a long time. But if you pick a direction that is important to you, you can just drive that way, and bring them all with you. You can move toward values and goals in your life even with the monsters still there, as loud as they may scream at you. You may even find that they quiet down when you stop fighting with them.

I once attended an ACT training with Kevin Polk, who illustrated this concept in a powerful way. He asked for a volunteer from the audience, and a young woman named Freesia came up to the front of the room. He asked her to identify one of her values, and she was able to say that moving toward a fulfilling career was important to her.

"Wonderful," Kevin said. "So, on your way to a fulfilling career, what might be a specific goal?"

"Getting a good job," Freesia replied.

"Okay. And what might be a goal on the way to getting a good job?"

"Going to a job interview."

"Great. Let's use that. Imagine this represents your job interview." Kevin grabbed a stool and placed it on the other side of the room, then came back. "So, you're standing here, about to go to a job interview, moving in the direction of a fulfilling career. What thoughts might come up for you that could get in your way?"

Freesia thought for a moment. "I don't have enough experience."

"I don't have enough experience," repeated Kevin, as he wrote that down on a piece of paper with a marker. He then asked for a volunteer from the audience, and handed the paper to him. He then turned back to Freesia. "What other thoughts might come up as you're about to go to that job interview?"

"I'm too young."

Kevin again wrote this down and handed it to a different audience member. "What else?"

Kevin wrote down about a dozen of Freesia's comments, which seemed to be getting more honest with time. He put the marker down and came back to stand next to her, and said, "Okay, so you're about to go to that job interview, and you hear … " Kevin waved for the volunteers with the papers to speak up.

A cacophony of voices arose from all around the room. "You're too young!" "You don't have enough experience!" "You're not good enough!" "You're going to fail!" "You're going to say something stupid!"

Hearing her own thoughts coming back at her from all around the room had a visible effect on Freesia. Her eyes widened and she seemed a bit taken aback.

Kevin, still standing next to her, asked, "So all these thoughts came up. What can you do?"

Freesia mustered her courage and decided to answer the thoughts back. "I am too good enough! I'm not that young! I already have some good experiences! I'm not going to fail! I can speak intelligently!"

Kevin waved for the audience to continue. Again, the room was filled with, "You're going to fail!" "You're too young!" "You don't have enough experience!" "You're not good enough!" "You're going to say something stupid!"

For a moment, Freesia became frustrated, and answered them more loudly. "I am a capable woman! I have to try or I can't succeed! I have lots of things to feel proud of!" But the voices simply continued as they had, relentlessly.

Kevin saw her frustration building. "So, answering them back is not changing them, and you need to get to your job interview over there. What else can you do?"

Freesia was frozen in place with a stunned look on her face as the voices continued. After a few moments, Kevin leaned over to her with a loud whisper, pointing to the stool. "Just walk over there!"

Freesia suddenly realized that the voices could not keep her in place. She walked over to the stool despite the negative thoughts, reaching her goal of getting to the job interview.

It is hard to express in writing how dramatic that moment felt, especially for Freesia. Our thoughts and habits can get us hooked, and we miss how much choice we may actually have in any given moment.

If we keep our values in sight, before making each choice, we can ask ourselves, "Is what I'm doing bringing me closer to or farther away from the things I value?"

This does not mean that we have to over-analyze each moment, or that we won't get sidetracked from time to time. Right now, writing this book, I am moving toward my values of career and of helping others, but am moving away from other values like friends and family. However, I will soon head back in the direction of those other values as well. Sometimes we make bee-lines for important values, sometimes we casually meander. The important thing is to notice when you are stuck in circles, and consciously choose the directions you want to take.

Finding your values

Many people are so busy trying to survive, pay the bills, and deal with urgent day-to-day problems that they are not in touch with what they really value. It is so easy to fall into a sort of hypnotic routine, and we forget how to dream. What do you value? What gives you fulfillment?

We sometimes hear people say, "I don't know where we're going, but we're making good time!" If you don't know where you're going, how will you get there? Our values provide our lives with a sense of direction, like a compass heading.

If you wait around for your life's meaning to drop from the sky, you may be waiting a long time. It will likely take focused effort. There are a number of ways you can get in touch with your values. One is simply to create more "space" in your life to explore them. You can think over what you wanted to be when you grew up. You can imagine what you might do if you won the lottery. How would you want to spend your life if you knew you only had a year to live? What would you want to be said about you at your funeral after living a full life?

Be careful about choosing values only to impress others. You don't have to live for something like curing cancer, unless you truly have decided that is your life path. In fact, if anyone asks, it will probably be hard to put into words why your values are important to you. If you can give me very specific reasons, I would question if you are merely repeating something you heard growing up from parents or society, or if you are choosing your values based on what you think you "should" value.

Though values can be very unique to you, they are often broad but simple, like family, health, spirituality, career, balance, learning, simplicity, and adventure. It is important to note that you never "arrive" at a value. It is a guide, a compass heading. If family is one of your values, imagine what would happen if you said, "Well, got family down, what's next?" You live

Sun above the clouds in Hawaii. © Olivia Ossege.

your life moving toward family. When you think you are "done" with family, it usually falls apart.

Once you know your compass heading, you can set and accomplish specific goals along the way.

Setting Your Goals

Goals are the stepping stones we walk upon as we move toward our values. Have you ever set a goal, achieved it, then wondered why it had seemed so important? Most likely, it was because it was not part of some larger value in your life. Goals can be modified along the way, in service of the bigger context of what you value. If family is a value, your goals may be very different when you are in your 20s as compared to when you are in your 70s.

Though there are many variations, a commonly used acronym for setting goals is SMART: specific, measurable, attainable, relevant, and time-bound. If one of your values is health, having a goal of "exercising more" is too vague to be helpful. How would you know when you are meeting your goal?

When your goal is specific, it will keep you focused. A goal of stretching 10 minutes, walking on the treadmill 20 minutes, and performing 15 pushups and 30 sit-ups three times a week is better than "exercising every week." Tracking your body mass index is easier to measure than "be in better shape." If you are new to exercise, a goal of exercising three hours a day is not attainable, and you will quickly lose motivation and quit. Better to start with something you know you can do, and increase your goals in the future. Making the goal relevant means ensuring that it is taking you closer to what you value. Adding a time component to your goal helps you pace yourself, otherwise it becomes too easy to keep putting it off.

As you develop and adapt your goals to move you toward what you value, watch out for "dead person goals," that is, something even a dead person could do, such as "stop eating sweets." It is better to frame them in terms of actions you can commit to, like "eating healthy foods."

The challenge of choosing

One of the benefits of practicing mindfulness is that we become more aware of automatic patterns, which gives us more choice. But choice can be scary. Sometimes one of the biggest obstacles to moving toward our values is the difficulty of making decisions about our goals.

We all want freedom to make choices, but actually making the choices can be difficult because choosing one thing often cuts off other options. If I choose to go back to school, or to have a child, I am choosing to give up a lot of sleep, money, leisure time, and the ability to travel for extended periods. Sometimes we don't want to make a choice, in an attempt to keep all of our options open, and the decision ends up being made for us.

A study was done once in which rats were taught two different directions in a maze that led to cheese. The researchers found that the rats would get stuck in indecision, fearing that if they took the time to move through the maze to get one piece, the other piece might not be there later, so they ended up hungry.

When we sit with an important decision, we can notice all the factors involved, consider our feelings, and make the best choice for us, freeing ourselves from getting caught up in past automatic patterns. But with freedom comes responsibility. When I become aware of how much choice I have in my life, it becomes harder to blame others when things go wrong.

A young college student once asked me what it meant to grow up and be an adult. One of the things that came to mind for me was the realization that I am the person most responsible for my own life. There is no end to blaming other people and other things for all the problems in our lives. Disliking and even hating all those people and life circumstances that have caused you suffering serves to distract you from the sting of your pain, and keeps you stuck. While it may well be true that people have caused you horrible anguish, tragic life circumstances have knocked you off your feet, and it was very unfair and undeserved, in this moment, there is no one more responsible than you for what your next action will be, what direction your life will take. This is at once both a frightening and liberating realization.

Of course, we get into bigger issues of diversity and social justice when we talk about how free we really are in modern society. We cannot deny the reality of the discrimination that still occurs due to things like race, gender, sexual orientation, religion, and ability. We still have a lot of work to do, especially those with the power and privilege. Yet, in this moment, I need to start from where I am.

Another aspect of freedom is becoming more aware of the impact our choices have on others. If what you are doing hurts others, is that working for you? While we don't have to please everyone with our decisions, especially when their displeasure is due to their own issues, we can learn to pay more attention to the consequences of our choices. Mindfulness helps us determine if what we are doing is compassionate or not, for ourselves and for others.

I once had a supervisor who said, "Everyone in that meeting I'm supposed to go to is so passive-aggressive. I'm just not going to show up today." It was completely lost on him that he himself was being passive-aggressive by doing that.

Being passive-aggressive is when you want to assert something, but don't do it directly. When we take responsibility, we have more options. We could still choose to be passive-aggressive, but we may find that being direct is more helpful. I remember when I was a teenager driving on a road trip during the winter, and someone in the back seat kept rolling her window down. The noise and wind bothered me, so I kept turning off the heat so she would get cold and roll it back up. This went on a number of times. It would have been much more effective to ask her to roll it up, or ask if it was too warm in the car. For all I knew, she was getting carsick and needed fresh air. I didn't say anything because I didn't want to upset her, and felt uncomfortable being direct, but the end result was more discomfort for everyone.

It can be very difficult to tease apart all the factors involved in making choices. Paying attention can help us be more clear about what the real factors are. We may be confusing the current situation with a past one, or we may be getting caught up in future "what ifs." We may be so focused on what others might think that we are not sure what we really want. We may even convince ourselves that we have no opinions, or that we are not worth imposing our wants for fear of appearing selfish.

Of course, we're not talking about whimsical wants. Once we identify our values, they can be compass headings to guide us each moment. Is this choice going to take us closer or further away from our values? We can certainly choose to make detours, or move toward other values, but we can always keep our long-term headings in sight.

Leisure Time

With all this talk so far about paying attention, dealing with challenges, and self-development, don't forget that all of us also need down time. That is, we need to allow ourselves to be completely unproductive, free to do (or not do) whatever we want for a little while each day. Sit and stare out of the window. Wander aimlessly through your house or yard. Flip through a magazine. Take a brief afternoon nap. Color with some crayons. Watch a television show or movie that you secretly enjoy, though you might not admit it to friends.

Your brain needs downtime, though don't make it another "thing to do" because it's good for you. As Alan Watts observed, "All work and no play makes Jack a dull boy. But if the only reason Jack is playing is so that he can work better afterwards, he's not really playing."[20]

Go ahead, give yourself permission to be unmindful sometimes. If it becomes a pattern of avoidance, you'll notice it, and you can go back over the earlier parts of this book. If old childhood messages keep popping up that you're lazy if you aren't working every moment you're awake, just watch them float on by. If feelings of guilt arise, just notice as they crest and pass away. Don't lose sight of your compass heading, but give yourself time to stop and smell the flowers on your journey toward your values.

Just This Moment

Ultimately, this moment is the only one we have in which to enrich our lives. Where else could you possibly go? When else could you possibly be present? No matter what you are experiencing, you can choose to drop into this moment and experience it in its fullness, even if you are in pain in this moment.

Alan Watts describes enlightenment as scraping a landscape painting off of a window to see the real beauty outside. We can begin to value the painting, a mere representation with flat limitations, more than the real thing. Our thoughts can be beautiful, but they put a layer of representation between us and reality. Go ahead and scrape a little off right now. What are you experiencing in this moment? My daughter's voice echoes through my home over the clack of my keyboard strokes, and I take a deep breath as I gaze out my window at the squirrels scurrying through the wet leaves.

So, now you have read about how to use mindfulness to both survive and to thrive. But how do you incorporate it consistently into your life? The first commitment will be to actually practice doing it regularly, fostering more awareness of your daily moments.

7

Building Your Mindfulness Muscles

Your brain pathways can be exercised and strengthened, just as your muscles can through physical exercise. What is your brain practicing most often?

I have been on many retreats over the years, but one of the richest I've experienced took place several years ago in India and Nepal, probably due to the historical significance of the places I went, the beauty of the awesome natural scenery, and the newness, and even bizarreness, of some of my experiences there.

I spent 17 nights in Bodh Gaya, India, the place where Siddhartha Gautama "woke up." Each morning, I got up at 5 a.m., walked across the city to the Japanese Zen temple, and sat in meditation. Afterwards, I would walk around the Mahabodhi monument, erected beside the Bodhi tree, under which Siddhartha was sitting when he had his breakthrough. I would then enjoy a good breakfast, explore various temples and places in the city, and enjoy a good lunch before walking around the Bodhi tree again. The afternoon was spent reading, writing, or meditating in my rented room before once again trekking across the city for the evening meditation at the Zen temple.

It was the end of January, so the days were mild, though the nights were chilly. No one used heaters, and my room had built-in openings near the

Mindfulness: Living through Challenges and Enriching Your Life in This Moment, First Edition. Richard W. Sears.
© 2014 John Wiley & Sons, Ltd. Published 2014 by John Wiley & Sons, Ltd.

ceiling since most of the year it was sweltering hot there. I bundled up in my hat, coat, and scarf every night when I went to bed.

It was mostly very dry and dusty there, but at one point, it rained continuously for three days. I simply maintained the same routine, though sometimes I had to creatively navigate around small lakes and rivers of mud.

Because everything was so new and different to me, it was much easier to pay attention to each moment I was in. Sickly, destitute families would be living under a tarp next to a splendid, lavish, golden temple. Wealthy, privileged tourists like myself would step over crippled children begging in the streets. I spent many hours swatting the countless mosquitoes that constantly made their way into my room to buzz my face, sorry to take their lives, but unwilling to trust their bites would be disease-free. Even procuring clean water, finding a computer terminal to check in on my doctoral students, and finding a satellite phone to call my family became mindfulness practices. I was only doing one thing at a time, and my mind became very clear.

After Bodh Gaya, I journeyed up to Kathmandu and Pokhara, Nepal, and sat in a Tibetan monastery for two weeks with my martial arts teacher and a couple of friends. The poverty of the populace was terrible (I earn more in one day than the average Nepalese earns in one year), yet the natural scenery was rich. I was drawn into each moment through all of my senses. Pounding drums and blaring horns played throughout the day, incense filled the air, shiny brocade and colorful images covered the walls, and special meals were prepared for us. Water came down through a pipe from the mountains, so we hoarded what bottled water we could obtain. One of the foods I ate must have been washed with that mountain water, as I was sick for a few days, though fortunately it was not too serious.

Even the pests were unique, and pulled me fully into the moment. On one occasion, I saw a couple of rather large cockroaches in my room. I watched one zoom under my bed, so I bent down to see where it went. As it crawled up one of the legs of the bed, I saw two big furry legs flash out and grab it. I'm not sure how long that massive spider had been living under my thin mattress, but instead of staying with my anxiety, I chose to dismantle the bed and liberate the poor creature.

I have quite a few troublesome squirrels around my home in the United States, but the wild monkeys living in Nepal make them seem quite tame. You had to be on your guard when out and about, as they were known to do hit-and-runs on passersby in search of some delicious goody. One morning, after leaving my laundry out to dry, I found my clothes scattered all over the side of the mountain. I consciously chose to avoid thinking about what they might have been doing with my underwear.

Perhaps the best moments of mindfulness were spent with my friends, walking in the foothills of the Himalayas, crossing over crystal clear

Monkeys in Nepal. © Richard Sears.

mountain streams on suspension bridges, passing by wild water buffaloes, discussing ancient practices and modern life.

Of course, I would not want to live like this every day. I enjoy spending time with my family, working with my colleagues, traveling and teaching, and helping others. I also appreciate having the comforts and conveniences of technology. While I respect, and I believe our society needs, those who choose to dedicate their lives to mind practices, one of my values is making these methods more available to everyone.

The goal is to be more present in all of our moments, but learning mindfulness in the midst of a stressful and chaotic life, as Marsha Linehan says, is like trying to put up a tent in the middle of a hurricane.[1] It helps to set a strong foundation by making dedicated time for training.

Even if your life is already going well, it is still nice to take vacations. No matter how present you are in your life, it can still be wonderful to go on retreats.

Although retreats can provide a unique opportunity to begin or deepen your practice, you don't need to leave your work and family to build your mindfulness muscles. The brain scan research discussed earlier showed measurable changes from a program like the one below with just eight weeks of practicing 45–60 minutes a day. You can have mini-retreats in your own home, time dedicated to fostering your own well-being.

This chapter will provide an outline for conducting your own mindfulness training sessions at home, using mindfulness recordings from my website or others, based on the mindfulness-based stress reduction and mindfulness-based cognitive therapy programs.[2] We will also discuss ways to work with barriers that arise, to keep up the momentum of the practices, and to incorporate more presence into your daily life.

Is Formal Practice Necessary?

Is it really necessary to formally practice mindfulness exercises? Some insist that it is, some insist that it isn't. However, no one can argue that the more you practice, the more refined and reliable your skills will become.

You don't need to practice scales when you are an expert musician – you can play anything and it sounds great. But if you pick up an instrument for the first time, unless you were born a musical genius, what you play will likely sound horrible. In the beginning, you focus on the best way to hold the instrument, repetitively play notes on various scales, and practice timing and rhythm. After years of discipline, you can then "play anything" as an expression of your inner creativity.

I once attended a traditional Japanese archery (kyudo) seminar for a weekend. Friends could not understand how it could take an entire weekend just to learn to shoot an arrow. They looked absolutely perplexed when I said that the teacher, an American named Rick Beal, had been studying kyudo for over 30 years. In traditional Japan, one might have to study with a teacher for three or four years before ever being allowed to shoot an actual bow. One would first develop the proper muscles through physical exercises, practice the proper form of the shooting sequence with a large rubber band, and learn the proper breathing techniques. Our teacher kindly let us shoot a few arrows that weekend, standing in front of us and helping us pull the massive bows open the first few times, but we were overwhelmed by the number of details we needed to know to even hit a target a few feet in front of us. Many times the arrow simply fell to the ground because we weren't yet fully aware of how we were holding the bow and the arrow in each and every moment. The teacher had a highly developed mindfulness practice that allowed him to coordinate every aspect of his body with the bow, arrow, and target. However, after all that practice, he could also quickly hit the bull's eye every time while casually walking around and talking to us if he chose to do so.

Author practicing kyudo. © Robert Denton.

Likewise, when you first learn mindfulness, it is very important to practice regularly. As you strengthen your practice, you become more aware, increasingly able to allow thoughts and feelings to flow more naturally as you participate more fully in your daily life.

Exercising your brain is similar to physical exercise. If you are out of shape, it's best to develop a regular routine to tone your muscles, ideally at a gym with a supportive trainer. Once you are in shape, you might stay in shape by incorporating exercise into your daily life by taking the stairs and walking more, though setting regular times to exercise is the best way to stay in shape.

Importance of Consistency

The ancient Zen teacher Chinul taught the idea of "sudden awakening, gradual cultivation." Reading this book, you may have had a few moments of clarity and insight. You can choose to "wake up" to the moment you are in anytime you wish. But because it took a lifetime of habits to get you where you are now, deeply cultivating more consistent presence in your life takes time.

As with physical exercise, consistency is important. Sometimes I hear someone get very excited about mindfulness, and say, "I'm going to get up at 5:00 am and meditate for two hours a day!" This is like someone who is out of shape starting out with a very intense physical exercise routine. Inevitably, enthusiasm wears off after a couple of days. It is much better to start with a few minutes a day, and gradually build up to a workable amount of time for you. Twenty minutes a day is both beneficial and sustainable. It is also better to do a little every day, rather than only practicing for hours on the weekends.

Posture

Many traditional schools emphasize the importance of the posture you use during mediation practice. There are actually good reasons for these recommendations, such as allowing the breath to flow naturally, putting the spine into its naturally curved position, and providing stability so you are not pulled out of your meditation state by body movements.

However, I find that beginners often get so caught up in trying to sit the "right" way that they can't focus on the exercise, or get frustrated and quit because they find it uncomfortable. I almost always sit in chairs when I teach mindfulness, as this is what most of the people I work with are accustomed to. Many traditional cultures did not have sofas and chairs, so sitting on the floor was very natural. I've been to many workshops where participants sat on the floor because the teacher did, only to spend the entire time shifting in pain and not concentrating much on what was being taught.

Most people find that leaning back feels too much like resting, so induces sleep. Leaning forward usually invokes a feeling of intensity, as when you are deeply engaged in a conversation with someone. Straightening our spine into a naturally upright posture, without strain, signals to your brain that you are going to pay more attention. Although you don't hear these terms much anymore, I find that this posture connotes a sense of dignity and integrity.

Lying down is of course okay, especially for the body scan, but it can lend itself to falling asleep, especially if you are sleep-deprived. For all mindfulness exercises, experiment to find the position that works best for you, especially if you are pregnant or suffer from chronic pain. The most important thing is to be as comfortable as you can so you can practice paying attention.

Likewise, experiment with doing these exercises with your eyes closed and with them open or shaded. Sometimes closed eyes helps concentration, sometimes it leads to mind-wandering or sleepiness. Eyes open a little, softly gazing at the ground or whatever is in front of you, is sometimes grounding and sometimes distracting. You can make noticing the effects of how you sit a part of your mindfulness practice.

Inquiry

You will find free, downloadable audio recordings of all the mindfulness exercises for this program on my website, www.psych-insights.com. There are also quite a few other good recordings available by Jon Kabat-Zinn, Zindel Segal, Susan Woods, and others. These recordings will allow you to practice the exercises exactly as group participants do.

Inquiring about how an exercise went is one of the most important learning processes in a mindfulness group, especially when you first learn a new exercise, but you can practice doing this for yourself. Inquiry helps to foster a sense of openness, exploration, curiosity, and wonder, crucial attitudes for the development of mindfulness.

Ask yourself the following three questions to get the most out of each mindfulness exercise.[3]

1 **What did I notice?** After the exercise, reflect back on your experience. What physical sensations were present in your body? What did you see, hear, taste, or smell? What emotions came up? What thoughts came and went? Were you pulled away by distractions, past memories, or thoughts about the future? Were you able to keep bringing your attention back where you wanted it to be? Pay attention to how your senses, emotions, and thoughts are distinctly separate but interrelated.

2 **How is this different from the way I normally do this activity?** Many of the exercises you will be doing are normal activities, so asking yourself this question helps distinguish being mindful from automatic pilot mode. Whether the activity involved eating, walking, or relating to your thoughts or feelings, what differences did you notice (if any) about doing it mindfully?

3 **What does this exercise have to do with what I want from this program?** Although you may reach a point where you understand the value of just being in each moment, in the beginning it is important to have a sense of why you are doing these exercises to keep yourself motivated. What do you think the mindfulness exercise has to do with reducing problems like stress, anxiety, depression, and chronic pain, or with moving toward what you value? Rather than always relying on someone else to tell you,

you will increasingly find that you can answer these questions through the attention that develops with your personal practice.

Setting Your Resolve

Completing an eight-week program like the one below is not easy for everyone. Set your intentions to finish, and prepare yourself for the challenges of sticking to practicing every day. Write down the date you will start (now is usually the best time), and map out how the next eight weeks will fit into your schedule.

Remember that how you deal with the challenges that come up with this practice often mirror how you handle (or avoid) difficulties in your life. What are the values in your life motivating you to do this program? Are you willing to be with the challenges and discomfort as you move toward those values?

Hopefully, you will also see this as a special treat you are giving yourself, and not as another "thing to do." Give yourself permission to set aside some personal time for being.

It is very important to note that this program is best done when you are in a fairly good place emotionally. If you have serious medical issues, you would consult with a physician before taking on an intense physical exercise program. Likewise, if you are currently experiencing serious emotional difficulties, you may not have the attentional capacity to do these exercises, and may not have the resources to work through what might come up. If this is true for you, seek professional guidance before embarking on a program like this.

An Eight-Week Home Practice Program

So, are you ready to build up your mindfulness muscles? The themes and practices below are based on the MBSR and MBCT programs, developed by Jon Kabat-Zinn, Zindel Segal, Mark Williams, John Teasdale, and others. I was so impressed when I started learning about these programs. At first I couldn't believe that people could achieve so much with a short, structured program, when it had taken me years of personal instruction. Yet, both the research and my personal experiences with hundreds of people have demonstrated remarkable results for those who do these practices.

Unfortunately, you will be missing a crucial ingredient of these groups – having others to go through these practices with. I have had countless participants say they had read books about mindfulness and dabbled in the practice for decades, but had amazing breakthroughs when they joined and completed our eight-week program. Even when I teach this course individually, I find the results are never quite as good as when these practices are taught in a group. There is something about sharing personal experiences, having the feedback of others, the accountability for keeping up the practice, normalizing the challenges, and sharing the human experience of it all that makes the material come to life in a more useful and practical way.

Although it would be best to find a formal MBSR, MBCT, or other similar group in your area led by a competent instructor, the program below will provide a solid foundation. After practicing regularly, you will find that you get a lot more out of re-reading this book, reading other books, or attending weekend workshops on mindfulness. You will also find it easier to internalize the ideas that make sense when you read them, but are challenging to put into daily life.

Below is an outline of weekly practices for building your mindfulness muscles. As you practice these exercises, it may be helpful to review some of the concepts in the previous chapters of this book. At the end of this outline, we will discuss common challenges encountered when doing these practices.

Week 1

The theme during this first week is "awareness and automatic pilot." Throughout the next seven days, see if you can notice when you are in automatic pilot mode. The two exercises we begin with are mindful eating and the body scan.

Mindful eating

Eating is something we very often do automatically, so it is a nice place to begin fostering mindfulness. Find a quiet place to sit down and pay attention to eating something small, like a raisin or a piece of chocolate. Take your time and notice as much as you can about the experience of eating. Look at the color, feel the texture, and smell the aroma of the food. Slowly place it in your mouth and notice what happens. Chew very slowly and experience the range of tastes throughout your mouth. Pay attention to thoughts, memories, and emotions that come and go, and separate them out from what you are actually experiencing while you are eating.

Throughout this first week, try to remember to consciously slow down and pay attention when you are eating. Ideally, try to eat one entire meal with mindful awareness.

Body scan

We often don't pay that much attention to our bodies, yet it is the foundation of all our interactions with the world and those around us. Practice the body scan once per day throughout this first week, listening to the recording to guide your attention systematically through your body. This will help you strengthen your ability to focus, hold, and shift your attention with very concrete physical sensations before we move into more subtle things like thoughts in later weeks.

Daily activities

As a way to start bridging practice to daily life, pick a routine activity that you will do more mindfully once a day this week, like brushing your teeth, taking a shower, or feeding your pets.

Week 2

After practicing for a week, you have probably become aware of the theme of the second week, which is "living in our heads." You likely noticed a wide variety of thoughts and feelings arising as you worked to begin the new habit of practicing mindfulness. Skip ahead to the list of potential barriers in the next section of this chapter and see how they might relate to your own practice as you continue this week.

Body scan

Continue practicing the body scan each day for one more week, paying particular attention to how you relate to the common challenges listed at the end of this chapter if and when they come up for you.

Mindful breathing

Because breathing is simple, portable, and a process that is both conscious and unconscious, it is a wonderful mindfulness exercise. Listen to a mindful breathing recording, or just set a timer for 10–15 minutes, and practice feeling your breath. You can stay with the sensations of your belly rising and falling, or feel the air as it moves in and out of your nostrils. When your mind wanders, simply escort your attention back to your breathing. If your mind wanders a thousand times, just bring it back a thousand times.

Pleasant experiences

Practice noticing at least one pleasant event each day. Pay attention to how your body is feeling during the experience, the qualities of your emotions, and what thoughts are present. It doesn't have to be anything profound – you might just look out your window at a tree blowing in the wind (if you find that pleasant).

Daily activities

Choose a new routine activity to pay attention to once a day throughout the coming week.

Week 3

After practicing a simple exercise like feeling the breath, you will have become aware of how much your mind wanders. This week's theme is "gathering the scattered mind." Throughout the next seven days, try to pay more attention to how often your mind wanders all over the place, and gently bring it more often to what you are doing in the moment.

Breath, body, and sounds

This exercise begins with the mindful breathing exercise you practiced last week. After a few minutes, expand your awareness to include the sensations of your entire body in space, all at once. Whenever your mind wanders, practice bringing it back to being present with your awareness of your body-as-a-whole. Next, shift your awareness to your sense of hearing. Notice the sounds around you, both near and far. Rather than straining, allow sounds to come to your ears. Be aware of your brain's tendency to label the sounds, and practice staying with the actual qualities of the sounds. Practice this exercise every other day in the coming week.

Mindful stretching

On the alternate days of the coming week, practice paying attention to the changing sensations, emotions, and thoughts that arise as you move through a yoga routine or through simple stretching exercises. This offers a chance to practice being mindful during movement, and to stay present during any mild discomfort that arises during some of the stretches.

Three-minute breathing space

This short exercise is designed to help ground you in the present. In the first minute, ask yourself, "What am I experiencing in this moment?" Do a quick check-in with your body sensations, emotions, and thoughts. In the second minute, practice mindful breathing as a way to gather your attention. In the third minute, expand your awareness to your entire body, perhaps reminding yourself, "Whatever I'm feeling, it's already here anyway, just let me feel it." Practice this exercise three times a day for the coming week.

Week 4

This week's theme is "recognizing aversion." Pay attention over the next seven days to the mind's tendency to push things away automatically, and notice if you are doing that unconsciously or if you are choosing to do it on purpose.

Sitting meditation

Begin this exercise with the breath, body, and sounds practice. When practicing the body-as-a-whole exercise, pay particular attention to how you relate to feelings of pain or discomfort if they arise. Practice consciously moving into and exploring unpleasant sensations as an alternative to automatically pushing them away. After the mindful hearing exercise, shift your awareness to your own thoughts, noticing how they arise, linger, and pass away. Practice this exercise every other day.

Mindful walking

On the alternate days, practice mindfully paying attention while you are walking. When we watch a baby learn to walk, or if we have a significant knee or back injury, we are reminded of how complicated the process is. When we grow older, and are in good health, we usually do it automatically. For this exercise, slow things down and become aware of the many sensations involved in taking each step, and notice any emotions or thoughts that arise.

Three-minute breathing space

Continue to practice the three-minute breathing space three times a day as you did in the previous week. In addition, try to notice when you become stressed or upset at any point during the day, and if you can, stop and do a three-minute breathing space. Don't necessarily expect anything to change or get better, just practice moving into your experiences.

Week 5

This week's theme is "allowing/letting be." Throughout the coming week, practice noticing our tendency to want things to be different than they are. Before we can change anything, we need to practice letting things be as we find them in this moment.

Sitting meditation

Each day this week, continue practicing mindfulness of breath, body, sounds, and thoughts. Then purposefully bring to mind a minor difficulty that you've been thinking about lately, or something unpleasant that has happened recently. Doing this allows us to practice staying with something difficult, instead of automatically pushing it away. When we let go of our compulsive internal struggles, we can relate more flexibly to our challenges, often discovering that we have many more options in our moments than we first realize.

Three-minute breathing space

Continue this practice three times a day, and whenever you become aware that you are feeling stressed.

Week 6

The theme this week is, "thoughts are not facts," with a subtitle of "even the ones that tell you they are." Throughout the week, pay attention to how strongly your thoughts try to convince you of their truth. Remind yourself that even though a thought might represent a reality, thoughts are different than the things or events they represent, so it is up to you to determine how accurate and how helpful they are.

Customize your practice

Of all the exercises you have done so far, begin to experiment with personalizing a practice routine that works well for you. Also, try practicing some of the exercises without using the recordings if you haven't already been doing so.

Relapse signatures

Now that you are becoming more aware, make a list of signs that might indicate that you are beginning to get overwhelmed, as discussed in Chapter 4, so that you can become more proactive at taking care of yourself before things get too bad.

Three-minute breathing space

Continue this practice three times a day, and whenever you become aware that you are feeling stressed or overwhelmed.

Week 7

Becoming more aware of when we are getting overwhelmed leads to asking ourselves "How can I best take care of myself?," which is this week's theme. Often we get so caught up in dealing with problems that we forget to ask this question. Pay attention over the next seven days to how you can take better care of yourself.

Customized practice

Continue to experiment with personalizing a routine that works well for you, so that you will be inspired to keep practicing after you finish this eight-week program.

Typical day exercise and self-care action plan

If you haven't already done so, go back over Chapter 4 and complete the typical day exercise, and create your own personal action plan for taking care of yourself when you notice that you are getting overwhelmed.

Three-minute breathing space

Continue this practice three times a day, and whenever you become aware that you are feeling stressed. As you may have noticed, this short exercise actually contains the essence of all forms of mindfulness practice.

Week 8

The final theme is "maintaining and extending new learning." If you have been able to practice consistently, congratulate yourself! If not, don't let the weight of the past discourage you from beginning fresh in this moment.

During this final week, think back over your experiences, how they fit with what you read in this and other books, how you will apply what you've learned in your life. Resolve to keep up at least a short practice each day to keep your mindfulness muscles in shape, and make plans for how you might support your practice (e.g., reading books, joining a local group, etc.).

Choiceless awareness

As your practice matures, you may enjoy something Jon Kabat-Zinn calls "choiceless awareness," which is called "just sitting" by Zen practitioners. This practice is very advanced because it is so simple. It involves maintaining the same state of openness and awareness you have been practicing, but without picking any one particular thing to pay attention to. If a sound comes, it is heard. If a thought or feeling arises, it is noticed as it arises and passes. During this practice, we don't chase after things and we don't push things away. Old reaction patterns begin to settle down, and we become more fully present in whatever moment we find ourselves in.

Working with Barriers

Mindfulness practice is about opening up and being with ourselves in this moment. Why is this difficult to do regularly? We can get into such a habit of keeping busy that we fear what might come up for us if we allow ourselves to feel. With our great intelligence, we can come up with many reasons to avoid practicing.

Everyone will experience challenges in their mindfulness practice. After all, we have been practicing mindlessness for most of our lives, so it will take intentional effort to develop new habits. Some of the barriers that come up seem so strong that we may be tempted to quit. If we can foster a mindful attitude of curiosity toward these barriers, they can be wonderful opportunities to learn about and change how we respond to difficulties in all of the aspects of our lives.

Finding time

One of the most common barriers to beginning or maintaining a mindfulness practice is the sense of not having enough time. In the fast-paced technological world we live in, this is a very realistic concern to address. However, if you don't have 15 minutes a day to pause and take care of yourself, you are probably not going to lead a very happy, healthy, or long life. The bigger question may be what is really important to you?

There are some things everyone makes time for, no matter how busy they are. No one ever tells me, "I never shower – that's 15 minutes a day I could be doing more important things!" Of course there are cultural differences in personal hygiene, but most of us simply decide that a shower is very important and make time for it. Yet, how often do we put our own self-care last?

You can make self-care a habit, too. If you make mindfulness a part of your daily routine, consistently practicing at a regular time and place, you won't have to stop and ask yourself in any given moment whether or not you should do it.

Deep down, we may feel that we don't deserve to make time for ourselves. We may feel selfish or guilty if we don't take care of everyone else first.

Whenever you find yourself choosing not to practice, make your experience in that moment the practice itself. What is stopping you? What sensations, emotions, and thoughts are present? Can you choose to move toward what you value anyway?

Falling asleep

Falling asleep is a common experience when learning mindfulness. Some people are so busy that they are not accustomed to sitting still, so when they stop moving, their brains think it must be time to sleep. It takes practice to foster a sense of "waking up."

It may be helpful to experiment with practicing at different times of the day to see what works best for you. Some people find it a nice way to end the day, yet others feel activated by it and then have a hard time sleeping if they practice in the evening.

Of course, lack of sufficient, deep, quality sleep is a ubiquitous problem in our modern culture. We need six to ten hours of good sleep every night to function at our best. Sleep problems such as apnea, a disorder in which you stop breathing multiple times per night, are often missed because your brain doesn't register a memory if you awaken for less than 30 seconds. Someone who briefly wakes up all night may not even know it.

Sleep is crucial for attention and concentration. A study was once done in which half of the kids diagnosed with attention-deficit/hyperactivity disorder (ADHD) no longer met criteria for the disorder when they got enough sleep (meaning they didn't really have ADHD in the first place, they were sleep-deprived).

Often participants in my mindfulness groups tell me, "I've had trouble sleeping for years – it's great how the body scan helps me fall asleep." By repeatedly returning attention to the body, ruminative thoughts that keep you awake all night lose their fuel, and it becomes easier to relax into sleep. This is okay, but be sure to consciously choose when you are using it to sleep, and be sure to also practice it at other times to become more alert. To keep my intention clear for myself, when I am practicing the body scan to be mindful, I start at my toes and move up. If I am using it to fall asleep, I start at my head and work my way down.

As with all of our experiences, we can even use sleepiness as an opportunity to foster attention. Years ago, I decided to go to a workshop with Elana Rosenbaum, one of the pioneers of mindfulness-based stress reduction. The workshop was about a five-hour drive away, and happened to be near the house of an old friend. I drove up the evening before, and chatted with my friend until the wee hours of the morning. He also happened to be an amateur wine maker, so he offered me a variety of his homemade tomato wines, beet wines, and others.

Needless to say, I was rather tired when I got to the workshop. Elana had us all lie down on the floor to do the body scan, and it didn't take me long to fall asleep. A nearby participant even mentioned that I snored some. Elana inquired about what people noticed during the exercise, and asked if anyone had fallen asleep. I raised my hand, and was surprised and embarrassed that no one else did, especially since I had thought of myself as a teacher already. True to the spirit of mindfulness, Elana made no judgments – she simply asked me, "Did you notice where you were in your body when you fell asleep?" By asking that question, she modeled that every experience can be an opportunity to notice what is happening in the moment.

This reminded me of a traditional practice of noticing if you were inhaling or exhaling when you fell asleep, and if you were inhaling or exhaling when you woke up in the morning. Of course, can go overboard with trying too hard to pay attention all the time, but you can learn a lot about how sleepiness comes on, and how often we add muscle tension as we struggle to stay awake, which only makes us more tired.

Not feeling anything

Unless you are an athlete, dancer, or yoga practitioner, you probably don't pay that much attention to your body unless it is hurting or feeling pleasure. Therefore, many who start practicing something like the body scan say that they are unable to feel much.

It is okay to use visualization to help you focus your attention, but one of the goals is to feel what is actually present, and to distinguish physical sensations from our thoughts and feelings about them. You can "imagine" how your knee is feeling, picturing it in your mind, but this is different from the reality – the picture in your head is only a representation of the knee. When you touch your knee, there is no question you are feeling it.

Physiologically, some parts of your body are easier to feel, because they have more nerve ends. Your lips, fingers, and genitalia are far more sensitive than your back and thighs. Also, our senses tend to habituate, or lose their novelty and go unnoticed, when the input doesn't change. When you hold hands with someone, you don't notice it as much after a while, so you give them a squeeze or caress to let them know you are still there.

Simply noticing that you are not aware of any sensations in a certain area is already being mindful of your present moment experience. It is also okay to move your body if it helps you ground your attention in an actual physical sensation. With time and practice, your brain will grow more connections, and you will be able to feel more.

Zoning out

Sometimes participants tell me that they immediately go off in their heads during a mindfulness exercise, such as into a deep state of meditation. There is nothing inherently wrong with this, but mindfulness is about consciously choosing to be more present. If you automatically zone out or try to avoid difficulties in your life and relationships, you end up creating long-term problems.

Strong feelings of boredom are another form of zoning out. We are so accustomed to distracting ourselves, that when we sit still, our brains can sometimes hunger for entertainment. This can even take the form of strange sensory experiences, like hallucinations, hearing things, and odd body sensations.

As with falling asleep, you can make these experiences part of your mindfulness practice. What were you thinking, feeling, and sensing in your body before you zoned out? What brought you back to the present moment?

Not doing it "right"

People sometimes are seeking a "good" session, and are disappointed if they don't get it, and may even choose to quit if every session isn't magical. Though you may sometimes have seemingly cosmic experiences, chasing after them will only push them away. What could be more cosmic than being present in this moment?

There is no "right" way to do mindfulness. It is not about achieving a special state, it is about paying attention to how things are. If you notice you are yawning and tired the whole time, you are being mindful. If you are upset, just allow yourself to feel it. Wherever you want to go in life, it's best to start from where you are now.

Conditions weren't right

Though it is ideal to have a quiet, inspiring space to practice mindfulness, the reality is that there will inevitably be complications, interruptions, and distractions.

Though you should proactively create a good environment if you can, ultimately, distractions are wonderful opportunities for practice. Pay attention to the thoughts and feelings that arise. You may notice funny thoughts like, "I wish those inconsiderate people would be quiet – I'm practicing acceptance and compassion over here!"

Over time, you will react less strongly to distractions, simply noticing them, instantly deciding if you need to attend to them or not, and gently bringing your attention back to your practice. Distractions can even deepen your practice. Remember, whatever you are able to notice is happening in the present moment.

Strong emotions

A lot of interesting things can happen when you finally choose to be still and pay attention. You may feel agitation when you don't have something to do, with thoughts that you are wasting time. You may even feel a strong urge to get up and "accomplish something." Thoughts may arise that our self-worth is dependent on getting something done.

Sitting still, dropping defenses, allows old feelings to surface. Random memories and emotions will arise, linger, and drift away. Old hurts and traumas may begin to bubble up. Your urge may be to push them away or stuff them back down, but you can choose to sit with them, to relate to them differently. If you notice recurrent, intense memories of old traumas arising, they need to be processed – their messages need to be heard and released, and this is best done under the guidance of a competent mental health professional.

All of this is part of the practice. Staying with your emotions, watching them rise and fall, allows them to flow through you, making it easier for you to do this all throughout the day.

Many find the practice of mindfulness to be complete unto itself. After all, what could exist outside of the moment you are in? However, for those of us who need tricks to help us get into the moment, there are a variety of other practices for developing the mind.

8

Beyond Mindfulness
More Ways to Train Your Mind

It is amazing how little we know about our own minds.

For many years, I read of the awe and reverence given to sacred sites in India, one of the places that developed such a rich and sophisticated science of the mind. My university allowed me an opportunity to present at the World Conference on Psychology and Spirituality in New Delhi. To my good fortune, my mentor Stephen K. Hayes was going to Nepal a month later to study an ancient practice for removing obstacles, and I would be able to meet him there. This allowed me three weeks with no agenda, so I chose to go to Bodh Gaya, the city where the historical Buddha attained enlightenment. I had heard that this city had temples of almost every tradition, which would allow me a wonderful opportunity for study and practice.

After spending a week in Delhi, and visiting the Taj Mahal, I got over the jet lag, and some of the culture shock. There was a lot more shock to come, however, as Bodh Gaya was in Bihar, the poorest state in India.

I flew into a tiny, run-down airport in Patna, the state capital. I approached the "tourist advisor," which consisted of a man sitting on a stool. He told me a bus would be arriving in about four hours that would take me directly to Bodh Gaya. However, I was eager to make the seven-hour journey, as I wanted to arrive before nightfall. Armed with my *Lonely Planet Guide*, I told the man I wanted a taxi to the Mithapur bus station. He looked bewildered

Mindfulness: Living through Challenges and Enriching Your Life in This Moment, First Edition. Richard W. Sears.
© 2014 John Wiley & Sons, Ltd. Published 2014 by John Wiley & Sons, Ltd.

for a moment, then concerned. He smiled politely, and did his best to explain to me in broken English that it was best to wait for the official bus. But after being in India for almost a whole week, I was attached to the idea that I would be fine, and wanted to get going. He reluctantly sold me a voucher for the taxi to the bus station.

The taxis from the airport were pre-paid, to prevent naive foreigners like me from being taken advantage of. I found a beat-up taxi waiting out front, and handed him the voucher. He looked at me and chuckled, said something incomprehensible, then motioned me to get inside. Many people in New Delhi spoke English, but it was much less common in the state of Bihar, especially outside of the major cities.

Along the way, the driver kept stopping and picking up people, later dropping them off, likely making the best use of my fixed taxi fare. I was becoming concerned about ever making it to the bus station. We began driving into tiny back alleys, and the thought occurred to me that the driver and his friends might just take me to an abandoned factory and rob me. Not wanting to offend them by having such a thought, but wanting to be ready, I opened the combination lock on the chain I used to secure my backpack, ready to intercept any weapon that might be directed at me.

Finally, we made it to the "bus station," which turned out to be a massive dirt field covered with hundreds of people and dozens of busses. Ten men swarmed me as soon as I stepped out, asking where I was going, and offering to carry my backpack. I selected the one closest to me, an elderly gentlemen dressed in rags, who smiled cheerfully and grabbed it from me. The driver tapped my arm and held his hand out. "I already gave you the voucher, right?" He moved his head as if to say, "Well, yeah, but … " so I dug into my wallet to give him a tip. Even though it was almost equal to the taxi fare, he seemed disappointed, and got back into his car.

When I turned around, I was alone in the crowd of hundreds. The man who took my backpack was nowhere in sight. I shouted at the top of my lungs, frantically running through the crowd, trying to ask if anyone saw the man who took my backpack. Most people either ignored me or looked at me with confusion. After a few minutes, a man passing by on a bus leaned out the window and pointed as he looked at me. Turning that direction, I saw what looked like my backpack about a hundred meters away, bobbing through the crowd on top of someone's head. I ran and dodged through the crowd as fast as I could, and my backpack disappeared behind one of the busses. When I got to the bus, he was loading it into the back. He saw me and smiled. The bus driver was standing there, and confirmed that this was the bus to Bodh Gaya. Fortunately, I had already figured out that in India, nodding one's head meant no, and shaking one's head meant yes, something that caused me a lot of confusion at first. As I went to sit down, I caught just enough Hindi to hear him teasing me under his breath that I was wearing a *mala* (beads for counting in meditation practice), so of course I was going to Bodh Gaya. I raised my arm and spoke up that I was in fact wearing two *malas*, and we both laughed.

It was becoming increasingly obvious why the tourist advisor at the airport was so concerned about my choice to travel this way. As I went to sit down, I discovered the seats had not been designed for tall people like me. The space between the seats was smaller than the distance from my knees to the back of my hips, so I was painfully wedged in. The bus quickly filled to capacity, so I could not turn sideways to relieve the pressure.

The bus moved slowly, and stopped frequently on the busy city streets. Vendors literally jumped onto the bus and moved up the aisle to try to sell things, jumping back off when the bus got rolling again. Dozens of human bodies jumped on and off the roof, bumpers, and windows all along the way.

Once we got out of the city, the bus became less crowded, and the scenery more beautiful. At every stop, I wondered if someone was going to walk off with my backpack, stored under the bus with everyone else's belongings. I kept asking, "Bodh Gaya?" and the driver would laugh and nod his head (meaning "no"). By the time we actually got there, almost everyone remaining on the bus kindly spoke up to make sure I knew this was my stop. My backpack was covered in dust from the road, but I was very happy to see it.

It turned out I was still a couple of miles outside of Bodh Gaya, so I was greeted by a swarm of "taxi" drivers. The first one who made it to me must have been about 12 years old, asked me where I was staying, and offered to take me there for 20 rupees. In the spirit of this haggling culture, I suggested 10, and he accepted. As I walked with the young man past the other taxi drivers in their small motorized carts, they tossed out teasing comments. I soon found out why. It turned out that the "taxi" was a donkey cart. It was hard to even get up onto, but I didn't want to go back on my word in giving the young man my business. The poor animal strained to pull the two of us, and I felt bad. Once we made it into town, he kept stopping, and saying "Here!" But before jumping out, I saw no signs of any kind, so I repeated the name of where I was staying. When we finally arrived, he held out his hand and demanded in a loud voice, "100 rupees!" I animatedly expressed outrage, engaging in the customary vociferous bartering. I only later realized that 100 rupees was only a little over two dollars.

I had such mixed feelings being in Bodh Gaya. In each of the three traditions into which I was ordained, I can trace my lineage back to Siddhartha Gautama himself, who had his initial awakening on a rock in the center of town, beneath a tree that still stands there, known at the "Bodhi" or awakening tree. I was filled with reverence and respect for the traditions that originated from this teacher 2,500 years ago.

Yet, this dusty, poverty-stricken town had become a tourist trap. The streets had been lined with gaudy lights and decorations, and swarms of peddlers would assault me as I walked through town, saying things like "Buddha would want you to buy flowers." Crippled children would fold up their legs for maximum effect as they walked around on their hands and begged for money.

The ancient texts often spoke of this place as magical, but seeing monks lift their robes and urinate on the sidewalk wherever they happened to be dampened my sense of awe.

If this was the only impression I had ever gotten of these ancient wisdom teachings, I would never have been interested in them. What could a culture so rife with poverty and suffering have to teach me about life?

At one point, as I sat under the Bodhi tree, taking it all in, I suddenly began laughing. Siddhartha never claimed to be anything more than a human being. If he were alive today, he would probably find it amusing that people were showing reverence to a rock where his rear end sat (along with some compassion for their need for inspiration). My own expectations, my need for something special, created my confusion.

Reverence and respect for culture and tradition are important, but I believe that the most traditional thing we can do is to be modern. In his day, the Buddha's teachings were cutting-edge ideas designed to help the people of his time and culture. There are timeless principles about how the human mind works, but to make those useful, we must always adapt them to the needs of the individuals in today's society.

The Dalai Lama has said, "My religion is compassion." In one of my Zen lineages, our family tradition is asking, "How may I help you?" Our Zen practice is asking "What is this moment?" In my clinical practice, I ask, "What brings you here today?"

This is a unique time in history, when advances in science allow us major breakthroughs in such things as understanding how the brain functions. It is also the first time when we have access to the wisdom teachings of all the world's cultures and what they have learned over the centuries about the nature of the mind. Science can investigate the questions of "how," and traditions can inform our questions of "why."

Mindfulness is only one method of developing the mind. In this chapter, we will explore a variety of other methods that have been used for centuries, which are also starting to get support from modern research.

In many traditions, mindfulness was seen as a tool for developing awareness, of honing the ability to notice more clearly, as a prerequisite for more "advanced" mind development exercises. Some traditions have found that just noticing is enough, allowing our own inner wisdom to guide us moment to moment. For those of us who think too much and miss the simplicity of each moment, "skillful means" were developed to help us as well, using sophisticated intellectual reasoning to demonstrate the limits of the intellect.

Loving-Kindness

When you begin to pay more attention to your own thoughts and feelings, it is not uncommon to discover some deep-rooted negative conceptions at the core of your identity. These may have come from messages instilled by parents, peers, or society itself, whether from intentionally abusive people or from those who thought they were "helping."

Loving-kindness meditation is a method of deliberately fostering a deeper sense of compassion for yourself and others. Though there are variations in how the practice is done, you basically begin by imagining someone or something which produces a warm, loving feeling within you. This could be an inspiring teacher or spiritual figure, a loved one, a child, a parent, a pet, or even a symbol. Let this feeling warm your heart. Then allow the sense of love and kindness to spread throughout your body. You might even repeat some words silently to yourself, such as "May I be happy, at peace, and free from suffering." You could choose to imagine yourself as a small child, and giving yourself that feeling of unconditional love that should be showered on every child. Gradually, allow that sense of loving-kindness to spread outside of you, encompassing all of your loved ones, then strangers, then even those who may have harmed you. You can silently repeat to yourself, "May she/he/they be happy, at peace, and free from suffering." You can even imagine this feeling of love and kindness spreading out to fill your city, eventually filling the entire world. Rest in this state for a while, then gradually bring it all back into your heart.

Practicing this regularly can help to counteract the countless negative messages ingrained in us, and fosters a more positive attitude toward ourselves and others. We can still be firm and set boundaries when needed, but we can more easily let go of the negative feelings that create unnecessary turmoil. Interestingly, studies of people practicing loving-kindness meditation have actually shown an improvement in vagal tone, a measure of the vagus nerve's ability to maintain homeostasis in the body. It had been thought this was something set at birth.

Analytical Meditations

With a clear mind, and the ability to allow your emotions to rise and fall, you can begin paying more attention to the patterns in nature, and to our place in the world. Two important topics for analysis are interdependence and impermanence.

It is crucial that these types of exercises be done when you are in a good place emotionally. Even though you are only looking at things as they are,

Baby deer. © Jeremy Rogers.

society actively works to ignore these characteristics of reality. Nothing you read here will be new to you, but we typically just don't think about these things much, and often push away the emotions they bring up. Mindfulness keeps us on the subject matter, anchoring us from drifting off into worries and ruminations if strong feelings arise. Purposefully bringing these subjects to mind, and sitting with the emotions, serves to inoculate us against the sting of suffering that ignorance of them can create, allowing us to be more resilient, patient, and kind.

Interdependence

Recognizing the interconnectedness of all things counters the feelings of isolation and frustration that can come up in our daily lives. Below are two examples of how these meditations might be done, one for food, and one for your own sense of who you are.

Food

Giving thanks for our food is a common practice in many cultures, but now that we can immediately buy food in a box and heat it up in seconds, we don't often appreciate where it comes from.

Plan a time when you can sit down and eat a meal at your own pace. As you look at your food, ponder all of the factors that came into play to bring it into existence and how it came to be in front of you. If there is a carrot on your plate, think about how it got there. It was grown on a farm. A farmer had to develop a patch of land and buy all of the equipment necessary to grow carrots. The nutrients in the soil came from fertilizer and bacteria. The sun, which ignited after billions of hydrogen atoms came together with enough gravity to spark nuclear fusion reactions, provided the light to foster photosynthesis. Rain nourished the carrot and entered its cells after the earth's water cycle carried the molecules all over the planet. The carrot was harvested, transported over roads that many human beings had to build and maintain, and arrived at the store or market where people work hard to maintain their business. Soon, the carrot will be eaten by you, its nutrients will be extracted and delivered to your body's cells, and it will literally become a part of you.

You can go deeper in any number of countless veins of thought on this topic. You will never fully know, or have time to ponder, all of the factors, but doing this for a few minutes will deepen your appreciation of how interconnected everything is.

Self

The very same analysis can also be done using the question, "Who am I?" You can ponder all the factors that brought you into and maintain your existence. As we are vastly more complex than a carrot, you may need a few years to sit with this one. When you begin to notice and appreciate the countless causes and conditions that contribute to who you are, your sense of self will be much less narrow and constricted. You will begin to feel that since you need so many other processes and people to exist, in a very real sense, all of this is you, not just the bag of skin you carry around.

Meditation on impermanence and death

With the recognition of interdependence comes the understanding that everything is changing as a result of continuous interactions with other things. These changes can be almost imperceptible sometimes, but close observation, especially at the microscopic level, shows intense activity and change. That which changes, by definition, is not permanent. Living beings too are always changing, and therefore are impermanent. The greatest change we know as human beings is called death.

We work hard to hold onto things and people, but no matter how hard we try, we cannot do so for very long, because everything is always changing, however subtly. Recognition of this truth allows us to let go of the mental struggle to grasp, and fosters appreciation of each material object we encounter, each human being we interact with, and each moment as it is.

If you have ever had a near-death experience, you know how wondrous all of your subsequent moments are – the ones you know you almost missed. Unfortunately, these insights tend to wear off as we gradually adjust back to life as we knew it before. Meditation on death, as morbid as it may sound at first, deepens our appreciation of life.

Modern society in general rarely speaks about death. We often pretend it isn't really going to happen, until we experience the loss of a loved one, and its reality slaps us in the face. Although being educated about death does not remove the pain of separation from a loved one, a little preparation helps us grieve more fully (whatever that means to each of us and our culture) without adding additional anxiety or worries about the grieving itself.

When you are in a good place, and are ready to sit with any anxieties or fears that come up, you can meditate on death systematically, pondering a number of aspects about it. One is the idea of the universality of death. Consider that all living creatures, without exception (including yourself), will one day die. This includes all loved ones, all pets, everyone who has ever lived or will ever live.

Another component of the practice is to consider the inevitability of death. In this phase, you contemplate the fact that there is no escape from death. Even those who are fabulously wealthy, healthy, and brilliant will die some-day. There is no one in the world who has ever permanently cheated death. You've never heard, "In the news today, a 6,000-year-old woman was found in the mountains that death forgot about." It will happen to us all.

Another consideration is that you do not know when death will occur. Sometimes children die before parents do. Sometimes babies die in their cribs. Not knowing when death will occur keeps us more appreciative of this moment, for the time that we do have to live and to share with loved ones.

A further consideration is that the manner of death for each person is uncertain. A person could die peacefully while sleeping, or die slowly and painfully of cancer.

As with anxiety, fears of death will rise and fall on their own as you stay with these ideas. The goal is not to completely overcome fears of death and change, but to spend less energy struggling to avoid thinking or worrying about them. You may even begin to see the world and your relationships with fresh eyes again.

Now, take a deep breath, feel whatever you are feeling in this moment, and take a look around you. Remind yourself how precious this moment is.

Getting Hooked

In the practice of Zen, teaching devices known as "*kōans*" are often used to help us recognize when our thinking gets us hooked into problems that don't exist in reality. *Kōans* are often described as unanswerable riddles, but in fact, the answers call for a simple, direct action in the present moment.

My fellow Zen teacher James Myo Gak Foster and I call our *kōan* work "mindfulness in dialogue" because the interactions with the teacher are designed to draw you into the moment, helping you to let go of all the ways your thinking makes things more complicated.

When I give mindfulness workshops to crowds of mental health professionals, I give them the following *kōan*:

What is the truth?

How would you answer if I were asking you that right now?

Typically, the entire room goes silent (no small feat for a room full of therapists). In that initial moment, their minds usually go blank. Zen calls this "beginner's mind" or "don't know mind" or "before thought." This is why traditional Zen students often start with a shout, a clap, or a slam on the floor. Out of this clear mind, an answer appropriate to the situation and the moment can arise.

For most participants, the blankness doesn't last very long, and their minds begin racing. We want to sound clever. We want to get the right answer. We don't want to sound foolish. We don't want to embarrass ourselves. We begin to second guess our guesses. We may even get angry for being put into such an awkward position.

Most people add extra ideas into the question, like thinking that what they heard was, "What is the ultimate truth from a philosophical perspective?" If someone says, "It depends on your perspective," I might say, "Okay, then give me your perspective."

Missing the directness I am asking for, they may come back with, "It's what you make of it," to which I might reply, "No, you're giving me philosophy. I want the truth."

Some take this up as an exciting challenge, and some are very irritated by me "shutting them down" and telling them they are wrong. It is amazing how much power our minds give to someone who appears to be in authority. But who gives authority? Why get so upset because someone has a different opinion? We can learn a great deal about how our minds operate and react in the process of working through a *kōan*.

Some people love this part of the workshop, but some people hate it. Every time I do this, however, the room comes alive. There is electricity in the air. People are very engaged and present in those moments, in contrast to when we are discussing ideas and theories in the other parts of the workshop.

Eventually I hear something like, "The truth is what's happening right now."

"Ah," I smile. "You're getting closer, but you're just giving me a menu when I'm hungry for dinner."

This is often followed up with something like, "The truth is what is."
"That's still a description. I want the truth itself." I may say, which some take as a hint, and some take as a taunt.

Silence often follows, then a correct answer springs into someone's mind. It is simply whatever you are seeing, hearing, feeling, tasting, or smelling in this moment. My favorite answer, given after an eight-hour workshop in a small hotel conference room with old, hard chairs, was, "Sore butt!" There was no arguing with that truth!

Truth is all around us. What could possibly be hidden? Yet, we feel unsatisfied, and continuously seek for some kind of special something that must be out there somewhere. We keep thinking there must be something secret, something complicated that we just can't figure out. Something profound, we think, must be hard to get.

But where else can you find the truth? How could you ever be anywhere and anyplace else, other than right here, right now? Everything else exists only in memory and thought. Can you give me tomorrow's newspaper? Can you show me yesterday? Sure, we can agree to compare calendars and talk about the past and the future, but you will never be in any other moment than now. When you realize you can't get out of this moment no matter how hard you try, you let go of a great deal of emotional struggle, and there is a tremendous release of energy.

The next time you feel stuck, or hooked by your thinking, just sit with it for a little while. You may just discover that a large part of the problem exists only in your head.

Becoming a New You

In mindfulness exercises, we practice accepting ourselves as we are in this moment. For some of us, this is very difficult to do, because we don't recognize our true nature.

Another option is to create a larger-than-life identity that represents a quality that we wish to more fully internalize and manifest. This is done through the "three secrets" of thought, word, and deed, which Stephen K. Hayes translates into the action words, "visualize, verbalize, and vitalize."[1]

If I wish to be a more compassionate person, I can visualize myself as compassionate, say compassionate things, and engage in compassionate actions. This is a proven approach in behavioral psychotherapy, colloquially known as "fake it till you make it." If you change what you do, and stick with it, your feelings will catch up later.

Though the concept is simple, traditional practices for doing this can be very sophisticated, taking hours or even days to complete. Visualizations could involve elaborate celestial images representing the qualities you wish to embody. Words might take the form of highly meaningful ancient phrases. Actions might take the form of symbolic hand gestures, body postures, or movements designed to trick your brain into believing that you really do possess the characteristics you wish to manifest.

Traditional practices involve creating a safe space, purifying and refining your inner qualities, gaining a broader perspective on your connection to the universe, then letting go of all concepts, sometimes even burning it all away symbolically with fire. Interestingly, the heart of many of these practices is to be more fully in the moment. By giving your brain amazingly complex concepts and activities, you arrive back to a very simple appreciation of now.

While exercises like these can be very useful, they must be practiced with caution. The elaborate historical practices were only done under the guidance of a wise mentor. Carefully consider why you would want to change your sense of identity. As the saying goes, be careful of what you wish for, you just might get it.

Breaking through Obstacles

Many people believe that all meditation practices are about becoming more peaceful. In a sense this is true, but truth does not always appear peaceful to us.

A peaceful and compassionate person can appear wrathful to others. A lioness may look terribly frightening when she is protecting her cub. A loving parent may firmly deny a child's demanding request for excessive candy, knowing that even though the child will enjoy it in the moment, it will cause long-term health problems. A good parent also knows that giving in to tantrums very often makes them worse. To that child, the parent looks very mean and uncaring in that moment.

Sometimes setting boundaries is the most loving thing we can do, both for ourselves and for others. In the Tibetan tradition, there is a very important practice in which obstacles are cleared away and negative emotions are transformed into wisdom and compassion. This is done through highly symbolic actions, such as nailing down representations of the obstacles with a three-sided dagger known as a *phurba*.

This type of practice is the specialty of the monks at Pema Ts'al in Nepal. Considering the images of death, skeletons, and knives all around us, the monks were amazingly kind people, with a wonderful sense of humor.

During our stay there, the head monk, Lama Kunga, led a very important New Year's ceremony lasting multiple days. My friends and I were honored with cushions up front next to him. He held a beautifully crafted wand, like those that conductor's use, with a long, iridescent peacock feather on the

Monk with *phurba*, Nepal. © Richard Sears.

end. He motioned the wand to guide the orchestra of monks in blowing their trumpets, long horns, bells, and drums. Once in a while, he extended the wand a little farther, shaking to signal that a note should be held, and he tickled my face. He smiled at me with a twinkle in his eye.

Sitting for hours in the morning cold, I would sometimes flick bits of the offering rice at the young orphan monks down the row. After a look of confusion, and a few more carefully aimed grains, they would catch me smiling, and try to sneakily fire some back at me.

It is important to be a mature, well-balanced person, and to keep a sense of humor, when undertaking assertive action to make changes. Obstacles have a way of continuing to come up, and of course, the most insidious obstacles are the ones within us.

What obstacles are currently in your own life? How might you nail them down, and transform the energy of your stress into wisdom and compassion?

Connecting with Nature

In these modern times, we human beings are losing our connection with the natural world. Not so long ago, our ancestors were intimately in touch with the earth and the sky. Now the weather is only noticed when it is particularly beautiful, or, more often, when it is inconvenient. Managing water and fire, which we now take for granted, were crucial to survival.

When I was a small child, I remember that no matter how upset I felt, I could find solace by sitting on my porch and looking at the trees. Even now, as I look out my window, seeing trees invokes a sense of peace. Most of us find it easier and more "natural" to be present in nature. Since we live most of our lives now in boxes and cubicles, is it any wonder we often feel so disconnected from the world? Even looking at pictures of nature seems to engender a feeling of simplicity and connection, which is why images of trees, leaves, rocks, or water are often associated with mindfulness.

As mentioned in Chapter 4, Shugendo, which literally means, "the way of training and testing," taught very dramatic ways to build up the power of intention. As with the concept in ACT of being willing to move toward your values even when there is chaos outside of and within you, engaging your will to move into intimidating trials is considered a path to enlightenment through nature.

Akin to what we know about exposure therapy for overcoming fear and anxiety, the Shugendo tradition utilized the common fears of water, fire, and heights as tools for training.

I first tried fire walking when I was 15 years old. My youth group had built a fire behind the church one evening, and since I lived about a mile away and was going to walk home, I stayed to watch the fire burn down. I had been reading a book by Stephen K. Hayes about his fire-walking experience in Japan,[2] which inspired me to rake out the burning coals with a stick to try walking over them myself. I took off my shoes and socks and stood at the edge for a few moments, feeling the heat, smelling the smoke, and watching the wavy patterns of light over the coals. I steeled my resolve, grasped my hands together over my chest, and walked over the coals quickly.

To my amazement, I was fine! I silently celebrated being brave enough to try it, and enjoyed the exuberance of accomplishing such a feat. Then I got a little cocky. My teacher said he had seen the adepts in Japan grinning and stomping across the coals, so I walked across again, stamping my feet on the fiery embers, full of confidence. Unfortunately, some of the coals stuck to my feet after I reached the other side, and I cried out in pain as I wiped my feet in the wet grass. Now thankful that no one had been watching, I carefully limped home on sore feet. It took two weeks for the blisters to heal.

Tree in the courtyard of Pema Ts'al, Nepal. © Richard Sears.

I later learned that there are some good scientific reasons why feet don't burn when you walk on coals properly, but even with that intellectual knowledge, it is still a test of will. I also learned the importance of having a mentor instead of trying to learn solely through books.

In ancient times, trainees were dangled from mountain cliffs by old rusty chains. In a modern adaptation, years ago I took a martial arts student who wanted to learn Shugendo up in an airplane shortly after I received my pilot's license.

In preparation for my license test, I repeatedly practiced recovering from a stall. A stall occurs when the air is not moving over the wing fast enough, or at the right angle, so lift is lost, and the plane falls down through the air like any other object would. By dropping the nose of the plane, it picks up speed and returns the wing to a better lift angle, allowing the pilot to pull out and level off. This is of course practiced from a safe altitude. In the plane

I was learning in, usually one of the wings would drop during a stall, which made for a pretty dramatic experience. It seemed perfect for my friend and student to practice facing fear.

As we climbed into the sky after takeoff, my friend was already nervous. He was gripping his hands tightly in a traditional symbolic gesture I had shown him to represent the experience of moving through fear. When we reached a safe altitude, I looked over at him, and asked if he was ready. He gripped his hands even more tightly and pulled them to his chest. "Ready as I'm going to be!"

As an added dramatic effect, I decided to perform a power-on stall. With the engine going almost full throttle, I pulled back on the yoke to make the airplane climb at a high angle, one you would not normally experience on an airplane, to induce the stall. It felt like we were flying up into space on a rocket, except we were slowing down as the engine strained to pull us up.

In my solo practice, the plane would smoothly drop back down to pick up speed. If a wing dropped, I simply pushed on the opposite rudder to balance it back out. What I did not expect with my friend, however, was the very rapid and dramatic drop the plane made. I realized later that since my friend was heavier than me, the weight inside the plane was almost triple what I was used to. The plane quickly dived straight down toward the ground, the engine roaring at full throttle, and both of us were pushed upwards. I had always preferred keeping my seat belt a little loose for comfort, which I now greatly regretted, as I was thrown back up so far that I could not reach the throttle or the control yoke, even with my arms reaching as far as they could. The ground was rapidly filling the windshield as our full-power dive increasingly sped us toward the earth.

I angled my body forward as much as I could by pushing back on the seat, and after what seemed like a very long time, I finally got enough of a grip on the yoke to pull it back and take us out of the dive, allowing me to settle into the seat and pull back the throttle. The horizon looked so beautiful.

My friend certainly got to experience his fear, and I learned some valuable lessons. I was definitely fully present in those moments, and have resolved to never repeat those mistakes.

In my youth, I sought dramatic experiences, hoping to find some breakthrough. Now I find that the wonder lies in all of our moments. Below is something I wrote a little while back while vacationing:

As I stand on the beach in Nags Head, in the Outer Banks of North Carolina, I watch as children play, and a few brave young people try to ride the waves on surf boards. My family plays in the cold blasting water, chuckling and shivering.

I do not feel compelled to jump in the water and battle nature this time. I have nothing left to prove to myself or anyone else. I laughingly acknowledge that my health and age are also natural processes with which I need not struggle.

Heron riding the waves. © Richard Sears.

I take a deep breath and enjoy and respect the moment as it is. I attempt to capture it with my new camera. Gulls and herons swoop down and appear to play and surf on the wave crests.

I feel the wind on my face, the same wind that is bringing in rain clouds, powering the waves, holding up the birds, and lifting the kites flown by the children on the beach.

I am slowly beginning to recognize that I am not in fact so separate from all of this. My own blood is much like the salt water. My bones are not so different than the shells under my feet. I too am a collection of ever-changing processes, dependent on all of the forces of nature to come into and continue my being.

All of the discipline, all of the efforts, all of the struggle, bring us back to the realization that discipline, effort, and struggle only take place in the realm of thinking. Struggling or not, the sun is shining right now, even if we can't see it. Aware of it or not, the air envelops the entire earth. We may curse the storms and praise the sunshine, but heat and water power the weather systems that sustain all life.

In just this moment, we are already connected to all of nature, and to all our fellow human beings.

Afterword

So, you have finished this book, exploring the various aspects of mindfulness and the challenges and opportunities of integrating it into your daily life. At the end of a Zen retreat, it would be traditional to ask a very simple question, which I will ask you now:

What have you attained?

If you were to tell me something you remembered about what you read, you would be falling into the past. If you tell me what you're going to do with this information, you're jumping into the future. What are you experiencing in this moment? What do you see, hear, feel, smell, and taste, right now? The past and the future only truly exist as memories and thoughts. What else could you possibly attain, outside of this very moment you are in?

I am looking outside my window at the morning sun shining through the leaves of the autumn trees, listening to my cat purring, and feeling honored to share these words with you.

Mindfulness: Living through Challenges and Enriching Your Life in This Moment, First Edition.
Richard W. Sears.
© 2014 John Wiley & Sons, Ltd. Published 2014 by John Wiley & Sons, Ltd.

Mindfulness Exercises

The best way to learn mindfulness is to practice it regularly. The following recordings are available for free from the author's website, www.psych-insights.com.

- Body scan
- Mindfulness of breath, body, sounds, and thoughts
- Three-minute breathing space
- Loving-kindness
- Embodying love visualization

Mindfulness: Living through Challenges and Enriching Your Life in This Moment, First Edition.
Richard W. Sears.
© 2014 John Wiley & Sons, Ltd. Published 2014 by John Wiley & Sons, Ltd.

References

Chapter 1: The Need for Mindfulness

1. Watts, A. (2004). *Learning the human game* [audio CD]. Louisville, CO: Sounds True.
2. Watts, A. (1957). *The way of Zen.* New York: Vintage Books.
3. Grepmair, L., Mietterlehner, F., Loew, T., Bachler, E., Rother, W., & Nickel, N. (2007). Promoting mindfulness in psychotherapists in training influences the treatment results of their patients: A randomized, double-blind, controlled study. *Psychotherapy and Psychosomatics, 76,* 332–338. doi:10.1159/000107560
4. Sagan, C. (1980). *Cosmos.* New York: Random House

Chapter 2: What Is Mindfulness?

1. Newberg, A., D'Aquili, E., & Rause, V. (2001). *Why God won't go away: Brain science and the biology of belief.* New York: Random House.
2. Kabat-Zinn, J. (2003). Mindfulness-based interventions in context: Past, present, and future. *Clinical Psychology: Science and Practice, 10*(2), 144–156.
3. Williams, M., Teasdale, J., Segal, Z., & Kabat-Zinn, J. (2007). *The mindful way through depression: Freeing yourself from chronic unhappiness.* New York: Guilford Press.
4. Watts, A. (1996). *Myth and religion: The edited transcripts.* Rutland, VT: Charles E. Tuttle Publishing.

Mindfulness: Living through Challenges and Enriching Your Life in This Moment, First Edition. Richard W. Sears.
© 2014 John Wiley & Sons, Ltd. Published 2014 by John Wiley & Sons, Ltd.

5. Sohlberg, M. M., & Mateer, C. A. (1989). *Introduction to cognitive rehabilitation: Theory and practice.* New York: Guilford Press.
6. Watts, A. (1999). *The Tao of philosophy.* Rutland, VT: Charles E. Tuttle Publishing.
7. Watts, A. (2004). *Learning the human game* [audio CD]. Louisville, CO: Sounds True.
8. Dutton, D. G., & Aron, A. P. (1974). Some evidence for heightened sexual attraction under conditions of high anxiety. *Journal of Personality and Social Psychology, 30*(4), 510–517. doi:10.1037/h0037031
9. Schachter, S., & Singer, J. (1962). Cognitive, social, and physiological determinants of emotional state. *Psychological Review, 69*, 379–399.
10. Watts, A. (2002). *Still the mind: An introduction to meditation.* Novato, CA: New World Library.
11. Hayes, S. C., Strohsahl, K., & Wilson, K. G. (2012). *Acceptance and commitment therapy: The process and practice of mindful change.* New York: Guilford Press.
12. Watts, A. (1957). *The way of Zen.* New York: Vintage Books.
13. Fraser, J. S. (1989). The strategic rapid intervention approach. In Charles Figley (Ed.), *Treating Stress In The Family* (ch. 5, pp. 122–157). New York: Brunner/Mazel.
14. Lazar, S. W., Kerr, C. E., Wasserman, R. H., Gray, J. R., Greve, D. N., Treadway, M. T., … Fischl, B. (2005). Meditation experience is associated with increased cortical thickness. *Neuroreport, 16*(17), 1893–1897.
15. Siegel, D. J. (2007). *The mindful brain: Reflection and attunement in the cultivation of well-being.* New York: W. W. Norton & Company.

Chapter 3: What Mindfulness Is Not

1. Sears, R., Rudisill, J., & Mason-Sears, C. (2006). *Consultation skills for mental health professionals.* New York: John Wiley & Sons.
2. Muesse, M. (2011). *Practicing mindfulness: An introduction to meditation* [audio CD]. Chantilly, VA: The Teaching Company.
3. Watts, A. (1966). *The book: On the taboo against knowing who you are.* New York: Random House.

Chapter 4: When Things Go Wrong: Responding to Challenges

1. Segal, Z. V., Williams, J. M. G., & Teasdale, J. D. (2013). *Mindfulness-based cognitive therapy for depression: Second edition.* New York: Guilford Press.
2. Ibid.
3. Ibid.

Chapter 5: When Things Go Terribly Wrong

1. Beck, A. T., Rush, A. J., Shaw, B. F., & Emery, G. (1979). *Cognitive therapy for depression* (p. 11). New York: The Guilford Press.
2. Bowen, S., Chawla, N., & Marlatt, G. A. (2010). *Mindfulness-based relapse prevention for addictive behaviors: A clinician's guide.* New York: The Guilford Press.
3. Albers, S. (2003). *Eating mindfully: How to end mindless eating and enjoy a balanced relationship with food.* Oakland, CA: New Harbinger Publications.
4. Kristeller, J. L., Baer, R. A., & Quillian, R. W. (2006). Mindfulness-based approaches to eating disorders. In R. A. Baer (Ed.), *Mindfulness and acceptance-based interventions: Conceptualization, application, and empirical support* (pp. 75–91). San Diego, CA: Elsevier.
5. Kristeller, J. L., & Wolever, R. Q. (2011). Mindfulness-based eating awareness training for treating binge eating disorder: The conceptual foundation. *Eating Disorders, 19*(1), 49–61. doi:10.1080/10640266.2011.533605

Chapter 6: Enriching Your Life

1. Kabat-Zinn, J. (1990). *Full catastrophe living: Using the wisdom of your body and mind to face stress, pain, and illness.* New York: Dell.
2. http://www.neweconomics.org/
3. Ibid.
4. Abrams Spring, J. (1997). *After the affair: Healing the pain and rebuilding trust when a partner has been unfaithful.* New York: William Morrow Paperbacks.
5. Franken, A. (2003). *Oh, the things I know.* New York: Plume.
6. Wile, D. (1995). *After the fight: Using your disagreements to build a stronger relationship.* New York: The Guilford Press.
7. Glasser, H., & Easley, J. (1998). *Transforming the difficult child: The nurtured heart approach.* Tucson, AZ: Center for the Difficult Child Publications.
8. Semple, R. J., & Lee, J. (2011). *Mindfulness-based cognitive therapy for anxious children: A manual for treating childhood anxiety.* Oakland, CA: New Harbinger Publications.
9. http://thehawnfoundation.org/mindup/
10. Duncan, L. G., & Bardacke, N. (2010). Mindfulness-based childbirth and parenting education: Promoting family mindfulness during the perinatal period. *Journal of Child & Family Studies, 19*, 190–202. doi:10.1007/s10826-009-9313-7
11. http://www.neweconomics.org/
12. Ibid.
13. Ibid.
14. Alexander, R. (2008). *Wise mind, open mind: Finding purpose and meaning in times of crisis, loss, & change.* Oakland, CA: New Harbinger Publications.
15. Matthiessen, P. (1999). *Zen and the writing life* [audio cassette]. Louisville, CO: Sounds True.

16. Niemiec, R. (2014). *Mindfulness and character strengths: A practical guide to flourishing*. Boston, MA: Hogrefe Publishing.

17. Peterson, C., & Seligman, M. E. P. (2004). *Character strengths and virtues: A handbook and classification*. New York: Oxford University Press and Washington, DC: American Psychological Association (www.viacharacter.org).

18. http://www.neweconomics.org/

19. Hayes, S. C., Strohsahl, K., & Wilson, K. G. (2012). *Acceptance and commitment therapy: The process and practice of mindful change*. New York: Guilford Press.

20. Watts, A. (1999). *The Tao of philosophy*. Rutland, VT: Charles E. Tuttle Publishing.

Chapter 7: Building Your Mindfulness Muscles

1. Linehan, M. M. (1993). *Skills training manual for treating borderline personality disorder*. New York: Guilford Press.

2. Kabat-Zinn, J. (1990). *Full catastrophe living: Using the wisdom of your body and mind to face stress, pain, and illness*. New York: Dell.

3. Segal, Z. V., Williams, J. M. G., & Teasdale, J. D. (2013). *Mindfulness-based cognitive therapy for depression*: Second edition. New York: Guilford Press.

Chapter 8: Beyond Mindfulness: More Ways to Train Your Mind

1. Hayes, S. K. (1992). *Action meditation: The Japanese diamond and lotus tradition*. Dayton, OH: SKH Quest Center.

2. Hayes, S. K. (1986). *Ninja realms of power: Spiritual roots and traditions of the shadow warrior*. Chicago: Contemporary Books.

Photo Credits

About the Author

Picture in Nepal. © Richard Sears.

Chapter 1: The Need for Mindfulness

Chapter opening image. © Richard Sears.

Page 4   Kids enjoying the beach. © Richard Sears.

Chapter 2: What Is Mindfulness?

Chapter opening image. © Richard Sears.

Page 25   Hawaiian beach. © Olivia Ossege.
Page 47   Boy in Nepal. © Richard Sears.

Chapter 3: What Mindfulness Is Not

Chapter opening image. © Richard Sears.

Page 62   Dalai Lama security team, 1996. Author is far left, Dr. Norbu far right. © David Piser.
Page 66   Dolphin leaping. © Olivia Ossege.
Page 76   Flower. © Jeremy Rogers.

Mindfulness: Living through Challenges and Enriching Your Life in This Moment, First Edition. Richard W. Sears.
© 2014 John Wiley & Sons, Ltd. Published 2014 by John Wiley & Sons, Ltd.

Chapter 4: When Things Go Wrong: Responding to Challenges

Chapter opening image. © Richard Sears.

Page 97   Vermont waterfall. Note people in upper left for scale. © Richard Sears.

Chapter 5: When Things Go Terribly Wrong

Chapter opening image. © Jeremy Rogers.

Page 162   Hawaii waves. © Olivia Ossege.

Chapter 6: Enriching Your Life

Chapter opening image. © Richard Sears.

Page 183   Father and daughter enjoying the beach. © Carrie Mason-Sears.
Page 186   Jumping at White Sands, New Mexico. © Carrie Mason-Sears.
Page 198   Sun above the clouds in Hawaii. © Olivia Ossege.

Chapter 7: Building Your Mindfulness Muscles

Chapter opening image. © Richard Sears.

Page 206   Monkeys in Nepal. © Richard Sears.
Page 208   Author practicing kyudo. © Robert Denton.

Chapter 8: Beyond Mindfulness: More Ways to Train Your Mind

Chapter opening image. © Richard Sears.

Page 229   Baby deer. © Jeremy Rogers.
Page 235   Monk with *phurba*, Nepal. © Richard Sears.
Page 237   Tree in the courtyard of Pema Ts'al, Nepal. © Richard Sears.
Page 239   Heron riding the waves. © Richard Sears.

Index

Mindfulness: Living through Challenges and Enriching Your Life in This Moment, First Edition.
Richard W. Sears.
© 2014 John Wiley & Sons, Ltd. Published 2014 by John Wiley & Sons, Ltd.